HISTORICAL AND MORAL ESSAYS

HISTORICAL AND MORAL ESSAYS

EDITED BY DANIEL J. HUGGER

ACTONINSTITUTE

ISBN 978-1-942503-52-1

Cover image: Picture of John Dalberg-Acton, 1st Baron Acton. Wikimedia Commons. Public Domain.

ACTONINSTITUTE

98 E. Fulton
Grand Rapids, Michigan 49503
616.454.3080
www.acton.org

Interior composition: Judy Schafer
Cover: Scaturro Design

Printed in the United States of America

CONTENTS

FOREWORD

When scholars discuss the nineteenth century of Western civilization, they automatically and reflexively conjure images of the three most profound and original minds of the period: Karl Marx, Charles Darwin, and Sigmund Freud. Sometimes, depending on the scholar, one might list Friedrich Nietzsche as well. This is obvious in the massive and tedious surveys of Western civilization as well as in the remaining and lingering canons of Great Books. None of this is false, of course, and the three (or four) men remembered certainly were among the greatest of minds to come into this world of sorrows.

One might, with equal accuracy and a bit more humanity and justice, create a different trinity. What about John Henry Newman, Alexis de Tocqueville, and Lord Acton? After all, as the great Russell Kirk once argued, "In every age, society has been relieved only by the endeavors of a few people moved by the grace of God."[1] With the possible exception of Darwin, neither the taken-for-granted trinity nor their followers were wont to taint themselves or their ideas with the airy notion of the "grace of God."

---

[1] Russell Kirk, *The Roots of American Order* (La Salle, IL: Open Court, 1974), 161.

As for the newly proposed trinity of nineteenth-century thinkers, these men and their followers would lovingly accept the grace of God. Even among these proposed three, however, Lord Acton—the author of the essays you now hold in your hands—remains the least known, the least studied, and the least understood. True, nearly every American with any education at all remembers his assertion that "power tends to corrupt." Other than this, though, he's largely forgotten or dismissed. It's as though his entire existence from 1834 to 1902 mattered only for that one sentence. Truly this is to both our discredit and our loss. Thanks to the Acton Institute and Daniel Hugger, we can begin to rectify this massive error near the beginning of the twenty-first century.

A profound thinker and essayist, Acton argued in his seminal piece of 1862, "Nationality": "Christianity rejoices at the mixture of races, as paganism identifies itself with their differences, because truth is universal, and errors various and particular."[2] The modern and rising nation-states, though, demand unity of thought, culture, and politics. In essence, Acton believed, the world was repaganizing, returning to its worship of the state as god. After all, he wrote, "in the ancient world idolatry and nationality went together, and the same term is applied in Scripture to both."[3]

While this is just one of many profound arguments that Acton advanced during his writing career, it is critical to see him not only as important in his own day and age, but also as the critical link in the arguments about natural rights, liberty, and human dignity between Edmund Burke and Thomas Jefferson, a century earlier, and Friedrich Hayek and Christopher Dawson, a century later.

In his own day and age, though, Acton tapped into something rather deep in the currents and movements of the Western tradition. Imagine for a moment the influence the original trinity mentioned above had on the West and on the world.

---

[2] Acton, "Nationality," in *Lord Acton: Historical and Moral Essays*, 117.
[3] Acton, "Nationality," 117.

When looking at the depth and intelligence and brilliance of their arguments, one can readily narrow down each to one fundamental element. For Darwin all things were biological and adaptive. For Marx they were economic. For Freud they were psychological. As Acton would well understand, none of these things were untrue. The problem with each was not falsity but lack of context. A human being is biological, economic, and psychological, but not singularly. Rather a human being is all of these plus a million other things. As with Burke before and Dawson after, Acton knew that humanity's greatness and its sin simultaneously resided in the immense complexity of each individual human person made uniquely in the infinite image of God. With Socrates as well as Hayek, Acton knew that we know very little and that, through humility, we recognize our limitations of knowledge.

Thus, one can readily picture Acton writing "Christianity rejoices at the mixture of and mysteries of human complexities, as Darwinism identifies itself with their biological adaptation." Or, "as Marxism identifies itself with their economic base." Or, "as Freudianism identifies itself with their psychological urges." Each of these can be answered, "yes, but there's more." Again, no matter how significant Darwin, Marx, and Freud were, Acton is more nuanced, broader, and thus, in the long run, more accurate and insightful. Unlike the three more famous men, Acton never demanded any gnostic sureties in this world or the next. Faith is, after all, not fact.

Of course, this book you now are reading is much deeper than what I've just given. Hugger has ably and, indeed, lovingly crafted a book of some of the best arguments Acton made in his life. From a philosophy of history to the history of liberty, from specific personalities to the grand movement of ideas, Acton looked at all with a Catholic and classical wisdom so often lacking in his day. We would do well to remember Acton. In so doing, we remember not just the man, but the insight of one man into a much larger and unfathomably complicated world. True, in choosing Acton over Darwin, Marx, and Freud, we choose an ignorance and humility that the world hates. But, then, the world has generally hated what's good for it. Have your ideologies if you must, but I'll take truth, beauty, and goodness anytime. Oh, and by the way, power does corrupt.

Bradley J. Birzer
The Imaginative Conservative
and Hillsdale College

INTRODUCTION

Daniel J. Hugger

The nature of liberty—that motive of good deeds and common pretext of crime—is contested: "No obstacle has been so constant, or so difficult to overcome, as uncertainty and confusion touching the nature of liberty."[1] It is contested to this day by liberals, conservatives, libertarians, and socialists, who all claim to be the champions of authentic freedom. From everywhere and everyone we hear calls for freedom on all sides of contentious issues.

Liberty is contested because it is complex. It is not merely a concern of political science or economy, an abstract philosophical concept, or a theological doctrine. It is all those things and many things besides; it is, as Lord Acton said, "the delicate fruit of a mature civilization."[2] On Mars Hill Saint Paul said of God, "in him we live, and move, and have our being" (Acts 17:28), and, as to our earthly life, civilization itself functions in much the same way. Civilization is the water in which we swim. To understand ourselves and our world we need historians, students of

---

[1] Acton, "The History of Freedom in Antiquity," in *Lord Acton: Historical and Moral Essays*, 2.

[2] Acton, "The History of Freedom in Antiquity," 1.

civilization. To understand liberty the best place to begin is with its foremost historian, Lord Acton.[3] Acton attempted several grand historical projects before settling on constructing a universal history of liberty: the trial of Galileo, a modern history of the popes, the origin of the American Constitution, and a history of the Index of Forbidden Books, to name but a few.[4] While these topics are of enduring historical interest and provide ample opportunity for moral reflection, they are primarily studies of events, persons, documents, and institutions. Acton's methodological commitments as a historian led him to an even more ambitious project centered wholly on an idea: "The history of institutions is often a history of deception and illusions; for their virtue depends on the ideas that produce and on the spirit that preserves them, and the form may remain unaltered when the substance has passed away."[5] Acton sought to discern and trace the substance of freedom as it emerged from the tensions, contradictions, and conflicts of the past, for "if the Past has been an obstacle and a burden, knowledge of the Past is the safest and the surest emancipation."[6] His efforts toward constructing a universal history of liberty, which consumed much of his life, were never synthesized into a single work. This is both a tragedy and a testament to the enormity and importance of the subject. What Paul Valéry said of literary works—that they are never finished but merely abandoned—is doubly true of historical works.[7]

---

[3] For a good explanation of how Acton himself viewed the role of the historian, see Josef L. Altholz, "Lord Acton on the Historian," in *Lord Acton: Historian and Moralist*, ed. Samuel Gregg (Grand Rapids: Acton Institute, 2017), 79–90.

[4] Gertrude Himmelfarb, *Lord Acton: A Study in Conscience and Politics* (1952; repr., Grand Rapids: Acton Institute, 2015), 116.

[5] Acton, "The History of Freedom in Antiquity," 2.

[6] Acton, "Inaugural Lecture on the Study of History," in *Lord Acton: Historical and Moral Essays*, 133.

[7] As recounted in Carl Fehrman, *Poetic Creation: Inspiration or Craft*, trans. Karin Petherick (Minneapolis: University of Minnesota Press, 1980), 92.

The purpose of this collection of historical and moral essays is to introduce the contemporary reader to the way that Lord Acton traced the emerging substance of the idea of liberty through history. The first three selections: "The History of Freedom in Antiquity" (1877), "The History of Freedom in Christianity" (1877), and Acton's review of Sir Erskine May's *Democracy in Europe* (1878) provide a primer on the history of freedom. They were grouped together by J. Rufus Fears in his *Selected Writings of Lord Acton* as "The History of Liberty," and of these selections Gertrude Himmelfarb wrote, "although the 'History of Liberty' has come down to us as 'the greatest book that was never written', it is possible to reproduce in broad outline the pattern of that history."[8] It is here that we find Acton's most enduring definition of liberty: "By liberty I mean the assurance that every man shall be protected in doing what he believes his duty, against the influence of authority and majorities, customs and opinion."[9] In these selections Acton teases out this definition of liberty from the ancient Israelites to the aftermath of the Revolutions of 1848 and the emergence of socialism as a political force in Europe.

The essay "Nationality" (1862) covers much of the same time period as Acton's review of Erskine May's *Democracy in Europe* (1878) but shifts the focus to the rise of nationalism and the threat it poses to liberty. From a twenty-first century perspective—a perspective shaped by the great conflicts of the twentieth century against fascism and communism—Acton appears positively prophetic. By the close of the First World War many in liberal nations had come to believe that a nation's borders should be commensurate with "lines of nationality."[10] After the Russian Revolution the state was reorganized into Soviet Socialist

---

[8] Himmelfarb, *Lord Acton*, 118.

[9] Acton, "The History of Freedom in Antiquity," 3. For a thorough examination and exploration of this definition, see Christoph Böhr, "Religious Foundations of the Liberal Society," in *Lord Acton: Historian and Moralist*, 55–78.

[10] See point nine of President Woodrow Wilson's famous "Fourteen Points" speech: "President Wilson's Address to Congress (Delivered in Joint Session)," in *U.S. Foreign Policy: A Documentary and Reference Guide,*

Republics as part of a policy of national delimitation. The horrors of the Nazis' race policy and those of similar fascist states were the logical end of the nationalist ideology according to Acton:

> By making the State and the nation commensurate with each other in theory, it reduces practically to a subject condition all other nationalities that may be within the boundary.... According, therefore, to the degree of humanity and civilisation in that dominant body which claims all the rights of the community, the inferior races are exterminated, or reduced to servitude, or outlawed, or put in a condition of dependence.[11]

As penetrating as his insights in this essay are, Acton's language of "inferior races," "races intellectually superior," and "barbarous or sunken nations" is alarming to contemporary readers. Acton is not without blemish, as few were, in his more Eurocentric age. It is clear, however, in the context of the essay, that Acton is using the language of race in the sense of a group of people sharing the same culture, history, and language, and not in the sense of populations with distinct physical characteristics. The temptations of prejudice, nationalism, and tribalism are perennial and when allowed to influence the policies of states, doubly dangerous. Our own is a time of growing influence for nationalist populism in many corners of the world. Acton's analysis is as prescient as ever.

Acton's "Inaugural Lecture on the Study of History" (1895) is his greatest statement on historical method and the moral responsibility of the historian. Delivered late in his life on the occasion of his appointment as the Regius Professor of Modern History at Cambridge,[12] it is a testament to both his academic scholarship and moral conscience. Here is the synthesis of Acton

---

ed. Akis Kalaitzidis and Gregory W. Streich (Santa Barbara: Greenwood, 2011), 71.

[11] Acton, "Nationality," in *Lord Acton: Historical and Moral Essays*, 123.

[12] For a detailed survey of Acton's career at Cambridge, see Owen Chadwick, "Professor Lord Acton," in *Lord Acton: Historian and Moralist*, 1–38.

the historian and the moralist. History is to be written with the goal of establishing the certainty of points of fact rather than merely pouring out a deluge of information; it is to be written dispassionately but never without reference to the enduring moral law. The historian must always be prepared to render moral judgment lest too much explaining end with too much excusing. Years earlier Acton had written to his former teacher Ignaz Döllinger that "the *History of Liberty* should indeed not be a history of the world, but rather a kind of philosophy of history."[13] The inaugural lecture is the closest extant expression of that synthesis, an ingenious mixture of the theory and practice of history. In this lecture Acton also returns to the themes of the earlier essays and unpacks how the reign of conscience, as it unfolded in history, has made possible the discipline of modern history.

The lecture "Beginning of the Modern State" (1899–1901) touches upon the origins of the claims of conscience in medieval civilization that shape the ebb and flow of modern history: "The line of march will prove, on the whole, to have been from force and cruelty to consent and association, to humanity, rational persuasion, and the persistent appeal to common, simple, and evident maxims."[14] Acton draws these lines from the Ottoman Conquest to the conflicts of emerging great powers over Italy and to the coronation of Emperor Charles V. In many ways this lecture is a return to and further development of the ideas within the earlier lectures, "The History of Freedom in Christianity" and "Inaugural Lecture on the Study of History."

In "The New World" (1899–1901) Acton turns his attention to the developments in the Western Hemisphere. While Acton wrote much about the United States and North American

---

[13] Acton to Döllinger, February 11, 1881, excerpted in *Selected Writings of Lord Acton*, ed. J. Rufus Fears, 3 vols. (Indianapolis: Liberty Fund, 1985–88), 3:494. For an account of Acton's education, including his time studying with Döllinger, see James C. Holland, "The Legacy of an Education," in *Lord Acton: Historian and Moralist*, 139–52.

[14] Acton, "Beginning of the Modern State," in *Lord Acton: Historical and Moral Essays*, 197.

colonial history, here is a unique lecture focused on early Spanish and Portuguese exploration and the colonial history of Latin America. From an examination of the economic motivations of Portuguese exploration, the cruel and entrepreneurial exploits of the conquistadors, to the beginnings of the slave trade, Acton brings to life the idea that "history is often made by energetic men, steadfastly following ideas, mostly wrong, that determine events."[15]

The final three selections, "The Rise of the Whigs" (1899–1901), Acton's review of Thomas Macknight's *The Life and Times of Edmund Burke* (1858), and "The American Revolution" (1899–1901), provide valuable insights into the Anglo-American tradition of liberty. "The Rise of the Whigs" documents the origins of English Liberalism in the thought and political action of English Nonconformists during the reign of Charles II. The experience of the English Civil War conditioned their moderate and practical approach to liberty: "Monarchy, Aristocracy, Prelacy, were things that could be made innocuous, that could be adjusted, limited, and preserved."[16] Out of religious dissent arose general and universal principles that Acton, both aristocratic and Catholic, made his own. This marriage between principled and practical politics was best embodied by Whig statesman Edmund Burke. Acton's first contribution to the *Rambler*, a brilliant and often controversial journal of Catholic opinion of which Acton would later be editor, was his review of Macknight's *The Life and Times of Edmund Burke*. Burke is of special interest to Catholics, "for Burke was the wisest, the most sincere, and the most disinterested of all the advocates of the Catholic cause."[17] Acton notes that this advocacy was not merely political but intellectual for, as a historian, Burke was free of the

---

[15] Acton, "The New World," in *Lord Acton: Historical and Moral Essays*, 232.

[16] Acton, "The Rise of the Whigs," in *Lord Acton: Historical and Moral Essays*, 243.

[17] Acton, "The Life and Times of Edmund Burke," in *Lord Acton: Historical and Moral Essays*, 245.

anti-medieval and anti-Catholic prejudice that shaped the writings of British historians of the time. Burke's approach served very much as a model for the young Acton.[18] The final selection in this collection, "The American Revolution" (1899–1901), is a succinct examination of the causes, principles, conduct, and legacy of that event. It delves into the revolution's relationship to the ancient cause of liberty and the proximate antecedents in the history of liberty in Britain in general and among the Whigs in particular. Acton is careful to note the shortcomings of the revolution but concludes, "And yet, by the development of the principle of Federalism, it has produced a community more powerful, more prosperous, more intelligent, and more free than any other which the world has seen."[19]

The texts presented in this collection are themselves drawn primarily from two early anthologies of Acton's writings, *The History of Freedom and Other Essays* and *Lectures on Modern History*, both edited by John Neville Figgis and Reginald Vere Laurence. Acton's review of Thomas Macknight's *The Life and Times of Edmund Burke* is reprinted from the *Rambler*. These essays were also checked against the later collection, *Selected Writings of Lord Acton*, edited by J. Rufus Fears. Acton's original text has been retained almost entirely here, but a few minor changes have been made to make spelling consistent across the selections.

My own thinking about and along with Acton has been shaped profoundly by Gertrude Himmelfarb's masterful biography *Lord Acton: A Study in Conscience and Politics*, which I would commend to any reader interested in the life and ideas of Lord Acton. The recently published *Lord Acton: Historian and Moralist*, edited by Samuel Gregg, is an excellent collection of essays by a wide variety of scholars on the life and thought of Lord Acton that

---

[18] On tensions between the thought of Burke and Acton's mature thought, see Russell Kirk, "Lord Acton on Revolution," in *Lord Acton: Historian and Moralist*, 125–38.

[19] Acton, "The American Revolution," in *Lord Acton: Historical and Moral Essays*, 262. For a discussion of Acton's thought on America, see Stephen J. Tonsor, "Quest for Liberty: America in Acton's Thought," in *Lord Acton: Historian and Moralist*, 113–23.

is also highly recommended to the reader. It is my hope that the present anthology will serve the reader well as a gateway to the writings and thought of Lord Acton the historian, moralist, and champion of liberty.

1

THE HISTORY OF FREEDOM
IN ANTIQUITY*

L iberty, next to religion, has been the motive of good deeds
and the common pretext of crime, from the sowing of the
seed at Athens, two thousand four hundred and sixty years ago,
until the ripened harvest was gathered by men of our race. It
is the delicate fruit of a mature civilisation; and scarcely a century has passed since nations, that knew the meaning of the
term, resolved to be free. In every age its progress has been
beset by its natural enemies, by ignorance and superstition, by
lust of conquest and by love of ease, by the strong man's craving for power, and the poor man's craving for food. During
long intervals it has been utterly arrested, when nations were
being rescued from barbarism and from the grasp of strangers,
and when the perpetual struggle for existence, depriving men
of all interest and understanding in politics, has made them
eager to sell their birthright for a pottage, and ignorant of the

---

*Published in Lord Acton, *The History of Freedom in Antiquity and The
History of Freedom in Christianity, Two Addresses delivered to the members of
the Bridgnorth Institute at the Agricultural Hall, February 26, and May 28,
1877* (Bridgnorth: C. Edkins, 1877). Reprinted in *The History of Freedom
and Other Essays*, ed. John Neville Figgis and Reginald Vere Laurence
(London: Macmillan, 1907), 1–29; *Selected Writings of Lord Acton*, ed.
J. Rufus Fears, 3 vols. (Indianapolis: Liberty Fund, 1985–88), 1:5–28.

treasure they resigned. At all times sincere friends of freedom have been rare, and its triumphs have been due to minorities, that have prevailed by associating themselves with auxiliaries whose objects often differed from their own; and this association, which is always dangerous, has been sometimes disastrous, by giving to opponents just grounds of opposition, and by kindling dispute over the spoils in the hour of success. No obstacle has been so constant, or so difficult to overcome, as uncertainty and confusion touching the nature of true liberty. If hostile interests have wrought much injury, false ideas have wrought still more; and its advance is recorded in the increase of knowledge, as much as in the improvement of laws. The history of institutions is often a history of deception and illusions; for their virtue depends on the ideas that produce and on the spirit that preserves them, and the form may remain unaltered when the substance has passed away.

A few familiar examples from modern politics will explain why it is that the burden of my argument will lie outside the domain of legislation. It is often said that our Constitution attained its formal perfection in 1679, when the Habeas Corpus Act was passed. Yet Charles II succeeded, only two years later, in making himself independent of Parliament. In 1789, while the States-General assembled at Versailles, the Spanish Cortes, older than Magna Charta and more venerable than our House of Commons, were summoned after an interval of generations, but they immediately prayed the King to abstain from consulting them, and to make his reforms of his own wisdom and authority. According to the common opinion, indirect elections are a safeguard of conservatism. But all the Assemblies of the French Revolution issued from indirect elections. A restricted suffrage is another reputed security for monarchy. But the Parliament of Charles X, which was returned by 90,000 electors, resisted and overthrew the throne; while the Parliament of Louis Philippe, chosen by a Constitution of 250,000, obsequiously promoted the reactionary policy of his Ministers, and in the fatal division which, by rejecting reform, laid the monarchy in the dust, Guizot's majority was obtained by the votes of 129 public functionaries. An unpaid legislature is, for obvious reasons, more independent than most of the Continental legislatures which receive pay. But it would be unreasonable in America to send a member as far as from here to Constantinople to live for twelve months at his own expense in the dearest of capital cities. Legally and to outward seeming the American President is the successor of Washington, and still enjoys powers devised and limited by the Convention of Philadelphia. In reality the new President differs from the Magistrate imagined by the Fathers of the Republic as widely as Monarchy from Democracy, for he is expected to make 70,000 changes in the public service; fifty years ago John Quincy Adams dismissed only two men. The purchase of judicial appointments is manifestly indefensible; yet in the old French monarchy that monstrous practice created the only corporation able to resist the king. Official corruption, which would ruin a commonwealth, serves in Russia as a salutary relief from the pressure of absolutism. There are conditions in which it is scarcely a hyperbole to say that slavery itself is a stage on the road to freedom. Therefore we are not so much concerned this evening with the dead letter of edicts and of statutes as with the living thoughts of men. A century ago it was perfectly well known that whoever had one audience of a Master in Chancery was made to pay for three, but no man heeded the enormity until it suggested to a young lawyer that it might be well to question and examine with rigorous suspicion every part of a system in which such things were done. The day on which that gleam lighted up the clear hard mind of Jeremy Bentham is memorable in the political calendar beyond the entire administration of many statesmen. It would be easy to point out a paragraph in St. Augustine, or a sentence of Grotius that outweighs in influence the Acts of fifty Parliaments, and our cause owes more to Cicero and Seneca, to Vinet and Tocqueville, than to the laws of Lycurgus or the Five Codes of France.

By liberty I mean the assurance that every man shall be protected in doing what he believes his duty against the influence of authority and majorities, custom and opinion. The State is competent to assign duties and draw the line between good and evil only in its immediate sphere. Beyond the limits of things necessary for its well-being, it can only give indirect help to fight the battle of life by promoting the influences which prevail against temptation,—religion, education, and the distribution of wealth. In ancient times the State absorbed authorities not its own, and intruded on the domain of personal freedom. In the Middle Ages it possessed too little authority, and suffered others to intrude. Modern States fall habitually into both excesses. The most certain test by which we judge whether a country is really free is the amount of security enjoyed by minorities. Liberty, by this definition, is the essential condition and guardian of religion; and it is in the history of the Chosen People, accordingly, that the first illustrations of my subject are obtained. The government of the Israelites was a Federation, held together by no political authority, but by the unity of race and faith, and founded, not on physical force, but on a voluntary covenant. The principle of self-government was carried out not only in each tribe, but in every group of at least 120 families; and there was neither privilege of rank nor inequality before the law. Monarchy was so alien to the primitive spirit of the community that it was resisted by Samuel in that momentous protestation and warning which all the kingdoms of Asia and many of the kingdoms of Europe have unceasingly confirmed. The throne was erected on a compact; and the king was deprived of the right of legislation among a people that recognised no lawgiver but God, whose highest aim in politics was to restore the original purity of the constitution, and to make its government conform to the ideal type that was hallowed by the sanctions of heaven. The inspired men who rose in unfailing succession to prophesy against the usurper and the tyrant, constantly proclaimed that the laws, which were divine, were paramount over sinful rulers, and appealed from the established authorities, from the king, the priests, and the princes of the people, to the healing forces that slept in the uncorrupted consciences of the masses. Thus the example of the Hebrew nation laid down the parallel lines on which all freedom has been won—the doctrine of national tradition and the doctrine of the higher law; the principle that a constitution grows from a root, by process of development, and not of essential change; and the principle that all political authorities must be tested and reformed according to a code which was not made by man. The operation of these principles, in unison, or in antagonism, occupies the whole of the space we are going over together.

The conflict between liberty under divine authority and the absolutism of human authorities ended disastrously. In the year 622 a supreme effort was made at Jerusalem to reform and preserve the State. The High Priest produced from the temple of Jehovah the book of the deserted and forgotten Law, and both king and people bound themselves by solemn oaths to observe it. But that early example of limited monarchy and of the supremacy of law neither lasted nor spread; and the forces by which freedom has conquered must be sought elsewhere. In the very year 586, in which the flood of Asiatic despotism closed over the city which had been, and was destined again to be, the sanctuary of freedom in the East, a new home was prepared for it in the West, where, guarded by the sea and the mountains, and by valiant hearts, that stately plant was reared under whose shade we dwell, and which is extending its invincible arms so slowly and yet so surely over the civilised world.

According to a famous saying of the most famous authoress of the Continent, liberty is ancient, and it is despotism that is new. It has been the pride of recent historians to vindicate the truth of that maxim. The heroic age of Greece confirms it, and it is still more conspicuously true of Teutonic Europe. Wherever we can trace the earlier life of the Aryan nations we discover germs which favouring circumstances and assiduous culture might have developed into free societies. They exhibit some sense of common interest in common concerns, little reverence for external authority, and an imperfect sense of the function and supremacy of the State. Where the division of property and labour is incomplete there is little division of classes and of power. Until societies are tried by the complex problems of civilisation they may escape despotism, as societies that are undisturbed by religious diversity avoid persecution. In general, the forms of the patriarchal age failed to resist the growth of absolute States when the difficulties and temptations of advancing life began to tell; and with one sovereign exception, which is not within my scope today, it is scarcely possible to trace their survival in the institutions of later times. Six hundred years before the birth of Christ absolutism held unbounded sway. Throughout the East it was propped by the unchanging influence of priests and armies. In the West, where there were no sacred books requiring trained interpreters, the priesthood acquired no preponderance, and when the kings were overthrown their powers passed to aristocracies of birth. What followed, during many generations, was the cruel domination of class over class, the oppression of the poor by the rich, and of the ignorant by the wise. The spirit of that domination found passionate utterance in the verses of the aristocratic poet Theognis, a man of genius and refinement, who avows that he longed to drink the blood of his political adversaries. From these oppressors the people of many cities sought deliverance in the less intolerable tyranny of revolutionary usurpers. The remedy gave new shape and energy to the evil. The tyrants were often men of surprising capacity and merit, like some of those who, in the fourteenth century, made themselves lords of Italian cities; but rights secured by equal laws and by sharing power existed nowhere.

From this universal degradation the world was rescued by the most gifted of the nations. Athens, which like other cities was distracted and oppressed by a privileged class, avoided violence and appointed Solon to revise its laws. It was the happiest choice that history records. Solon was not only the wisest man to be found in Athens, but the most profound political genius of antiquity; and the easy, bloodless, and pacific revolution by which he accomplished the deliverance of his country was the first step in a career which our age glories in pursuing, and instituted a power which has done more than anything, except revealed religion, for the regeneration of society. The upper class had possessed the right of making and administering the laws, and he left them in possession, only transferring to wealth what had been the privilege of birth. To the rich, who alone had the means of sustaining the burden of public service in taxation and war, Solon gave a share of power proportioned to the demands made on their resources. The poorest classes were exempt from direct taxes, but were excluded from office. Solon gave them a voice in electing magistrates from the classes above them, and the right of calling them to account. This concession, apparently so slender, was the beginning of a mighty change. It introduced the idea that a man ought to have a voice in selecting those to whose rectitude and wisdom he is compelled to trust his fortune, his family, and his life. And this idea completely inverted the notion of human authority, for it inaugurated the reign of moral influence where all political power had depended on moral force. Government by consent superseded government by compulsion, and the pyramid which had stood on a point was made to stand upon its base. By making every citizen the guardian of his own interest Solon admitted the element of Democracy into the State. The greatest glory of a ruler, he said, is to create a popular government. Believing that no man can be entirely trusted, he subjected all who exercised power to the vigilant control of those for whom they acted.

The only resource against political disorders that had been known till then was the concentration of power. Solon undertook to effect the same object by the distribution of power. He gave to the common people as much influence as he thought them able to employ, that the State might be exempt from arbitrary government. It is the essence of Democracy, he said, to obey no master but the law. Solon recognised the principle that political forms are not final or inviolable, and must adapt themselves to facts; and he provided so well for the revision of his constitution, without breach of continuity or loss of stability, that for centuries after his death the Attic orators attributed to him, and quoted by his name, the whole structure of Athenian law. The direction of its growth was determined by the fundamental doctrine of Solon, that political power ought to be commensurate with public service. In the Persian war the services of the Democracy eclipsed those of the Patrician orders, for the fleet that swept the Asiatics from the Aegean Sea was manned by the poorer Athenians. That class, whose valour had saved the State and had preserved European civilisation, had gained a title to increase of influence and privilege. The offices of State, which had been a monopoly of the rich, were thrown open to the poor, and in order to make sure that they should obtain their share, all but the highest commands were distributed by lot.

Whilst the ancient authorities were decaying, there was no accepted standard of moral and political right to make the framework of society fast in the midst of change. The instability that had seized on the forms threatened the very principles of government. The national beliefs were yielding to doubt, and doubt was not yet making way for knowledge. There had been a time when the obligations of public as well as private life were identified with the will of the gods. But that time had passed. Pallas, the ethereal goddess of the Athenians, and the Sun god whose oracles, delivered from the temple between the twin summits of Parnassus, did so much for the Greek nationality, aided in keeping up a lofty ideal of religion; but when the enlightened men of Greece learnt to apply their keen faculty of reasoning to the system of their inherited belief, they became quickly conscious that the conceptions of the gods corrupted the life and degraded the minds of the public. Popular morality could not be sustained by the popular religion. The moral instruction which was no longer supplied by the gods could not yet be found in books. There was no venerable code expounded by experts, no doctrine proclaimed by men of reputed sanctity like those teachers of the far East whose words still rule the fate of nearly half mankind. The effort to account for things by close observation and exact reasoning began by destroying. There came a time when the philosophers of the Porch and the Academy wrought the dictates of wisdom and virtue into a system so consistent and profound that it has vastly shortened the task of the Christian divines. But that time had not yet come.

The epoch of doubt and transition during which the Greeks passed from the dim fancies of mythology to the fierce light of science was the age of Pericles, and the endeavour to substitute certain truth for the prescriptions of impaired authorities, which was then beginning to absorb the energies of the Greek intellect, is the grandest movement in the profane annals of mankind, for to it we owe, even after the immeasurable progress accomplished by Christianity, much of our philosophy and far the better part of the political knowledge we possess. Pericles, who was at the head of the Athenian Government, was the first statesman who encountered the problem which the rapid weakening of traditions forced on the political world. No authority in morals or in politics remained unshaken by the motion that was in the air. No guide could be confidently trusted; there was no available criterion to appeal to, for the means of controlling or denying convictions that prevailed among the people. The popular sentiment as to what was right might be mistaken, but it was subject to no test. The people were, for practical purposes, the seat of the knowledge of good and evil. The people, therefore, were the seat of power.

The political philosophy of Pericles consisted of this conclusion. He resolutely struck away all the props that still sustained the artificial preponderance of wealth. For the ancient doctrine that power goes with land, he introduced the idea that power ought to be so equitably diffused as to afford equal security to all. That one part of the community should govern the whole, or that one class should make laws for another, he declared to be tyrannical. The abolition of privilege would have served only to transfer the supremacy from the rich to the poor, if Pericles had not redressed the balance by restricting the right of citizenship to Athenians of pure descent. By this measure the class which formed what we should call the third estate was brought down to 14,000 citizens, and became about equal in numbers with the higher ranks. Pericles held that every Athenian who neglected to take his part in the public business inflicted an injury on the commonwealth. That none might be excluded by poverty, he caused the poor to be paid for their attendance out of the funds of the State; for his administration of the federal tribute had brought together a treasure of more than two million sterling. The instrument of his sway was the art of speaking. He governed by persuasion. Everything was decided by argument in open deliberation, and every influence bowed before the ascendency of mind. The idea that the object of constitutions is not to confirm the predominance of any interest, but to prevent it; to preserve with equal care the independence of labour and the security of property; to make the rich safe against envy, and the poor against oppression, marks the highest level attained by the statesmanship of Greece. It hardly survived the great patriot who conceived it; and all history has been occupied with the endeavour to upset the balance of power by giving the advantage to money, land, or numbers. A generation followed that has never been equalled in talent—a generation of men whose works, in poetry and eloquence, are still the envy of the world, and in history, philosophy, and politics remain unsurpassed. But it produced no successor to Pericles, and no man was able to wield the sceptre that fell from his hand.

It was a momentous step in the progress of nations when the principle that every interest should have the right and the means of asserting itself was adopted by the Athenian Constitution. But for those who were beaten in the vote there was no redress. The law did not check the triumph of majorities or rescue the minority from the dire penalty of having been outnumbered. When the overwhelming influence of Pericles was removed, the conflict between classes raged without restraint, and the slaughter that befell the higher ranks in the Peloponnesian war gave an irresistible preponderance to the lower. The restless and inquiring spirit of the Athenians was prompt to unfold the reason of every institution and the consequences of every principle, and their Constitution ran its course from infancy to decrepitude with unexampled speed.

Two men's lives span the interval from the first admission of popular influence, under Solon, to the downfall of the State. Their history furnishes the classic example of the peril of Democracy under conditions singularly favourable. For the Athenians were not only brave and patriotic and capable of generous sacrifice, but they were the most religious of the Greeks. They venerated the Constitution which had given them prosperity, and equality, and freedom, and never questioned the fundamental laws which regulated the enormous power of the Assembly. They tolerated considerable variety of opinion and great licence of speech; and their humanity towards their slaves roused the indignation even of the most intelligent partisan of aristocracy. Thus they became the only people of antiquity that grew great by democratic institutions. But the possession of unlimited power, which corrodes the conscience, hardens the heart, and confounds the understanding of monarchs, exercised its demoralising influence on the illustrious democracy of Athens. It is bad to be oppressed by a minority, but it is worse to be oppressed by a majority. For there is a reserve of latent power in the masses which, if it is called into play, the minority can seldom resist. But from the absolute will of an entire people there is no appeal, no redemption, no refuge but treason. The humblest and most numerous class of the Athenians united the legislative, the judicial, and, in part, the executive power. The philosophy that was then in the ascendant taught them that there is no law superior to that of the State—the lawgiver is above the law.

It followed that the sovereign people had a right to do whatever was within its power, and was bound by no rule of right or wrong but its own judgment of expediency. On a memorable occasion the assembled Athenians declared it monstrous that they should be prevented from doing whatever they chose. No force that existed could restrain them; and they resolved that no duty should restrain them, and that they would be bound by no laws that were not of their own making. In this way the emancipated people of Athens became a tyrant; and their Government, the pioneer of European freedom, stands condemned with a terrible unanimity by all the wisest of the ancients. They ruined their city by attempting to conduct war by debate in the marketplace. Like the French Republic, they put their unsuccessful commanders to death. They treated their dependencies with such injustice that they lost their maritime Empire. They plundered the rich until the rich conspired with the public enemy, and they crowned their guilt by the martyrdom of Socrates.

When the absolute sway of numbers had endured for near a quarter of a century, nothing but bare existence was left for the State to lose; and the Athenians, wearied and despondent, confessed the true cause of their ruin. They understood that for liberty, justice, and equal laws, it is as necessary that Democracy should restrain itself as it had been that it should restrain the Oligarchy. They resolved to take their stand once more upon the ancient ways, and to restore the order of things which had subsisted when the monopoly of power had been taken from the rich and had not been acquired by the poor. After a first restoration had failed, which is only memorable because Thucydides, whose judgment in politics is never at fault, pronounced it the best Government Athens had enjoyed, the attempt was renewed with more experience and greater singleness of purpose. The hostile parties were reconciled, and proclaimed an amnesty, the first in history. They resolved to govern by concurrence. The laws, which had the sanction of tradition, were reduced to a code; and no act of the sovereign assembly was valid with which they might be found to disagree. Between the sacred lines of the Constitution which were to remain inviolate, and the decrees which met from time to time the needs and notions of the day, a broad distinction was drawn; and the fabric of a law which had been the work of generations was made independent of momentary variations in the popular will. The repentance of the Athenians came too late to save the Republic. But the lesson of their experience endures for all times, for it teaches that government by the whole people, being the government of the most numerous and most powerful class, is an evil of the same nature as unmixed monarchy, and requires, for nearly the same reasons, institutions that shall protect it against itself, and shall uphold the permanent reign of law against arbitrary revolutions of opinion.

Parallel with the rise and fall of Athenian freedom, Rome was employed in working out the same problems, with greater constructive sense, and greater temporary success, but ending at last in a far more terrible catastrophe. That which among the ingenious Athenians had been a development carried forward by the spell of plausible argument, was in Rome a conflict between rival forces. Speculative politics had no attraction for the grim and practical genius of the Romans. They did not consider what would be the cleverest way of getting over a difficulty, but what way was indicated by analogous cases; and they assigned less influence to the impulse and spirit of the moment, than to precedent and example. Their peculiar character prompted them to ascribe the origin of their laws to early times, and in their desire to justify the continuity of their institutions, and to get rid of the reproach of innovation, they imagined the legendary history of the kings of Rome. The energy of their adherence to traditions made their progress slow, they advanced only under compulsion of almost unavoidable necessity, and the same questions recurred often, before they were settled. The constitutional history of the Republic turns on the endeavours of the aristocracy, who claimed to be the only true Romans, to retain in their hands the power they had wrested from the kings, and of the plebeians to get an equal share in it. And this controversy, which the eager and restless Athenians went through in one generation, lasted for more than two centuries, from a time when the *plebs* were excluded from the government of the city, and were taxed, and made to serve without pay, until, in the year 285, they were admitted to political equality. Then followed one hundred and fifty years of unexampled prosperity and glory; and then, out of the original conflict which had been compromised, if not theoretically settled, a new struggle arose which was without an issue.

The mass of poorer families, impoverished by incessant service in war, were reduced to dependence on an aristocracy of about two thousand wealthy men, who divided among themselves the immense domain of the State. When the need became intense the Gracchi tried to relieve it by inducing the richer classes to allot some share in the public lands to the common people. The old and famous aristocracy of birth and rank had made a stubborn resistance, but it knew the art of yielding. The later and more selfish aristocracy was unable to learn it. The character of the people was changed by the sterner motives of dispute. The fight for political power had been carried on with the moderation which is so honourable a quality of party contests in England. But the struggle for the objects of material existence grew to be as ferocious as civil controversies in France. Repulsed by the rich, after a struggle of twenty-two years, the people, three hundred and twenty thousand of whom depended on public rations for food, were ready to follow any man who promised to obtain for them by revolution what they could not obtain by law.

For a time the Senate, representing the ancient and threatened order of things, was strong enough to overcome every popular leader that arose, until Julius Caesar, supported by an army which he had led in an unparalleled career of conquest, and by the famished masses which he won by his lavish liberality, and skilled beyond all other men in the art of governing, converted the Republic into a Monarchy by a series of measures that were neither violent nor injurious.

The Empire preserved the Republican forms until the reign of Diocletian; but the will of the Emperors was as uncontrolled as that of the people had been after the victory of the Tribunes. Their power was arbitrary even when it was most wisely employed, and yet the Roman Empire rendered greater services to the cause of liberty than the Roman Republic. I do not mean by reason of the temporary accident that there were emperors who made good use of their immense opportunities, such as Nerva, of whom Tacitus says that he combined monarchy and liberty, things otherwise incompatible; or that the Empire was what its panegyrists declared it, the perfection of Democracy. In truth it was at best an ill-disguised and odious despotism. But Frederic the Great was a despot; yet he was a friend to toleration and free discussion. The Bonapartes were despotic; yet no liberal ruler was ever more acceptable to the masses of the people than the First Napoleon, after he had destroyed the Republic, in 1805, and the Third Napoleon at the height of his power in 1859. In the same way, the Roman Empire possessed merits which, at a distance, and especially at a great distance of time, concern men more deeply than the tragic tyranny which was felt in the neighbourhood of the Palace. The poor had what they had demanded in vain of the Republic. The rich fared better than during the Triumvirate. The rights of Roman citizens were extended to the people of the provinces. To the imperial epoch belong the better part of Roman literature and nearly the entire Civil Law; and it was the Empire that mitigated slavery, instituted religious toleration, made a beginning of the law of nations, and created a perfect system of the law of property. The Republic which Caesar overthrew had been anything but a free State. It provided admirable securities for the rights of citizens; it treated with savage disregard the rights of men; and allowed the free Roman to inflict atrocious wrongs on his children, on debtors and dependants, on prisoners and slaves. Those deeper ideas of right and duty, which are not found on the tables of municipal law, but with which the generous minds of Greece were conversant, were held of little account, and the philosophy which dealt with such speculations was repeatedly proscribed, as a teacher of sedition and impiety.

At length, in the year 155, the Athenian philosopher Carneades appeared at Rome, on a political mission. During an interval of official business he delivered two public orations, to give the unlettered conquerors of his country a taste of the disputations that flourished in the Attic schools. On the first day he discoursed of natural justice. On the next he denied its existence, arguing that all our notions of good and evil are derived from positive enactment. From the time of that memorable display, the genius of the vanquished held its conquerors in thrall. The most eminent of the public men of Rome, such as Scipio and Cicero, formed their minds on Grecian models, and her jurists underwent the rigorous discipline of Zeno and Chrysippus.

If, drawing the limit in the second century, when the influence of Christianity becomes perceptible, we should form our judgment of the politics of antiquity by its actual legislation, our estimate would be low. The prevailing notions of freedom were imperfect, and the endeavours to realise them were wide of the mark. The ancients understood the regulation of power better than the regulation of liberty. They concentrated so many prerogatives in the State as to leave no footing from which a man could deny its jurisdiction or assign bounds to its activity. If I may employ an expressive anachronism, the vice of the classic State was that it was both Church and State in one. Morality was undistinguished from religion and politics from morals; and in religion, morality, and politics there was only one legislator and one authority. The State, while it did deplorably little for education, for practical science, for the indigent and helpless, or for the spiritual needs of man, nevertheless claimed the use of all his faculties and the determination of all his duties. Individuals and families, associations and dependencies were so much material that the sovereign power consumed for its own purposes. What the slave was in the hands of his master, the citizen was in the hands of the community. The most sacred obligations vanished before the public advantage. The passengers existed

15

for the sake of the ship. By their disregard for private interests, and for the moral welfare and improvement of the people, both Greece and Rome destroyed the vital elements on which the prosperity of nations rests, and perished by the decay of families and the depopulation of the country. They survive not in their institutions, but in their ideas, and by their ideas, especially on the art of government, they are—

> The dead, but sceptred sovereigns who still rule
> Our spirits from their urns.

To them, indeed, may be tracked nearly all the errors that are undermining political society—Communism, Utilitarianism, the confusion between tyranny and authority, and between lawlessness and freedom.

The notion that men lived originally in a state of nature, by violence and without laws, is due to Critias. Communism in its grossest form was recommended by Diogenes of Sinope. According to the Sophists, there is no duty above expediency and no virtue apart from pleasure. Laws are an invention of weak men to rob their betters of the reasonable enjoyment of their superiority. It is better to inflict than to suffer wrong; and as there is no greater good than to do evil without fear of retribution, so there is no worse evil than to suffer without the consolation of revenge. Justice is the mask of a craven spirit; injustice is worldly wisdom; and duty, obedience, self-denial are the impostures of hypocrisy. Government is absolute, and may ordain what it pleases, and no subject can complain that it does him wrong, but as long as he can escape compulsion and punishment, he is always free to disobey. Happiness consists in obtaining power and in eluding the necessity of obedience; and he that gains a throne by perfidy and murder, deserves to be truly envied.

Epicurus differed but little from the propounders of the code of revolutionary despotism. All societies, he said, are founded on contract for mutual protection. Good and evil are conventional terms, for the thunderbolts of heaven fall alike on the just and the unjust. The objection to wrongdoing is not the act, but in its consequences to the wrongdoer. Wise men contrive laws, not to bind, but to protect themselves; and when they prove to be unprofitable they cease to be valid. The illiberal sentiments of even the most illustrious metaphysicians are disclosed in the saying of Aristotle, that the mark of the worst governments is that they leave men free to live as they please.

If you will bear in mind that Socrates, the best of the pagans, knew of no higher criterion for men, of no better guide of conduct, than the laws of each country; that Plato, whose sublime doctrine was so near an anticipation of Christianity that celebrated theologians wished his works to be forbidden, lest men should be content with them, and indifferent to any higher dogma—to whom was granted that prophetic vision of the Just Man, accused, condemned and scourged, and dying on a Cross— nevertheless employed the most splendid intellect ever bestowed on man to advocate the abolition of the family and the exposure of infants; that Aristotle, the ablest moralist of antiquity, saw no harm in making raids upon a neighbouring people, for the sake of reducing them to slavery—still more, if you will consider that, among the moderns, men of genius equal to these have held political doctrines not less criminal or absurd—it will be apparent to you how stubborn a phalanx of error blocks the paths of truth; that pure reason is as powerless as custom to solve the problem of free government; that it can only be the fruit of long, manifold, and painful experience; and that the tracing of the methods by which divine wisdom has educated the nations to appreciate and to assume the duties of freedom, is not the least part of that true philosophy that studies to

> Assert eternal Providence,
> And justify the ways of God to men.

But, having sounded the depth of their errors, I should give you a very inadequate idea of the wisdom of the ancients if I allowed it to appear that their precepts were no better than their practice. While statesmen and senates and popular assemblies supplied examples of every description of blunder, a noble literature arose, in which a priceless treasure of political knowledge was stored, and in which the defects of the existing institutions were exposed with unsparing sagacity. The point on which the ancients were most nearly unanimous is the right of the people to govern, and their inability to govern alone. To meet this difficulty, to give to the popular element a full share without a monopoly of power, they adopted very generally the theory of a mixed Constitution. They differed from our notion of the same thing, because modern Constitutions have been a device for limiting monarchy; with them they were invented to curb democracy. The idea arose in the time of Plato—though he repelled it—when the early monarchies and oligarchies had vanished, and it continued to be cherished long after all democracies had been absorbed in the Roman Empire. But whereas a sovereign prince who surrenders part of his authority yields to the argument of superior force, a sovereign people, relinquishing its own prerogative succumbs to the influence of reason. And it has in all times proved more easy to create limitations by the use of force than by persuasion.

The ancient writers saw very clearly that each principle of government standing alone is carried to excess and provokes a reaction. Monarchy hardens into despotism. Aristocracy contracts into oligarchy. Democracy expands into the supremacy of numbers. They therefore imagined that to restrain each element by combining it with the others would avert the natural process of self-destruction, and endow the State with perpetual youth. But this harmony of monarchy, aristocracy, and democracy blended together, which was the ideal of many writers, and which they supposed to be exhibited by Sparta, by Carthage, and by Rome, was a chimera of philosophers never realised by antiquity. At last Tacitus, wiser than the rest, confessed that the mixed Constitution, however admirable in theory, was difficult to establish and impossible to maintain. His disheartening avowal is not disowned by later experience.

The experiment has been tried more often than I can tell, with a combination of resources that were unknown to the ancients—with Christianity, parliamentary government, and a free press. Yet there is no example of such a balanced Constitution having lasted a century. If it has succeeded anywhere it has been in our favoured country and in our time; and we know not yet how long the wisdom of the nation will preserve the equipoise. The Federal check was as familiar to the ancients as the Constitutional. For the type of all their Republics was the government of a city by its own inhabitants meeting in the public place. An administration embracing many cities was known to them only in the form of the oppression which Sparta exercised over the Messenians, Athens over her Confederates, and Rome over Italy. The resources which, in modern times, enabled a great people to govern itself through a single centre did not exist. Equality could be preserved only by Federalism; and it occurs more often amongst them than in the modern world. If the distribution of power among the several parts of the State is the most efficient restraint on monarchy, the distribution of power among several States is the best check on democracy. By multiplying centres of government and discussion it promotes the diffusion of political knowledge and the maintenance of healthy and independent opinion. It is the protectorate of minorities, and the consecration of self-government. But although it must be enumerated among the better achievements of practical genius in antiquity, it arose from necessity, and its properties were imperfectly investigated in theory.

When the Greeks began to reflect on the problems of society, they first of all accepted things as they were, and did their best to explain and defend them. Inquiry, which with us is stimulated by doubt, began with them in wonder. The most illustrious of the early philosophers, Pythagoras, promulgated a theory for the preservation of political power in the educated class, and ennobled a form of government which was generally founded on popular ignorance and on strong class interests. He preached authority and subordination, and dwelt more on duties than on rights, on religion than on policy; and his system perished in the revolution by which oligarchies were swept away. The revolution afterwards developed its own philosophy, whose excesses I have described.

But between the two eras, between the rigid didactics of the early Pythagoreans and the dissolving theories of Protagoras, a philosopher arose who stood aloof from both extremes, and whose difficult sayings were never really understood or valued until our time. Heraclitus, of Ephesus, deposited his book in the temple of Diana. The book has perished, like the temple and the worship, but its fragments have been collected and interpreted with incredible ardour, by the scholars, the divines, the philosophers, and politicians who have been engaged the most intensely in the toil and stress of this century. The most renowned logician of the last century adopted every one of his propositions; and the most brilliant agitator among Continental Socialists composed a work of eight hundred and forty pages to celebrate his memory.

Heraclitus complained that the masses were deaf to truth, and knew not that one good man counts for more than thousands; but he held the existing order in no superstitious reverence. Strife, he says, is the source and the master of all things. Life is perpetual motion, and repose is death. No man can plunge twice into the same current, for it is always flowing and passing, and is never the same. The only thing fixed and certain in the midst of change is the universal and sovereign reason, which all men may not perceive, but which is common to all. Laws are sustained by no human authority, but by virtue of their derivation from the one law that is divine. These sayings, which recall the grand outlines of political truth which we have found in the Sacred Books, and carry us forward to the latest teaching of our most enlightened contemporaries, would bear a good deal of elucidation and comment. Heraclitus is, unfortunately, so obscure that Socrates could not understand him, and I won't pretend to have succeeded better.

If the topic of my address was the history of political science, the highest and the largest place would belong to Plato and Aristotle. The *Laws* of the one, the *Politics* of the other, are, if I may trust my own experience, the books from which we may learn the most about the principles of politics. The penetration with which those great masters of thought analysed the institutions of Greece, and exposed their vices, is not surpassed by anything in later literature; by Burke or Hamilton, the best political writers of the last century; by Tocqueville or Roscher, the most eminent of our own. But Plato and Aristotle were philosophers, studious not of unguided freedom, but of intelligent government. They saw the disastrous effects of ill-directed striving for liberty; and they resolved that it was better not to strive for it, but to be content with a strong administration, prudently adapted to make men prosperous and happy.

Now liberty and good government do not exclude each other; and there are excellent reasons why they should go together. Liberty is not a means to a higher political end. It is itself the highest political end. It is not for the sake of a good public administration that it is required, but for security in the pursuit of the highest objects of civil society, and of private life. Increase of freedom in the State may sometimes promote mediocrity, and give vitality to prejudice; it may even retard useful legislation, diminish the capacity for war, and restrict the boundaries of Empire. It might be plausibly argued that, if many things would be worse in England or Ireland under an intelligent despotism, some things would be managed better; that the Roman Government was more enlightened under Augustus and Antoninus than under the Senate, in the days of Marius or of Pompey. A generous spirit prefers that his country should be poor, and weak, and of no account, but free, rather than powerful, prosperous, and enslaved. It is better to be the citizen of a humble commonwealth in the Alps, without a prospect of influence beyond the narrow frontier, than a subject of the superb autocracy that overshadows half of Asia and of Europe. But it may be urged, on the other side, that liberty is not the sum or the substitute of all the things men ought to live for; that to be real it must be circumscribed, and that the limits of circumscription vary; that advancing civilisation invests the State with increased rights and duties, and imposes increased burdens and constraint on the subject; that a highly instructed and intelligent community may perceive the benefit of compulsory obligations which, at a lower stage, would be thought unbearable; that liberal progress is not vague or indefinite, but aims at a point where the public is subject to no restrictions but those of which it feels the advantage; that a free country may be less capable of doing much for the advancement of religion, the prevention of vice, or the relief of suffering, than one that does not shrink from confronting great emergencies by some sacrifice of individual rights, and some concentration of power; and that the supreme political object ought to be sometimes postponed to still higher moral objects. My argument involves no collision with these qualifying reflections. We are dealing, not with the effects of freedom, but with its causes. We are seeking out the influences which brought arbitrary government under control, either by the diffusion of power, or by the appeal to an authority which transcends all government, and among those influences the greatest philosophers of Greece have no claim to be reckoned.

It is the Stoics who emancipated mankind from its subjugation to despotic rule, and whose enlightened and elevated views of life bridged the chasm that separates the ancient from the Christian state, and led the way to freedom. Seeing how little security there is that the laws of any land shall be wise or just, and that the unanimous will of a people and the assent of nations are liable to err, the Stoics looked beyond those narrow barriers, and above those inferior sanctions, for the principles that ought to regulate the lives of men and the existence of society. They made it known that there is a will superior to the collective will of man, and a law that overrules those of Solon and Lycurgus. Their test of good government is its conformity to principles that can be traced to a higher legislator. That which we must obey, that to which we are bound to reduce all civil authorities, and to sacrifice every earthly interest, is that immutable law which is perfect and eternal as God Himself, which proceeds from His nature, and reigns over heaven and earth and over all the nations.

The great question is to discover, not what governments prescribe, but what they ought to prescribe; for no prescription is valid against the conscience of mankind. Before God, there is neither Greek nor barbarian, neither rich nor poor, and the slave is as good as his master, for by birth all men are free; they are citizens of that universal commonwealth which embraces all the world, brethren of one family, and children of God. The true guide of our conduct is no outward authority, but the voice of God, who comes down to dwell in our souls, who knows all our thoughts, to whom are owing all the truth we know, and all the good we do; for vice is voluntary, and virtue comes from the grace of the heavenly spirit within.

What the teaching of that divine voice is, the philosophers who had imbibed the sublime ethics of the Porch went on to expound: It is not enough to act up to the written law, or to give all men their due; we ought to give them more than their due, to be generous and beneficent, to devote ourselves for the good of others, seeking our reward in self-denial and sacrifice, acting from the motive of sympathy and not of personal advantage. Therefore we must treat others as we wish to be treated by them, and must persist until death in doing good to our enemies, regardless of unworthiness and ingratitude. For we must be at war with evil, but at peace with men, and it is better to suffer than to commit injustice. True freedom, says the most eloquent of the Stoics, consists in obeying God. A State governed by such principles as these would have been free far beyond the measure of Greek or Roman freedom; for they open a door to religious toleration, and close it against slavery. Neither conquest nor purchase, said Zeno, can make one man the property of another.

These doctrines were adopted and applied by the great jurists of the Empire. The law of nature, they said, is superior to the written law, and slavery contradicts the law of nature. Men have no right to do what they please with their own, or to make profit out of another's loss. Such is the political wisdom of the ancients, touching the foundations of liberty, as we find it in its highest development, in Cicero, and Seneca, and Philo, a Jew of Alexandria. Their writings impress upon us the greatness of the work of preparation for the Gospel which had been accomplished among men on the eve of the mission of the Apostles. St. Augustine, after quoting Seneca, exclaims: "What more could a Christian say than this Pagan has said?" The enlightened pagans had reached nearly the last point attainable without a new dispensation, when the fulness of time was come. We have seen the breadth and the splendour of the domain of Hellenic thought, and it has brought us to the threshold of a greater kingdom.

The best of the later classics speak almost the language of Christianity, and they border on its spirit.

But in all that I have been able to cite from classical literature, three things are wanting,—representative government, the emancipation of the slaves, and liberty of conscience. There were, it is true, deliberative assemblies, chosen by the people; and confederate cities, of which, both in Asia and Africa, there were so many leagues, sent their delegates to sit in Federal Councils. But government by an elected Parliament was even in theory a thing unknown. It is congruous with the nature of Polytheism to admit some measure of toleration. And Socrates, when he avowed that he must obey God rather than the Athenians, and the Stoics, when they set the wise man above the law, were very near giving utterance to the principle. But it was first proclaimed and established by enactment, not in polytheistic and philosophical Greece, but in India, by Asoka, the earliest of the Buddhist kings, two hundred and fifty years before the birth of Christ.

Slavery has been, far more than intolerance, the perpetual curse and reproach of ancient civilisation, and although its rightfulness was disputed as early as the days of Aristotle, and was implicitly, if not definitely, denied by several Stoics, the moral philosophy of the Greeks and Romans, as well as their practice, pronounced decidedly in its favour. But there was one extraordinary people who, in this as in other things, anticipated the purer precept that was to come. Philo of Alexandria is one of the writers whose views on society were most advanced. He applauds not only liberty but equality in the enjoyment of wealth. He believes that a limited democracy, purged of its grosser elements, is the most perfect government, and will extend itself gradually over all the world. By freedom he understood the following of God. Philo, though he required that the condition of the slave should be made compatible with the wants and claims of his higher nature, did not absolutely condemn slavery. But he has put on record the customs of the Essenes of Palestine, a people who, uniting the wisdom of the Gentiles with the faith of the Jews, led lives which were uncontaminated by the surrounding civilisation, and were the first to reject slavery both in principle and practice. They formed a religious community rather than a State, and their numbers did not exceed 4000. But their example testifies to how great a height religious men were able to raise their conception of society even without the succour of the New Testament, and affords the strongest condemnation of their contemporaries.

This, then, is the conclusion to which our survey brings us: There is hardly a truth in politics or in the system of the rights of man that was not grasped by the wisest of the Gentiles and the Jews, or that they did not declare with a refinement of thought and a nobleness of expression that later writers could never surpass. I might go on for hours, reciting to you passages on the law of nature and the duties of man, so solemn and religious that though they come from the profane theatre on the Acropolis, and from the Roman Forum, you would deem that you were listening to the hymns of Christian Churches and the discourse of ordained divines. But although the maxims of the great classic teachers, of Sophocles, and Plato, and Seneca, and the glorious examples of public virtue were in the mouths of all men, there was no power in them to avert the doom of that civilisation for which the blood of so many patriots and the genius of such incomparable writers had been wasted in vain. The liberties of the ancient nations were crushed beneath a hopeless and inevitable despotism, and their vitality was spent, when the new power came forth from Galilee, giving what was wanting to the efficacy of human knowledge to redeem societies as well as men.

It would be presumptuous if I attempted to indicate the numberless channels by which Christian influence gradually penetrated the State. The first striking phenomenon is the slowness with which an action destined to be so prodigious became manifest. Going forth to all nations, in many stages of civilisation and under almost every form of government, Christianity had none of the character of a political apostolate, and in its absorbing mission to individuals did not challenge public authority. The early Christians avoided contact with the State, abstained from the responsibilities of office, and were even reluctant to serve in the army. Cherishing their citizenship of a kingdom not of this world, they despaired of an empire which seemed too powerful to be resisted and too corrupt to be converted, whose institutions, the work and the pride of untold centuries of paganism, drew their sanctions from the gods whom the Christians accounted devils, which plunged its hands from age to age in the blood of martyrs, and was beyond the hope of regeneration and foredoomed to perish. They were so much overawed as to imagine that the fall of the State would be the end of the Church and of the world, and no man dreamed of the boundless future of spiritual and social influence that awaited their religion among the race of destroyers that were bringing the empire of Augustus and of Constantine to humiliation and ruin. The duties of government were less in their thoughts than the private virtues and duties of subjects; and it was long before they became aware of the burden of power in their faith. Down almost to the time of Chrysostom, they shrank from contemplating the obligation to emancipate the slaves.

Although the doctrine of self-reliance and self-denial, which is the foundation of political economy, was written as legibly in the New Testament as in the *Wealth of Nations*, it was not recognised until our age. Tertullian boasts of the passive obedience of the Christians. Melito writes to a pagan Emperor as if he were incapable of giving an unjust command; and in Christian times Optatus thought that whoever presumed to find fault with his sovereign exalted himself almost to the level of a god. But this political quietism was not universal. Origen, the ablest writer of early times, spoke with approval of conspiring for the destruction of tyranny.

After the fourth century the declarations against slavery are earnest and continual. And in a theological but yet pregnant sense, divines of the second century insist on liberty, and divines of the fourth century on equality. There was one essential and inevitable transformation in politics. Popular governments had existed, and also mixed and federal governments, but there had been no limited government, no State the circumference of whose authority had been defined by a force external to its own. That was the great problem which philosophy had raised, and which no statesmanship had been able to solve. Those who proclaimed the assistance of a higher authority had indeed drawn a metaphysical barrier before the governments, but they had not known how to make it real. All that Socrates could effect by way of protest against the tyranny of the reformed democracy was to die for his convictions. The Stoics could only advise the wise man to hold aloof from politics, keeping the unwritten law in his heart. But when Christ said: "Render unto Caesar the things that are Caesar's, and unto God the things that are God's," those words, spoken on His last visit to the Temple, three days before His death, gave to the civil power, under the protection of conscience, a sacredness it had never enjoyed, and bounds it had never acknowledged; and they were the repudiation of absolutism and the inauguration of freedom. For our Lord not only delivered the precept, but created the force to execute it. To maintain the necessary immunity in one supreme sphere, to reduce all political authority within defined limits, ceased to be an aspiration of patient reasoners, and was made the perpetual charge and care of the most energetic institution and the most universal association in the world. The new law, the new spirit, the new authority, gave to liberty a meaning and a value it had not possessed in the philosophy or in the constitution of Greece or Rome before the knowledge of the truth that makes us free.

2

THE HISTORY OF FREEDOM
IN CHRISTIANITY*

When Constantine the Great carried the seat of empire from Rome to Constantinople he set up in the marketplace of the new capital a porphyry pillar which had come from Egypt, and of which a strange tale is told. In a vault beneath he secretly buried the seven sacred emblems of the Roman State, which were guarded by the virgins in the temple of Vesta, with the fire that might never be quenched. On the summit he raised a statue of Apollo, representing himself, and enclosing a fragment of the Cross; and he crowned it with a diadem of rays consisting of the nails employed at the Crucifixion, which his mother was believed to have found at Jerusalem.

The pillar still stands, the most significant monument that exists of the converted empire; for the notion that the nails which had pierced the body of Christ became a fit ornament

---

*Published in Lord Acton, *The History of Freedom in Antiquity and The History of Freedom in Christianity, Two Addresses delivered to the members of the Bridgnorth Institute at the Agricultural Hall, February 26, and May 28, 1877* (Bridgnorth: C. Edkins, 1877). Reprinted in *The History of Freedom and Other Essays,* ed. John Neville Figgis and Reginald Vere Laurence (London: Macmillan, 1907), 30–60; *Selected Writings of Lord Acton,* ed. J. Rufus Fears, 3 vols. (Indianapolis: Liberty Fund, 1985–88), 1:29–53.

for a heathen idol as soon as it was called by the name of a living emperor indicates the position designed for Christianity in the imperial structure of Constantine. Diocletian's attempt to transform the Roman Government into a despotism of the Eastern type had brought on the last and most serious persecution of the Christians; and Constantine, in adopting their faith, intended neither to abandon his predecessor's scheme of policy nor to renounce the fascinations of arbitrary authority, but to strengthen his throne with the support of a religion which had astonished the world by its power of resistance, and to obtain that support absolutely and without a drawback he fixed the seat of his government in the East, with a patriarch of his own creation.

Nobody warned him that by promoting the Christian religion he was tying one of his hands, and surrendering the prerogative of the Caesars. As the acknowledged author of the liberty and superiority of the Church, he was appealed to as the guardian of her unity. He admitted the obligation; he accepted the trust; and the divisions that prevailed among the Christians supplied his successors with many opportunities of extending that protectorate, and preventing any reduction of the claims or of the resources of imperialism.

Constantine declared his own will equivalent to a canon of the Church. According to Justinian, the Roman people had formally transferred to the emperors the entire plentitude of its authority, and, therefore, the Emperor's pleasure, expressed by edict or by letter, had force of law. Even in the fervent age of its conversion the Empire employed its refined civilisation, the accumulated wisdom of ancient sages, the reasonableness and sublety of Roman law, and the entire inheritance of the Jewish, the Pagan, and the Christian world, to make the Church serve as a gilded crutch of absolutism. Neither an enlightened philosophy, nor all the political wisdom of Rome, nor even the faith and virtue of the Christians availed against the incorrigible tradition of antiquity. Something was wanted beyond all the gifts of reflection and experience—a faculty of self-government and self-control, developed like its language in the fibre of a nation, and growing with its growth. This vital element, which many centuries of warfare, of anarchy, of oppression had extinguished in the countries that were still draped in the pomp of ancient civilisation, was deposited on the soil of Christendom by the fertilising stream of migration that overthrew the empire of the West.

In the height of their power the Romans became aware of a race of men that had not abdicated freedom in the hands of a monarch; and the ablest writer of the empire pointed to them with a vague and bitter feeling that, to the institutions of these barbarians, not yet crushed by despotism, the future of the world belonged. Their kings, when they had kings, did not preside at their councils; they were sometimes elective; they were sometimes deposed; and they were bound by oath to act in obedience with the general wish. They enjoyed real authority only in war. This primitive Republicanism, which admits monarchy as an occasional incident, but holds fast to the collective supremacy of all free men, of the constituent authority over all constituted authorities, is the remote germ of Parliamentary government. The action of the State was confined to narrow limits; but, besides his position as head of the State, the king was surrounded by a body of followers attached to him by personal or political ties. In these, his immediate dependants, disobedience or resistance to orders was no more tolerated than in a wife, a child, or a soldier; and a man was expected to murder his own father if his chieftain required it. Thus these Teutonic communities admitted an independence of government that threatened to dissolve society; and a dependence on persons that was dangerous to freedom. It was a system very favourable to corporations, but offering no security to individuals. The State was not likely to oppress its subjects; and was not able to protect them.

The first effect of the great Teutonic migration into the regions civilised by Rome was to throw back Europe many centuries to a condition scarcely more advanced than that from which the institutions of Solon had rescued Athens. Whilst the Greeks preserved the literature, the arts, and the science of antiquity and all the sacred monuments of early Christianity with a completeness of which the rended fragments that have come down to us give no commensurate idea, and even the peasants of Bulgaria knew the New Testament by heart, Western Europe lay under the grasp of masters the ablest of whom could not write their names. The faculty of exact reasoning, of accurate observation, became extinct for five hundred years, and even the sciences most needful to society, medicine and geometry, fell into decay, until the teachers of the West went to school at the feet of Arabian masters. To bring order out of chaotic ruin, to rear a new civilisation and blend hostile and unequal races into a nation, the thing wanted was not liberty but force. And for centuries all progress is attached to the action of men like Clovis, Charlemagne, and William the Norman, who were resolute and peremptory, and prompt to be obeyed.

The spirit of immemorial paganism which had saturated ancient society could not be exorcised except by the combined influence of Church and State; and the universal sense that their union was necessary created the Byzantine despotism. The divines of the Empire who could not fancy Christianity flourishing beyond its borders, insisted that the State is not in the Church, but the Church in the State. This doctrine had scarcely been uttered when the rapid collapse of the Western Empire opened a wider horizon; and Salvianus, a priest at Marseilles, proclaimed that the social virtues, which were decaying amid the civilised Romans, existed in greater purity and promise among the Pagan invaders. They were converted with ease and rapidity; and their conversion was generally brought about by their kings.

Christianity, which in earlier times had addressed itself to the masses, and relied on the principle of liberty, now made its appeal to the rulers, and threw its mighty influence into the scale of authority. The barbarians, who possessed no books, no secular knowledge, no education, except in the schools of the clergy, and who had scarcely acquired the rudiments of religious instruction, turned with childlike attachment to men whose minds were stored with the knowledge of Scripture, of Cicero, of St. Augustine; and in the scanty world of their ideas, the Church was felt to be something infinitely vaster, stronger, holier than their newly founded States. The clergy supplied the means of conducting the new governments, and were made exempt from taxation, from the jurisdiction of the civil magistrate, and of the political administrator. They taught that power ought to be conferred by election; and the Councils of Toledo furnished the framework of the Parliamentary system of Spain, which is, by a long interval, the oldest in the world. But the monarchy of the Goths in Spain, as well as that of the Saxons in England, in both of which the nobles and the prelates surrounded the throne with the semblance of free institutions, passed away; and the people that prospered and overshadowed the rest were the Franks, who had no native nobility, whose law of succession to the Crown became for one thousand years the fixed object of an unchanging superstition, and under whom the feudal system was developed to excess.

Feudalism made land the measure and the master of all things. Having no other source of wealth than the produce of the soil, men depended on the landlord for the means of escaping starvation; and thus his power became paramount over the liberty of the subject and the authority of the State. Every baron, said the French maxim, is sovereign in his own domain. The nations of the West lay between the competing tyrannies of local magnates and of absolute monarchs, when a force was brought upon the scene which proved for a time superior alike to the vassal and his lord.

In the days of the Conquest, when the Normans destroyed the liberties of England, the rude institutions which had come with the Saxons, the Goths, and the Franks from the forests of Germany were suffering decay, and the new element of popular government afterwards supplied by the rise of towns and the formation of a middle class was not yet active. The only influence capable of resisting the feudal hierarchy was the ecclesiastical hierarchy; and they came into collision, when the process of feudalism threatened the independence of the Church by subjecting the prelates severally to that form of personal dependence on the kings which was peculiar to the Teutonic state.

To that conflict of four hundred years we owe the rise of civil liberty. If the Church had continued to buttress the thrones of the king whom it anointed, or if the struggle had terminated speedily in an undivided victory, all Europe would have sunk down under a Byzantine or Muscovite despotism. For the aim of both contending parties was absolute authority. But although liberty was not the end for which they strove, it was the means by which the temporal and the spiritual power called the nations to their aid. The towns of Italy and Germany won their franchises, France got her States-General, and England her Parliament out of the alternate phases of the contest; and as long as it lasted it prevented the rise of divine right. A disposition existed to regard the crown as an estate descending under the law of real property in the family that possessed it. But the authority of religion, and especially of the papacy, was thrown on the side that denied the indefeasible title of kings. In France what was afterwards called the Gallican theory maintained that the reigning house was above the law, and that the sceptre was not to pass away from it as long as there should be princes of the royal blood of St. Louis. But in other countries the oath of fidelity itself attested that it was conditional, and should be kept only during good behaviour; and it was in conformity with the public law to which all monarchs were held subject, that King John was declared a rebel against the barons, and that the men who raised Edward III to the throne from which they had deposed his father invoked the maxim *Vox populi Vox Dei.*

And this doctrine of the divine right of the people to raise up and pull down princes, after obtaining the sanctions of religion, was made to stand on broader grounds, and was strong enough to resist both Church and king. In the struggle between the House of Bruce and the House of Plantagenet for the possession of Scotland and Ireland, the English claim was backed by the censures of Rome. But the Irish and the Scots refused it, and the address in which the Scottish Parliament informed the Pope of their resolution shows how firmly the popular doctrine had taken root. Speaking of Robert Bruce, they say:

> Divine Providence, the laws and customs of the country, which we will defend till death, and the choice of the people, have made him our king. If he should ever betray his principles, and consent that we should be subjects of the English king, then we shall treat him as an

enemy, as the subverter of our rights and his own, and shall elect another in his place. We care not for glory or for wealth, but for that liberty which no true man will give up but with his life.

This estimate of royalty was natural among men accustomed to see those whom they most respected in constant strife with their rulers. Gregory VII had begun the disparagement of civil authorities by saying that they are the work of the devil; and already in his time both parties were driven to acknowledge the sovereignty of the people, and appealed to it as the immediate source of power.

Two centuries later this political theory had gained both in definiteness and in force among the Guelphs, who were the Church party, and among the Ghibellines, or Imperialists. Here are the sentiments of the most celebrated of all the Guelphic writers:

A king who is unfaithful to his duty forfeits his claim to obedience. It is not rebellion to depose him, for he is himself a rebel whom the nation has a right to put down. But it is better to abridge his power, that he may be unable to abuse it. For this purpose, the whole nation ought to have a share in governing itself; the Constitution ought to combine a limited and elective monarchy, with an aristocracy of merit, and such an admixture of democracy as shall admit all classes to office, by popular election. No government has a right to levy taxes beyond the limit determined by the people. All political authority is derived from popular suffrage, and all laws must be made by the people or their representatives. There is no security for us as long as we depend on the will of another man.

This language, which contains the earliest exposition of the Whig theory of the revolution, is taken from the works of St. Thomas Aquinas, of whom Lord Bacon says that he had the largest heart of the school divines. And it is worthwhile to observe that he wrote at the very moment when Simon de Montfort summoned the Commons; and that the politics of the Neapolitan friar are centuries in advance of the English statesman's.

The ablest writer of the Ghibelline party was Marsilius of Padua. "Laws," he said,

> derive their authority from the nation, and are invalid without its assent. As the whole is greater than any part, it is wrong that any part should legislate for the whole; and as men are equal, it is wrong that one should be bound by laws made by another. But in obeying laws to which all men have agreed, all men, in reality, govern themselves. The monarch, who is instituted by the legislature to execute its will, ought to be armed with a force sufficient to coerce individuals, but not sufficient to control the majority of the people. He is responsible to the nation, and subject to the law; and the nation that appoints him, and assigns him his duties, has to see that he obeys the Constitution, and has to dismiss him if he breaks it. The rights of citizens are independent of the faith they profess; and no man may be punished for his religion.

This writer, who saw in some respects farther than Locke or Montesquieu, who, in regard to the sovereignty of the nation, representative government, the superiority of the legislature over the executive, and the liberty of conscience, had so firm a grasp of the principles that were to sway the modern world, lived in the reign of Edward II, five hundred and fifty years ago.

It is significant that these two writers should agree on so many of the fundamental points which have been, ever since, the topic of controversy; for they belonged to hostile schools, and one of them would have thought the other worthy of death. St. Thomas would have made the papacy control all Christian governments. Marsilius would have had the clergy submit to the law of the land; and would have put them under restrictions both as to property and numbers. As the great debate went on, many things gradually made themselves clear, and grew into settled convictions. For these were not only the thoughts of prophetic minds that surpassed the level of contemporaries; there was some prospect that they would master the practical world. The ancient reign of the barons was seriously threatened. The opening of the East by the Crusades had imparted a great stimulus to industry. A stream set in from the country to the towns, and there was no room for the government of towns in the feudal machinery. When men found a way of earning a livelihood without depending for it on the good will of the class that owned the land, the landowner lost much of his importance, and it began to pass to the possessors of moveable wealth. The townspeople not only made themselves free from the control of prelates and barons, but endeavoured to obtain for their own class and interest the command of the State.

The fourteenth century was filled with the tumult of this struggle between democracy and chivalry. The Italian towns, foremost in intelligence and civilisation, led the way with democratic constitutions of an ideal and generally an impracticable type. The Swiss cast off the yoke of Austria. Two long chains of free cities arose, along the valley of the Rhine, and across the heart of Germany. The citizens of Paris got possession of the king, reformed the State, and began their tremendous career of experiments to govern France. But the most healthy and vigorous growth of municipal liberties was in Belgium, of all countries on the Continent, that which has been from immemorial ages the most stubborn in its fidelity to the principle of self-government. So vast were the resources concentrated in the Flemish towns, so widespread was the movement of democracy, that it was long doubtful whether the new interest would not prevail, and whether the ascendency of the military aristocracy would not pass over to the wealth and intelligence of the men that lived by trade. But Rienzi, Marcel, Artevelde, and the other champions of the unripe democracy of those days, lived and died in vain. The upheaval of the middle class had disclosed the need, the passions, the aspirations of the suffering poor below; ferocious insurrections in France and England caused a reaction that retarded for centuries the readjustment of power, and the red spectre of social revolution arose in the track of democracy. The armed citizens of Ghent were crushed by the French chivalry; and monarchy alone reaped the fruit of the change that was going on in the position of classes, and stirred the minds of men.

Looking back over the space of a thousand years, which we call the Middle Ages, to get an estimate of the work they had done, if not towards perfection in their institutions, at least towards attaining the knowledge of political truth, this is what we find: Representative government, which was unknown to the ancients, was almost universal. The methods of election were crude; but the principle that no tax was lawful that was not granted by the class that paid it—that is, that taxation was inseparable from representation—was recognised, not as the privilege of certain countries, but as the right of all. Not a prince in the world, said Philip de Commines, can levy a penny without the consent of the people. Slavery was almost everywhere extinct; and absolute power was deemed more intolerable and more criminal than slavery. The right of insurrection was not only admitted but defined, as a duty sanctioned by religion. Even the principles of the Habeas Corpus Act, and the method of the Income Tax, were already known. The issue of ancient politics was an absolute state planted on slavery. The political produce of the Middle Ages was a system of states in which authority was restricted by the representation of powerful classes, by privileged associations, and by the acknowledgment of duties superior to those which are imposed by man.

As regards the realisation in practice of what was seen to be good, there was almost everything to do. But the great problems of principle had been solved, and we come to the question, How did the sixteenth century husband the treasure which the Middle Ages had stored up? The most visible sign of the times was the decline of the religious influence that had reigned so long. Sixty years passed after the invention of printing, and thirty thousand books had issued from European presses, before anybody undertook to print the Greek Testament. In the days when every State made the unity of faith its first care, it came to be thought that the rights of men, and the duties of neighbours and of rulers towards them, varied according to their religion; and society did not acknowledge the same obligations to a Turk or a Jew, a pagan or a heretic, or a devil worshipper, as to an orthodox Christian. As the ascendency of religion grew weaker, this privilege of treating its enemies on exceptional principles was claimed by the State for its own benefit; and the idea that the ends of government justify the means employed was worked into system by Machiavelli. He was an acute politican, sincerely anxious that the obstacles to the intelligent government of Italy should be swept away. It appeared to him that the most vexatious obstacle to intellect is conscience, and that the vigorous use of statecraft necessary for the success of difficult schemes would never be made if governments allowed themselves to be hampered by the precepts of the copy-book.

His audacious doctrine was avowed in the succeeding age by men whose personal character stood high. They saw that in critical times good men have seldom strength for their goodness, and yield to those who have grasped the meaning of the maxim that you cannot make an omelette if you are afraid to break the eggs. They saw that public morality differs from private, because no Government can turn the other cheek, or can admit that mercy is better than justice. And they could not define the difference or draw the limits of exception; or tell what other standard for a nation's acts there is than the judgment which Heaven pronounces in this world by success.

Machiavelli's teaching would hardly have stood the test of Parliamentary government, for public discussion demands at least the profession of good faith. But it gave an immense impulse to absolutism by silencing the consciences of very religious kings, and made the good and the bad very much alike. Charles V offered 5000 crowns for the murder of an enemy. Ferdinand I and Ferdinand II, Henry III and Louis XIII, each caused his most powerful subject to be treacherously despatched. Elizabeth and Mary Stuart tried to do the same to each other. The way was paved for absolute monarchy to triumph over the spirit and institutions of a better age, not by isolated acts of wickedness, but by a studied philosophy of crime and so thorough a perversion of the moral sense that the like of it had not been since the Stoics reformed the morality of paganism.

The clergy, who had in so many ways served the cause of freedom during the prolonged strife against feudalism and slavery, were associated now with the interest of royalty. Attempts had been made to reform the Church on the Constitutional model; they had failed, but they had united the hierarchy and the crown against the system of divided power as against a common enemy. Strong kings were able to bring the spirituality under subjection in France and Spain, in Sicily and in England. The absolute monarchy of France was built up in the two following centuries by twelve political cardinals. The kings of Spain obtained the same effect almost at a single stroke by reviving and appropriating to their own use the tribunal of the Inquisition, which had been growing obsolete, but now served to arm them with terrors which effectually made them despotic. One generation beheld the change all over Europe, from the anarchy of the days of the Roses to the passionate submission, the gratified acquiescence in tyranny that marks the reign of Henry VIII and the kings of his time.

The tide was running fast when the Reformation began at Wittenberg, and it was to be expected that Luther's influence would stem the flood of absolutism. For he was confronted everywhere by the compact alliance of the Church with the State; and a great part of his country was governed by hostile potentates who were prelates of the Court of Rome. He had, indeed, more to fear from temporal than from spiritual foes. The leading German bishops wished that the Protestant demands should be conceded; and the Pope himself vainly urged on the Emperor a conciliatory policy. But Charles V had outlawed Luther, and attempted to waylay him; and the Dukes of Bavaria were active in beheading and burning his disciples, whilst the democracy of the towns generally took his side. But the dread of revolution was the deepest of his political sentiments; and the gloss by which the Guelphic divines had got over the passive obedience of the apostolic age was characteristic of that medieval method of interpretation which he rejected. He swerved for a moment in his later years; but the substance of his political teaching was eminently conservative, the Lutheran States became the stronghold of rigid immobility, and Lutheran writers constantly condemned the democratic literature that arose in the second age of the Reformation. For the Swiss reformers were bolder than the Germans in mixing up their cause with politics. Zürich and Geneva were Republics, and the spirit of their governments influenced both Zwingli and Calvin.

Zwingli indeed did not shrink from the medieval doctrine that evil magistrates must be cashiered; but he was killed too early to act either deeply or permanently on the political character of Protestantism. Calvin, although a Republican, judged that the people are unfit to govern themselves, and declared the popular assembly an abuse that ought to be abolished. He desired an aristocracy of the elect, armed with the means of punishing not only crime but vice and error. For he thought that the severity of the medieval laws was insufficient for the need of the times; and he favoured the most irresistible weapon which the inquisitorial procedure put into the hand of the Government, the right of subjecting prisoners to intolerable torture, not because they were guilty, but because their guilt could not be proved. His teaching, though not calculated to promote popular institutions, was so adverse to the authority of the surrounding monarchs, that he softened down the expression of his political views in the French edition of his *Institutes*.

The direct political influence of the Reformation effected less than has been supposed. Most States were strong enough to control it. Some, by intense exertion, shut out the pouring flood. Others, with consummate skill, diverted it to their own uses. The Polish Government alone at that time left it to its course. Scotland was the only kingdom in which the Reformation triumphed over the resistance of the State; and Ireland was the only instance where it failed, in spite of Government support. But in almost every other case, both the princes that spread their canvas to the gale and those that faced it, employed the zeal, the alarm, the passions it aroused as instruments for the increase of power. Nations eagerly invested their rulers with every prerogative needed to preserve their faith, and all the care to keep Church and State asunder, and to prevent the confusion of their powers, which had been the work of ages, was renounced in the intensity of the crisis. Atrocious deeds were done, in which religious passion was often the instrument, but policy was the motive.

Fanaticism displays itself in the masses, but the masses were rarely fanaticised, and the crimes ascribed to it were commonly due to the calculations of dispassionate politicians. When the King of France undertook to kill all the Protestants, he was obliged to do it by his own agents. It was nowhere the spontaneous act of the population, and in many towns and in entire provinces the magistrates refused to obey. The motive of the Court was so far from mere fanaticism that the Queen immediately challenged Elizabeth to do the like to the English Catholics. Francis I and Henry II sent nearly a hundred Huguenots to the stake, but they were cordial and assiduous promoters of the Protestant religion in Germany. Sir Nicholas Bacon was one of the ministers who suppressed the mass in England. Yet when the Huguenot refugees came over he liked them so little that he reminded Parliament of the summary way in which Henry V at Agincourt dealt with the Frenchmen who fell into his hands. John Knox thought that every Catholic in Scotland ought to be put to death, and no man ever had disciples of a sterner or more relentless temper. But his counsel was not followed.

All through the religious conflict policy kept the upper hand. When the last of the Reformers died, religion, instead of emancipating the nations, had become an excuse for the criminal art of despots. Calvin preached and Bellarmine lectured, but Machiavelli reigned. Before the close of the century three events occurred which mark the beginning of a momentous change. The massacre of St. Bartholomew convinced the bulk of Calvinists of the lawfulness of rebellion against tyrants, and they became advocates of that doctrine in which the Bishop of Winchester had led the way and which Knox and Buchanan had received, through their master at Paris, straight from the medieval schools. Adopted out of aversion to the King of France, it was soon put in practice against the King of Spain. The revolted Netherlands, by a solemn Act, deposed Philip II, and made themselves independent under the Prince of Orange, who had been, and continued to be, styled his Lieutenant. Their example was important, not only because subjects of one religion deposed a monarch of another, for that had been seen in Scotland, but because, moreover, it put a republic in the place of a monarchy, and forced the public law of Europe to recognise the accomplished revolution. At the same time, the French Catholics, rising against Henry III, who was the most contemptible of tyrants, and against his heir, Henry of Navarre, who, as a Protestant, repelled the majority of the nation, fought for the same principles with sword and pen.

Many shelves might be filled with the books which came out in their defence during half a century, and they include the most comprehensive treatises on laws ever written. Nearly all are vitiated by the defect which disfigured political literature in the Middle Ages. That literature, as I have tried to show, is extremely remarkable, and its services in aiding human progress are very great. But from the death of St. Bernard until the appearance of Sir Thomas More's *Utopia*, there was hardly a writer who did not make his politics subservient to the interest of either Pope or King. And those who came after the Reformation were always thinking of laws as they might affect Catholics or Protestants. Knox thundered against what he called *the Monstrous Regiment of Women*, because the Queen went to mass, and Mariana praised the assassin of Henry III because the King was in league with Huguenots. For the belief that it is right to murder tyrants, first taught among Christians, I believe, by John of Salisbury, the most distinguished English writer of the twelfth century, and confirmed by Roger Bacon, the most celebrated Englishman of the thirteenth, had acquired about this time a fatal significance. Nobody sincerely thought of politics as a law for the just and the unjust, or tried to find out a set of principles that should hold good alike under all changes of religion. Hooker's *Ecclesiastical Polity* stands almost alone among the works I am speaking of, and is still read with admiration by every thoughtful man as the earliest and one of the finest prose classics in our language. But though few of the others have survived, they contributed to hand down masculine notions of limited authority and conditional obedience from the epoch of theory to generations of free men. Even the coarse violence of Buchanan and Boucher was a link in the chain of tradition that connects the Hildebrandine controversy with the Long Parliament, and St. Thomas with Edmund Burke.

That men should understand that governments do not exist by divine right, and that arbitrary government is the violation of divine right, was no doubt the medicine suited to the malady under which Europe languished. But although the knowledge of this truth might become an element of salutary destruction, it could give little aid to progress and reform. Resistance to tyranny implied no faculty of constructing a legal government in its place. Tyburn tree may be a useful thing, but it is better still that the offender should live for repentance and reformation. The principles which discriminate in politics between good and evil, and make States worthy to last, were not yet found.

The French philosopher Charron was one of the men least demoralised by party spirit, and least blinded by zeal for a cause. In a passage almost literally taken from St. Thomas, he describes our subordination under a law of nature, to which all legislation must conform; and he ascertains it not by the light of revealed religion, but by the voice of universal reason, through which God enlightens the consciences of men. Upon this foundation Grotius drew the lines of real political science. In gathering the materials of international law, he had to go beyond national treaties and denominational interests for a principle embracing all mankind. The principles of law must stand, he said, even if we suppose that there is no God. By these inaccurate terms he meant that they must be found independently of revelation. From that time it became possible to make politics a matter of principle and of conscience, so that men and nations differing in all other things could live in peace together, under the sanctions of a common law. Grotius himself used his discovery to little purpose, as he deprived it of immediate effect by admitting that the right to reign may be enjoyed as a freehold, subject to no conditions.

When Cumberland and Pufendorf unfolded the true significance of his doctrine, every settled authority, every triumphant interest recoiled aghast. None were willing to surrender advantages won by force or skill, because they might be in contradiction, not with the Ten Commandments, but with an unknown code, which Grotius himself had not attempted to draw up, and touching which no two philosophers agreed. It was manifest that all persons who had learned that political science is an affair of conscience rather than of might or expediency, must regard their adversaries as men without principle, that the controversy between them would perpetually involve morality, and could not be governed by the plea of good intentions, which softens down the asperities of religious strife. Nearly all the greatest men of the seventeenth century repudiated the innovation. In the eighteenth, the two ideas of Grotius, that there are certain political truths by which every State and every interest must stand or fall, and that society is knit together by a series of real and hypothetical contracts, became, in other hands, the lever that displaced the world. When, by what seemed the operation of an irresistible and constant law, royalty had prevailed over all enemies and all competitors, it became a religion. Its ancient rivals, the baron and the prelate, figured as supporters by its side. Year after year, the assemblies that represented the self-government of provinces and of privileged classes, all over the Continent, met for the last time and passed away, to the satisfaction of the people, who had learned to venerate the throne as the constructor of their unity, the promoter of prosperity and power, the defender of orthodoxy, and the employer of talent.

The Bourbons, who had snatched the crown from a rebellious democracy, the Stuarts, who had come in as usurpers, set up the doctrine that States are formed by the valour, the policy, and the appropriate marriages of the royal family; that the king is consequently anterior to the people, that he is its maker rather than its handiwork, and reigns independently of consent. Theology followed up divine right with passive obedience. In the golden age of religious science, Archbishop Ussher, the most learned of Anglican prelates, and Bossuet, the ablest of the French, declared that resistance to kings is a crime, and that they may lawfully employ compulsion against the faith of their subjects. The philosophers heartily supported the divines. Bacon fixed his hope of all human progress on the strong hand of kings. Descartes advised them to crush all those who might be able to resist their power. Hobbes taught that authority is always in the right. Pascal considered it absurd to reform laws, or to set up an ideal justice against actual force. Even Spinoza, who was a Republican and a Jew, assigned to the State the absolute control of religion.

Monarchy exerted a charm over the imagination, so unlike the unceremonious spirit of the Middle Ages, that, on learning the execution of Charles I, men died of the shock; and the same thing occurred at the death of Louis XVI and of the Duke of Enghien. The classic land of absolute monarchy was France. Richelieu held that it would be impossible to keep the people down if they were suffered to be well off. The Chancellor affirmed that France could not be governed without the right of arbitrary arrest and exile; and that in case of danger to the State it may be well that a hundred innocent men should perish. The Minister of Finance called it sedition to demand that the Crown should keep faith. One who lived on intimate terms with Louis XIV says that even the slightest disobedience to the royal will is a crime to be punished with death. Louis employed these precepts to their fullest extent. He candidly avows that kings are no more bound by the terms of a treaty than by the words of a compliment; and that there is nothing in the possession of their subjects which they may not lawfully take from them. In obedience to this principle, when Marshal Vauban, appalled by the misery of the people, proposed that all existing imposts should be repealed for a single tax that would be less onerous, the King took his advice, but retained all the old taxes whilst he imposed the new. With half the present population, he maintained an army of 450,000 men; nearly twice as large as that which the late Emperor Napoleon assembled to attack Germany. Meanwhile the people starved on grass. France, said Fénelon, is one enormous hospital. French historians believe that in a single generation six millions of people died of want. It would be easy to find tyrants more violent, more malignant, more odious than Louis XIV, but there was not one who ever used his power to inflict greater suffering or greater wrong; and the admiration with which he inspired the most illustrious men of his time denotes the lowest depth to which the turpitude of absolutism has ever degraded the conscience of Europe.

The Republics of that day were, for the most part, so governed as to reconcile men with the less opprobrious vices of monarchy. Poland was a State made up of centrifugal forces. What the nobles called liberty was the right of each of them to veto the acts of the Diet, and to persecute the peasants on his estates—rights which they refused to surrender up to the time of the partition, and thus verified the warning of a preacher spoken long ago: "You will perish, not by invasion or war, but by your infernal liberties." Venice suffered from the opposite evil of excessive concentration. It was the most sagacious of Governments, and would rarely have made mistakes if it had not imputed to others motives as wise as its own, and had taken account of passions and follies of which it had little cognisance. But the supreme power of the nobility had passed to a committee, from the committee to a Council of Ten, from the Ten to three Inquisitors of State; and in this intensely centralised form it became, about the year 1600, a frightful despotism. I have shown you how Machiavelli supplied the immoral theory needful for the consummation of royal absolutism; the absolute oligarchy of Venice required the same assurance against the revolt of conscience. It was provided by a writer as able as Machiavelli, who analysed the wants and resources of aristocracy, and made known that its best security is poison. As late as a century ago, Venetian senators of honourable and even religious lives employed assassins for the public good with no more compunction than Philip II or Charles IX.

The Swiss Cantons, especially Geneva, profoundly influenced opinion in the days preceding the French Revolution, but they had had no part in the earlier movement to inaugurate the reign of law. That honour belongs to the Netherlands alone among the Commonwealths. They earned it, not by their form of government, which was defective and precarious, for the Orange party perpetually plotted against it, and slew the two most eminent of the Republican statesmen, and William III himself intrigued for English aid to set the crown upon his head; but by the freedom of the press, which made Holland the vantage-ground from which, in the darkest hour of oppression, the victims of the oppressors obtained the ear of Europe.

The ordinance of Louis XIV, that every French Protestant should immediately renounce his religion, went out in the year in which James II became king. The Protestant refugees did what their ancestors had done a century before. They asserted the deposing power of subjects over rulers who had broken the original contract between them, and all the Powers, excepting France, countenanced their argument, and sent forth William of Orange on that expedition which was the faint dawn of a brighter day.

It is to this unexampled combination of things on the Continent, more than to her own energy, that England owes her deliverance. The efforts made by the Scots, by the Irish, and at last by the Long Parliament to get rid of the misrule of the Stuarts had been foiled, not by the resistance of Monarchy, but by the helplessness of the Republic. State and Church were swept away; new institutions were raised up under the ablest ruler that had ever sprung from a revolution; and England, seething with the toil of political thought, had produced at least two writers who in many directions saw as far and as clearly as we do now. But Cromwell's Constitution was rolled up like a scroll; Harrington and Lilburne were laughed at for a time and forgotten, the country confessed the failure of its striving, disavowed its aims, and flung itself with enthusiasm, and without any effective stipulations, at the feet of a worthless king.

If the people of England had accomplished no more than this to relieve mankind from the pervading pressure of unlimited monarchy, they would have done more harm than good. By the fanatical treachery with which, violating the Parliament and the law, they contrived the death of King Charles, by the ribaldry of the Latin pamphlet with which Milton justified the act before the world, by persuading the world that the Republicans were hostile alike to liberty and to authority, and did not believe in themselves, they gave strength and reason to the current of Royalism, which, at the Restoration, overwhelmed their work. If there had been nothing to make up for this defect of certainty and of constancy in politics England would have gone the way of other nations.

At that time there was some truth in the old joke which describes the English dislike of speculation by saying that all our philosophy consists of a short catechism in two questions: "What is mind? No matter. What is matter? Never mind." The only accepted appeal was to tradition. Patriots were in the habit of saying that they took their stand upon the ancient ways, and would not have the laws of England changed. To enforce their argument they invented a story that the constitution had come from Troy, and that the Romans had allowed it to subsist untouched. Such fables did not avail against Strafford; and the oracle of precedent sometimes gave responses adverse to the popular cause. In the sovereign question of religion, this was decisive, for the practice of the sixteenth century, as well as of the fifteenth, testified in favour of intolerance. By royal command, the nation had passed four times in one generation from one faith to another, with a facility that made a fatal impression on Laud. In a country that had proscribed every religion in turn, and had submitted to such a variety of penal measures against Lollard and Arian, against Augsburg and Rome, it seemed there could be no danger in cropping the ears of a Puritan.

But an age of stronger conviction had arrived; and men resolved to abandon the ancient ways that led to the scaffold and the rack, and to make the wisdom of their ancestors and the statutes of the land bow before an unwritten law. Religious liberty had been the dream of great Christian writers in the age of Constantine and Valentinian, a dream never wholly realised in the Empire, and rudely dispelled when the barbarians found that it exceeded the resources of their art to govern civilised populations of another religion, and unity of worship was imposed by laws of blood and by theories more cruel than the laws. But from St. Athanasius and St. Ambrose down to Erasmus and More, each age heard the protest of earnest men in behalf of the liberty of conscience, and the peaceful days before the Reformation were full of promise that it would prevail.

In the commotion that followed, men were glad to get tolerated themselves by way of privilege and compromise, and willingly renounced the wider application of the principle. Socinus was the first who, on the ground that Church and State ought to be separated, required universal toleration. But Socinus disarmed his own theory, for he was a strict advocate of passive obedience.

The idea that religious liberty is the generating principle of civil, and that civil liberty is the necessary condition of religious, was a discovery reserved for the seventeenth century. Many years before the names of Milton and Taylor, of Baxter and Locke were made illustrious by their partial condemnation of intolerance, there were men among the Independent congregations who grasped with vigour and sincerity the principle that it is only by abridging the authority of States that the liberty of Churches can be assured. That great political idea, sanctifying freedom and consecrating it to God, teaching men to treasure the liberties of others as their own, and to defend them for the love of justice and charity more than as a claim of right, has been the soul of what is great and good in the progress of the last two hundred years. The cause of religion, even under the unregenerate influence of worldly passion, had as much to do as any clear notions of policy in making this country the foremost of the free. It had been the deepest current in the movement of 1641, and it remained the strongest motive that survived the reaction of 1660.

The greatest writers of the Whig party, Burke and Macaulay, constantly represented the statesmen of the Revolution as the legitimate ancestors of modern liberty. It is humiliating to trace a political lineage to Algernon Sidney, who was the paid agent of the French king; to Lord Russell, who opposed religious toleration at least as much as absolute monarchy; to Shaftesbury, who dipped his hands in the innocent blood shed by the perjury of Titus Oates; to Halifax, who insisted that the plot must be supported even if untrue; to Marlborough, who sent his comrades to perish on an expedition which he had betrayed to the French; to Locke, whose notion of liberty involves nothing more spiritual than the security of property, and is consistent with slavery and persecution; or even to Addison, who conceived that the right of voting taxes belonged to no country but his own. Defoe affirms that from the time of Charles II to that of George I he never knew a politician who truly held the faith of either party; and the perversity of the statesmen who led the assault against the later Stuarts threw back the cause of progress for a century.

When the purport of the secret treaty became suspected by which Louis XIV pledged himself to support Charles II with an army for the destruction of Parliament, if Charles would overthrow the Anglican Church, it was found necessary to make concession to the popular alarm. It was proposed that whenever James should succeed, great part of the royal prerogative and patronage should be transferred to Parliament. At the same time, the disabilities of Nonconformists and Catholics would have been removed. If the Limitation Bill, which Halifax supported with signal ability, had passed, the Monarchical constitution would have advanced, in the seventeenth century, farther than it was destined to do until the second quarter of the nineteenth. But the enemies of James, guided by the Prince of Orange, preferred a Protestant king who should be nearly absolute, to a constitutional king who should be a Catholic. The scheme failed. James succeeded to a power which, in more cautious hands, would have been practically uncontrolled, and the storm that cast him down gathered beyond the sea.

By arresting the preponderance of France, the Revolution of 1688 struck the first real blow at Continental despotism. At home it relieved Dissent, purified justice, developed the national energies and resources, and ultimately, by the Act of Settlement, placed the crown in the gift of the people. But it neither introduced nor determined any important principle, and, that both parties might be able to work together, it left untouched the fundamental question between Whig and Tory. For the divine right of kings it established, in the words of Defoe, the divine right of freeholders; and their domination extended for seventy years, under the authority of John Locke, the philosopher of government by the gentry. Even Hume did not enlarge the bounds of his ideas; and his narrow materialistic belief in the connection between liberty and property captivated even the bolder mind of Fox.

By his idea that the powers of government ought to be divided according to their nature, and not according to the division of classes, which Montesquieu took up and developed with consummate talent, Locke is the originator of the long reign of

English institutions in foreign lands. And his doctrine of resistance, or, as he finally termed it, the appeal to Heaven, ruled the judgment of Chatham at a moment of solemn transition in the history of the world. Our Parliamentary system, managed by the great revolution families, was a contrivance by which electors were compelled, and legislators were induced to vote against their convictions; and the intimidation of the constituencies was rewarded by the corruption of their representatives. About the year 1770 things had been brought back, by indirect ways, nearly to the condition which the Revolution had been designed to remedy forever. Europe seemed incapable of becoming the home of free States. It was from America that the plain ideas that men ought to mind their own business, and that the nation is responsible to Heaven for the acts of the State,—ideas long locked in the breast of solitary thinkers, and hidden among Latin folios,—burst forth like a conqueror upon the world they were destined to transform, under the title of the Rights of Man. Whether the British legislature had a constitutional right to tax a subject colony was hard to say, by the letter of the law. The general presumption was immense on the side of authority; and the world believed that the will of the constituted ruler ought to be supreme, and not the will of the subject people. Very few bold writers went so far as to say that lawful power may be resisted in cases of extreme necessity. But the colonisers of America, who had gone forth not in search of gain, but to escape from laws under which other Englishmen were content to live, were so sensitive even to appearances that the Blue Laws of Connecticut forbade men to walk to church within ten feet of their wives. And the proposed tax, of only £12,000 a year, might have been easily borne. But the reasons why Edward I and his Council were not allowed to tax England were reasons why George III and his Parliament should not tax America. The dispute involved a principle, namely, the right of controlling government. Furthermore, it involved the conclusion that the Parliament brought together by a derisive election had no just right over the unrepresented nation, and it called on the people of England to take back its power. Our best statesmen saw that whatever might be the law, the rights of the nation were at stake. Chatham, in speeches better remembered than any that have been delivered in Parliament, exhorted America to be firm. Lord Camden, the late Chancellor, said: "Taxation and representation are inseparably united. God hath joined them. No British Parliament can separate them."

From the elements of that crisis Burke built up the noblest political philosophy in the world. "I do not know the method," said he, "of drawing up an indictment against a whole people. The natural rights of mankind are indeed sacred things, and if any public measure is proved mischievously to affect them, the objection ought to be fatal to that measure, even if no charter at all could be set up against it. Only a sovereign reason, paramount to all forms of legislation and administration, should dictate." In this way, just a hundred years ago, the opportune reticence, the politic hesitancy of European statesmanship, was at last broken down; and the principle gained ground, that a nation can never abandon its fate to an authority it cannot control. The Americans placed it at the foundation of their new government. They did more; for having subjected all civil authorities to the popular will, they surrounded the popular will with restrictions that the British legislature would not endure.

During the revolution in France the example of England, which had been held up so long, could not for a moment compete with the influence of a country whose institutions were so wisely framed to protect freedom even against the perils of democracy. When Louis Philippe became king, he assured the old Republican, Lafayette, that what he had seen in the United States had convinced him that no government can be so good as a Republic. There was a time in the Presidency of Monroe, about fifty-five years ago, which men still speak of as "the era of good feeling," when most of the incongruities that had come down from the Stuarts had been reformed, and the motives of later divisions were yet inactive. The causes of old-world trouble,— popular ignorance, pauperism, the glaring contrast between rich and poor, religious strife, public debts, standing armies and war,—were almost unknown. No other age or country had solved so successfully the problems that attend the growth of free societies, and time was to bring no further progress.

But I have reached the end of my time, and have hardly come to the beginning of my task. In the ages of which I have spoken, the history of freedom was the history of the thing that was not. But since the Declaration of Independence, or, to speak more justly, since the Spaniards, deprived of their king, made a new government for themselves, the only known forms of liberty, Republics and Constitutional Monarchy, have made their way over the world. It would have been interesting to trace the reaction of America on the Monarchies that achieved its independence; to see how the sudden rise of political economy suggested the idea of applying the methods of science to the art of government; how Louis XVI, after confessing that despotism was useless, even to make men happy by compulsion, appealed to the nation to do what was beyond his skill, and thereby resigned his sceptre to the middle class, and the intelligent men of France, shuddering at the awful recollections of their own experience, struggled to shut out the past, that they might deliver their children from the prince of the world and rescue the living from the clutch of the dead, until the finest opportunity ever given to the world was thrown away, because the passion for equality made vain the hope of freedom.

And I should have wished to show you that the same deliberate rejection of the moral code which smoothed the paths of absolute monarchy and of oligarchy, signalised the advent of the democratic claim to unlimited power,—that one of its leading champions avowed the design of corrupting the moral sense of men, in order to destroy the influence of religion, and a famous apostle of enlightenment and toleration wished that the last king might be strangled with the entrails of the last priest. I would have tried to explain the connection between the doctrine of Adam Smith, that labour is the original source of all wealth, and the conclusion that the producers of wealth virtually compose the nation, by which Sieyès subverted historic France; and to show that Rousseau's definition of the social compact as a voluntary association of equal partners conducted Marat, by short and unavoidable stages, to declare that the poorer classes were absolved, by the law of self-preservation, from the conditions of a contract which awarded to them misery and death; that they were at war with society, and had a right to all they could get by exterminating the rich, and that their inflexible theory of equality, the chief legacy of the Revolution, together with the avowed inadequacy of economic science to grapple with problems of the poor, revived the idea of renovating society on the principle of self-sacrifice, which had been the generous aspiration of the Essenes and the early Christians, of Fathers and Canonists and Friars; of Erasmus, the most celebrated precursor of the Reformation; of Sir Thomas More, its most illustrious victim; and of Fénelon, the most popular of bishops, but which, during the forty years of its revival, has been associated with envy and hatred and bloodshed, and is now the most dangerous enemy lurking in our path.

Last, and most of all, having told so much of the unwisdom of our ancestors, having exposed the sterility of the convulsion that burned what they adored, and made the sins of the Republic mount up as high as those of the monarchy, having shown that Legitimacy, which repudiated the Revolution, and Imperialism, which crowned it, were but disguises of the same element of violence and wrong, I should have wished, in order that my address might not break off without a meaning or a moral, to relate by whom, and in what connection, the true law of the formation of free States was recognised, and how that discovery, closely akin to those which, under the names of development, evolution, and continuity, have given a new and deeper method to other sciences, solved the ancient problem between stability and change, and determined the authority of tradition on the progress of thought; how that theory, which Sir James Mackintosh expressed by saying that Constitutions are not made, but grow; the theory that custom and the national qualities of the governed, and not the will of the government, are the makers of the law; and therefore that the nation, which is the source of its own organic institutions, should be charged with the perpetual custody of their integrity, and with the duty of bringing the form into harmony with the spirit, was made, by the singular co-operation of the purest Conservative intellect with red-handed revolution, of Niebuhr with Mazzini, to yield the idea of nationality, which, far more than the idea of liberty, has governed the movement of the present age.

I do not like to conclude without inviting attention to the impressive fact that so much of the hard fighting, the thinking, the enduring that has contributed to the deliverance of man from the power of man, has been the work of our countrymen, and of their descendants in other lands. We have had to contend, as much as any people, against monarchs of strong will and of resources secured by their foreign possession, against men of rare capacity, against whole dynasties of born tyrants. And yet that proud prerogative stands out on the background of our history. Within a generation of the Conquest, the Normans were compelled to recognise, in some grudging measure, the claims of the English people. When the struggle between Church and State extended to England, our Churchmen learned to associate themselves with the popular cause; and, with few exceptions, neither the hierarchical spirit of the foreign divines, nor the monarchical bias peculiar to the French, characterised the writers of the English school. The Civil Law, transmitted from the degenerate Empire to be the common prop of absolute power, was excluded from England. The Canon Law was restrained, and this country never admitted the Inquisition, nor fully accepted the use of torture which invested Continental royalty with so many terrors. At the end of the Middle Ages foreign writers acknowledged our superiority, and pointed to these causes. After that, our gentry maintained the means of local self-government such as no other country possessed. Divisions in religion forced toleration. The confusion of the common law taught the people that their best safeguard was the independence and the integrity of the judges.

All these explanations lie on the surface, and are as visible as the protecting ocean; but they can only be successive effects of a constant cause which must lie in the same native qualities of perseverance, moderation, individuality, and the manly sense of duty, which give to the English race its supremacy in the stern art of labour, which has enabled it to thrive as no other can on inhospitable shores, and which (although no great people has less of the bloodthirsty craving for glory and an army of 50,000 English soldiers has never been seen in battle) caused Napoleon to exclaim, as he rode away from Waterloo, "It has always been the same since Crecy."

Therefore, if there is reason for pride in the past, there is more for hope in the time to come. Our advantages increase, while other nations fear their neighbours or covet their neighbours' goods. Anomalies and defects there are, fewer and less intolerable, if not less flagrant than of old.

But I have fixed my eyes on the spaces that Heaven's light illuminates, that I may not lay too heavy a strain on the indulgence with which you have accompanied me over the dreary and heart-breaking course by which men have passed to freedom; and because the light that has guided us is still unquenched, and the causes that have carried us so far in the van of free nations have not spent their power; because the story of the future is written in the past, and that which hath been is the same thing that shall be.

3

Scarcely thirty years separate the Europe of Guizot and Metternich from these days of universal suffrage both in France and in United Germany; when a condemned insurgent of 1848 is the constitutional Minister of Austria; when Italy, from the Alps to the Adriatic, is governed by friends of Mazzini; and statesmen who recoiled from the temerities of Peel have doubled the electoral constituency of England. If the philosopher who proclaimed the law that democratic progress is constant and irrepressible had lived to see old age, he would have been startled by the fulfilment of his prophecy. Throughout these years of revolutionary change Sir Thomas Erskine May has been more closely and constantly connected with the centre of public affairs than any other Englishman, and his place, during most of the time, has been at the table of the House of Commons, where he has sat, like Canute, and watched the

*Published as "Sir Erskine May's *Democracy in Europe*," review of *Democracy in Europe: A History*, by Thomas Erskine May, *Quarterly Review* 145 (January 1878): 112–42. Reprinted in Lord Acton, *The History of Freedom and Other Essays*, ed. John Neville Figgis and Reginald Vere Laurence (London: Macmillan, 1907), 61–100; *Selected Writings of Lord Acton*, ed. J. Rufus Fears, 3 vols. (Indianapolis: Liberty Fund, 1985–88), 1:54–85.

rising tide. Few could be better prepared to be the historian of European Democracy than one who, having so long studied the mechanism of popular government in the most illustrious of assemblies at the height of its power, has written its history, and taught its methods to the world.

It is not strange that so delicate and laborious a task should have remained unattempted. Democracy is a gigantic current that has been fed by many springs. Physical and spiritual causes have contributed to swell it. Much has been done by economic theories, and more by economic laws. The propelling force lay sometimes in doctrine and sometimes in fact, and error has been as powerful as truth. Popular progress has been determined at one time by legislation, at others by a book, an invention, or a crime; and we may trace it to the influence of Greek metaphysicians and Roman jurists, of barbarian custom and ecclesiastical law, of the reformers who discarded the canonists, the sectaries who discarded the reformers, and the philosophers who discarded the sects. The scene has changed, as nation succeeded nation, and during the most stagnant epoch of European life the new world stored up the forces that have transformed the old.

A history that should pursue all the subtle threads from end to end might be eminently valuable, but not as a tribute to peace and conciliation. Few discoveries are more irritating than those which expose the pedigree of ideas. Sharp definitions and unsparing analysis would displace the veil beneath which society dissembles its divisions, would make political disputes too violent for compromise and political alliances too precarious for use, and would embitter politics with all the passion of social and religious strife. Sir Erskine May writes for all who take their stand within the broad lines of our constitution. His judgment is averse from extremes. He turns from the discussion of theories, and examines his subject by the daylight of institutions, believing that laws depend much on the condition of society, and little on notions and disputations unsupported by reality. He avows his disbelief even in the influence of Locke, and cares little to inquire how much self-government owes to Independency, or equality to the Quakers; and how democracy was affected by the doctrine that society is founded on contract, that happiness is the end of all government, or labour the only source of wealth; and for this reason, because he always touches ground, and brings to bear, on a vast array of sifted fact, the light of sound sense and tried experience rather than dogmatic precept, all men will read his book with profit, and almost all without offence.

Although he does not insist on inculcating a moral, he has stated in his introductory pages the ideas that guide him; and, indeed, the reader who fails to recognise the lesson of the book in every chapter will read in vain. Sir Erskine May is persuaded that it is the tendency of modern progress to elevate the masses of the people, to increase their part in the work and the fruit of civilisation, in comfort and education, in self-respect and independence, in political knowledge and power. Taken for a universal law of history, this would be as visionary as certain generalisations of Montesquieu and Tocqueville; but with the necessary restrictions of time and place, it cannot fairly be disputed. Another conclusion, supported by a far wider induction, is that democracy, like monarchy, is salutary within limits and fatal in excess; that it is the truest friend of freedom or its most unrelenting foe, according as it is mixed or pure; and this ancient and elementary truth of constitutional government is enforced with every variety of impressive and suggestive illustration from the time of the Patriarchs down to the revolution which, in 1874, converted federal Switzerland into an unqualified democracy governed by the direct voice of the entire people.

The effective distinction between liberty and democracy, which has occupied much of the author's thoughts, cannot be too strongly drawn. Slavery has been so often associated with democracy, that a very able writer pronounced it long ago essential to a democratic state; and the philosophers of the Southern Confederation have urged the theory with extreme fervour. For slavery operates like a restricted franchise, attaches power to property, and hinders Socialism, the infirmity that attends mature democracies. The most intelligent of Greek tyrants, Periander, discouraged the employment of slaves; and Pericles designates the freedom from manual labour as the distinguishing prerogative of Athens. At Rome a tax on manumissions immediately followed the establishment of political equality by Licinius. An impeachment of England for having imposed slavery on America was carefully expunged from the Declaration of Independence; and the French Assembly, having proclaimed the Rights of Man, declared that they did not extend to the colonies. The abolition controversy has made everybody familiar with Burke's saying, that men learn the price of freedom by being masters of slaves.

From the best days of Athens, the days of Anaxagoras, Protagoras, and Socrates, a strange affinity has subsisted between democracy and religious persecution. The bloodiest deed committed between the wars of religion and the revolution was due to the fanaticism of men living under the primitive republic in the Rhaetian Alps; and of six democratic cantons only one tolerated Protestants, and that after a struggle which lasted the better part of two centuries. In 1578 the fifteen Catholic provinces would have joined the revolted Netherlands but for the furious bigotry of Ghent; and the democracy of Friesland was the most intolerant of the States. The aristocratic colonies in America defended toleration against their democratic neighbours, and its triumph in Rhode Island and Pennsylvania was the work not of policy but of religion. The French Republic came to ruin because it found the lesson of religious liberty too hard to learn. Down to the eighteenth century, indeed, it was understood in monarchies more often than in free commonwealths. Richelieu acknowledged the principle whilst he was constructing the despotism of the Bourbons; so did the electors of Brandenburg, at the time when they made themselves absolute; and after the fall of Clarendon, the notion of Indulgence was inseparable from the design of Charles II to subvert the constitution.

A government strong enough to act in defiance of public feeling may disregard the plausible heresy that prevention is better than punishment, for it is able to punish. But a government entirely dependent on opinion looks for some security what that opinion shall be, strives for the control of the forces that shape it, and is fearful of suffering the people to be educated in sentiments hostile to its institutions. When General Grant attempted to grapple with polygamy in Utah, it was found necessary to pack the juries with Gentiles; and the Supreme Court decided that the proceedings were illegal, and that the prisoners must be set free. Even the murderer Lee was absolved, in 1875, by a jury of Mormons.

Modern democracy presents many problems too various and obscure to be solved without a larger range of materials than Tocqueville obtained from his American authorities or his own observation. To understand why the hopes and the fears that it excites have been always inseparable, to determine under what conditions it advances or retards the progress of the people and the welfare of free states, there is no better course than to follow Sir Erskine May upon the road which he has been the first to open.

In the midst of an invincible despotism, among paternal, military, and sacerdotal monarchies, the dawn rises with the deliverance of Israel out of bondage, and with the covenant which began their political life. The tribes broke up into smaller communities, administering their own affairs under the law they had sworn to observe, but which there was no civil power to enforce. They governed themselves without a central authority, a legislature, or a dominant priesthood; and this polity, which, under the forms of primitive society, realised some aspirations of developed democracy, resisted for above three hundred years the constant peril of anarchy and subjugation. The monarchy itself was limited by the same absence of a legislative power, by the submission of the king to the law that bound his subjects, by the perpetual appeal of prophets to the conscience of the people as its appointed guardian, and by the ready resource of deposition. Later still, in the decay of the religious and national constitution, the same ideas appeared with intense energy, in an extraordinary association of men who lived in austerity and self-denial, rejected slavery, maintained equality, and held their property in common, and who constituted in miniature an almost perfect Republic. But the Essenes perished with the city and the Temple, and for many ages the example of the Hebrews was more serviceable to authority than to freedom. After the Reformation, the sects that broke resolutely with the traditions of Church and State as they came down from Catholic times, and sought for their new institutions a higher authority than custom, reverted to the memory of a commonwealth founded on a voluntary contract, on self-government, federalism, equality, in which election was preferred to inheritance, and monarchy was an emblem of the heathen; and they conceived that there was no better model for themselves than a nation constituted by religion, owning no lawgiver but Moses, and obeying no king but God. Political thought had until then been guided by pagan experience.

Among the Greeks, Athens, the boldest pioneer of republican discovery, was the only democracy that prospered. It underwent the changes that were the common lot of Greek society, but it met them in a way that displayed a singular genius for politics. The struggle of competing classes for supremacy, almost everywhere a cause of oppression and bloodshed, became with them a genuine struggle for freedom; and the Athenian constitution grew, with little pressure from below, under the intelligent action of statesmen who were swayed by political reasoning more than by public opinion. They avoided violent and convulsive change, because the rate of their reforms kept ahead of the popular demand. Solon, whose laws began the reign of mind over force, instituted democracy by making the people, not indeed the administrators, but the source of power. He committed the Government not to rank or birth, but to land; and he regulated the political influence of the landowners by their share in the burdens of the public service. To the lower class, who neither bore arms nor paid taxes, and were excluded from the Government, he granted the privilege of choosing and of calling to account the men by whom they were governed, of confirming or rejecting the acts of the legislature and the judgments of the courts. Although he charged the Areopagus with the preservation of his laws, he provided that they might be revised according to need; and the ideal before his mind was government by all free citizens. His concessions to the popular element were narrow, and were carefully guarded. He yielded no more than was necessary to guarantee the attachment of the whole people to the State. But he admitted principles that went further than the claims which he conceded. He took only one step towards democracy, but it was the first of a series.

When the Persian wars, which converted aristocratic Athens into a maritime state, had developed new sources of wealth and a new description of interests, the class which had supplied many of the ships and most of the men that had saved the national independence and founded an empire, could not be excluded from power. Solon's principle, that political influence should be commensurate with political service, broke through the forms in which he had confined it, and the spirit of his constitution was too strong for the letter. The fourth estate was admitted to office, and in order that its candidates might obtain their share, and no more than their share, and that neither interest nor numbers might prevail, many public functionaries were appointed by lot. The Athenian idea of a Republic was to substitute the impersonal supremacy of law for the government of men. Mediocrity was a safeguard against the pretensions of superior capacity, for the established order was in danger, not from the average citizens, but from men, like Miltiades, of exceptional renown. The people of Athens venerated their constitution as a gift of the gods, the source and title of their power, a thing too sacred for wanton change. They had demanded a code, that the unwritten law might no longer be intrepreted at will by Archons and Areopagites; and a well-defined and authoritative legislation was a triumph of the democracy.

So well was this conservative spirit understood, that the revolution which abolished the privileges of the aristocracy was promoted by Aristides and completed by Pericles, men free from the reproach of flattering the multitude. They associated all the free Athenians with the interest of the State, and called them, without distinction of class, to administer the powers that belonged to them. Solon had threatened with the loss of citizenship all who showed themselves indifferent in party conflicts, and Pericles declared that every man who neglected his share of public duty was a useless member of the community. That wealth might confer no unfair advantage, that the poor might not take bribes from the rich, he took them into the pay of the State during their attendance as jurors. That their numbers might give them no unjust superiority, he restricted the right of citizenship to those who came from Athenian parents on both sides; and thus he expelled more than 4000 men of mixed descent from the Assembly. This bold measure, which was made acceptable by a distribution of grain from Egypt among those who proved their full Athenian parentage, reduced the fourth class to an equality with the owners of real property. For Pericles, or Ephialtes—for it would appear that all their reforms had been carried in the year 460, when Ephialtes died—is the first democratic statesman who grasped the notion of political equality. The measures which made all citizens equal might have created a new inequality between classes, and the artificial privilege of land might have been succeeded by the more crushing preponderance of numbers. But Pericles held it to be intolerable that one portion of the people should be required to obey laws which others have the exclusive right of making; and he was able, during thirty years, to preserve the equipoise, governing by the general consent of the community, formed by free debate. He made the undivided people sovereign; but he subjected the popular initiative to a court of revision, and assigned a penalty to the proposer of any measure which should be found to be unconstitutional. Athens, under Pericles, was the most successful Republic that existed before the system of representation; but its splendour ended with his life.

The danger to liberty from the predominance either of privilege or majorities was so manifest, that an idea arose that equality of fortune would be the only way to prevent the conflict of class interests. The philosophers, Phaleas, Plato, Aristotle, suggested various expedients to level the difference between rich and poor. Solon had endeavoured to check the increase of estates; and Pericles had not only strengthened the public resources by bringing the rich under the control of an assembly in which they were not supreme, but he had employed those resources in improving the condition and the capacity of the masses. The grievance of those who were taxed for the benefit of others was easily borne so long as the tribute of the confederates filled the treasury. But the Peloponnesian war increased the strain on the revenue and deprived Athens of its dependencies. The balance was upset; and the policy of making one class give, that another might receive, was recommended not only by the interest of the poor, but by a growing theory, that wealth and poverty make bad citizens, that the middle class is the one most easily led by reason, and that the way to make it predominate is to depress whatever rises above the common level, and to raise whatever falls below it. This theory, which became inseparable from democracy, and contained a force which alone seems able to destroy it, was fatal to Athens, for it drove the minority to treason. The glory of the Athenian democrats is, not that they escaped the worst consequences of their principle, but that, having twice cast out the usurping oligarchy, they set bounds to their own power. They forgave their vanquished enemies; they abolished pay for attendance in the assembly; they established the supremacy of law by making the code superior to the people; they distinguished things that were constitutional from things that were legal, and resolved that no legislative act should pass until it had been pronounced consistent with the constitution.

The causes which ruined the Republic of Athens illustrate the connection of ethics with politics rather than the vices inherent to democracy. A State which has only 30,000 full citizens in a population of 500,000, and is governed, practically, by about 3000 people at a public meeting, is scarcely democratic. The short triumph of Athenian liberty, and its quick decline, belong to an age which possessed no fixed standard of right and wrong. An unparalleled activity of intellect was shaking the credit of the gods, and the gods were the givers of the law. It was a very short step from the suspicion of Protagoras, that there were no gods, to the assertion of Critias that there is no sanction for laws. If nothing was certain in theology, there was no certainty in ethics and no moral obligation. The will of man, not the will of God, was the rule of life, and every man and body of men had the right to do what they had the means of doing. Tyranny was no wrong, and it was hypocrisy to deny oneself the enjoyment it affords. The doctrine of the Sophists gave no limits to power and no security to freedom; it inspired that cry of the Athenians, that they must not be hindered from doing what they pleased, and the speeches of men like Athenagoras and Euphemus, that the democracy may punish men who have done no wrong, and that nothing that is profitable is amiss. And Socrates perished by the reaction which they provoked.

The disciples of Socrates obtained the ear of posterity. Their testimony against the government that put the best of citizens to death is enshrined in writings that compete with Christianity itself for influence on the opinions of men. Greece has governed the world by her philosophy, and the loudest note in Greek philosophy is the protest against Athenian democracy. But although Socrates derided the practice of leaving the choice of magistrates to chance, and Plato admired the bloodstained tyrant Critias, and Aristotle deemed Theramenes a greater statesman than Pericles, yet these are the men who laid the first stones of a purer system, and became the lawgivers of future commonwealths.

The main point in the method of Socrates was essentially democratic. He urged men to bring all things to the test of incessant inquiry, and not to content themselves with the verdict of authorities, majorities, or custom; to judge of right and wrong, not by the will or sentiment of others, but by the light which God has set in each man's reason and conscience. He proclaimed that authority is often wrong, and has no warrant to silence or to impose conviction. But he gave no warrant to resistance. He emancipated men for thought, but not for action. The sublime history of his death shows that the superstition of the State was undisturbed by his contempt for its rulers.

Plato had not his master's patriotism, nor his reverence for the civil power. He believed that no State can command obedience if it does not deserve respect; and he encouraged citizens to despise their government if they were not governed by wise men. To the aristocracy of philosophers he assigned a boundless prerogative; but as no government satisfied that test, his plea for despotism was hypothetical. When the lapse of years roused him from the fantastic dream of his Republic, his belief in divine government moderated his intolerance of human freedom. Plato would not suffer a democratic polity; but he challenged all existing authorities to justify themselves before a superior tribunal; he desired that all constitutions should be thoroughly remodelled, and he supplied the greatest need of Greek democracy, the conviction that the will of the people is subject to the will of God, and that all civil authority, except that of an imaginary state, is limited and conditional. The prodigious vitality of his writings has kept the glaring perils of popular government constantly before mankind; but it has also preserved the belief in ideal politics and the notion of judging the powers of this world by a standard from heaven. There has been no fiercer enemy of democracy; but there has been no stronger advocate of revolution.

In the *Ethics* Aristotle condemns democracy, even with a property qualification, as the worst of governments. But near the end of his life, when he composed his *Politics*, he was brought, grudgingly, to make a memorable concession. To preserve the sovereignty of law, which is the reason and the custom of generations, and to restrict the realm of choice and change, he conceived it best that no class of society should preponderate, that one man should not be subject to another, that all should command and all obey. He advised that power should be distributed to high and low; to the first according to their property, to the others according to numbers; and that it should centre in the middle class. If aristocracy and democracy were fairly combined and balanced against each other, he thought that none would be interested to disturb the serene majesty of impersonal government. To reconcile the two principles, he would admit even the poorer citizens to office and pay them for the discharge of public duties; but he would compel the rich to take their share, and would appoint magistrates by election and not by lot. In his indignation at the extravagance of Plato, and his sense of the significance of facts, he became, against his will, the prophetic exponent of a limited and regenerated democracy. But the *Politics*, which, to the world of living men, is the most valuable of his works, acquired no influence on antiquity, and is never quoted before the time of Cicero. Again it disappeared for many centuries; it was unknown to the Arabian commentators, and in Western Europe it was first brought to light by St. Thomas Aquinas, at the very time when an infusion of popular elements was modifying feudalism, and it helped to emancipate political philosophy from despotic theories and to confirm it in the ways of freedom.

The three generations of the Socratic school did more for the future reign of the people than all the institutions of the States of Greece. They vindicated conscience against authority, and subjected both to a higher law; and they proclaimed that doctrine of a mixed constitution, which has prevailed at last over absolute monarchy, and still has to contend against extreme Republicans and Socialists, and against the masters of a hundred legions. But their views of liberty were based on expediency, not on justice. They legislated for the favoured citizens of Greece, and were conscious of no principle that extended the same rights to the stranger and the slave. That discovery, without which all political science was merely conventional, belongs to the followers of Zeno.

The dimness and poverty of their theological speculation caused the Stoics to attribute the government of the universe less to the uncertain design of gods than to a definite law of nature. By that law, which is superior to religious traditions and national authorities, and which every man can learn from a guardian angel who neither sleeps nor errs, all are governed alike, all are equal, all are bound in charity to each other, as members of one community and children of the same God. The unity of mankind implied the existence of rights and duties common to all men, which legislation neither gives nor takes away. The Stoics held in no esteem the institutions that vary with time and place, and their ideal society resembled a universal Church more than an actual State. In every collision between authority and conscience they preferred the inner to the outer guide; and, in the words of Epictetus, regarded the laws of the gods, not the wretched laws of the dead. Their doctrine of equality, of fraternity, of humanity; their defence of individualism against public authority; their repudiation of slavery, redeemed democracy from the narrowness, the want of principle and of sympathy, which are its reproach among the Greeks. In practical life they preferred a mixed constitution to a purely popular government. Chrysippus thought it impossible to please both gods and men; and Seneca declared that the people is corrupt and incapable, and that nothing was wanting, under Nero, to the fulness of liberty, except the possibility of destroying it. But their lofty conception of freedom, as no exceptional privilege but the birthright of mankind, survived in the law of nations and purified the equity of Rome.

Whilst Dorian oligarchs and Macedonian kings crushed the liberties of Greece, the Roman Republic was ruined, not by its enemies, for there was no enemy it did not conquer, but by its own vices. It was free from many causes of instability and dissolution that were active in Greece—the eager quickness, the philosophic thought, the independent belief, the pursuit of unsubstantial grace and beauty. It was protected by many subtle contrivances against the sovereignty of numbers and against legislation by surprise. Constitutional battles had to be fought over and over again; and progress was so slow, that reforms were often voted many years before they could be carried into effect. The authority allowed to fathers, to masters, to creditors, was as incompatible with the spirit of freedom as the practice of the servile East. The Roman citizen revelled in the luxury of power; and his jealous dread of every change that might impair its enjoyment portended a gloomy oligarchy. The cause which transformed the domination of rigid and exclusive patricians into the model Republic, and which out of the decomposed Republic built up the archetype of all despotism, was the fact that the Roman Commonwealth consisted of two States in one. The constitution was made up of compromises between independent bodies, and the obligation of observing contracts was the standing security for freedom. The plebs obtained self-government and an equal sovereignty, by the aid of the tribunes of the people, the peculiar, salient, and decisive invention of Roman statecraft. The powers conferred on the tribunes, that they might be the guardians of the weak, were ill defined, but practically were irresistible. They could not govern, but they could arrest all government. The first and the last step of plebeian progress was gained neither by violence nor persuasion, but by seceding; and, in like manner, the tribunes overcame all the authorities of the State by the weapon of obstruction. It was by stopping public business for five years that Licinius established

71

democratic equality. The safeguard against abuse was the right of each tribune to veto the acts of his colleagues. As they were independent of their electors, and as there could hardly fail to be one wise and honest man among the ten, this was the most effective instrument for the defence of minorities ever devised by man. After the Hortensian law, which in the year 287 gave to the plebeian assembly co-ordinate legislative authority, the tribunes ceased to represent the cause of a minority, and their work was done.

A scheme less plausible or less hopeful than one which created two sovereign legislatures side by side in the same community would be hard to find. Yet it effectually closed the conflict of centuries, and gave to Rome an epoch of constant prosperity and greatness. No real division subsisted in the people, corresponding to the artificial division in the State. Fifty years passed away before the popular assembly made use of its prerogative, and passed a law in opposition to the senate. Polybius could not detect a flaw in the structure as it stood. The harmony seemed to be complete, and he judged that a more perfect example of composite government could not exist. But during those happy years the cause which wrought the ruin of Roman freedom was in full activity; for it was the condition of perpetual war that brought about the three great changes which were the beginning of the end—the reforms of the Gracchi, the arming of the paupers, and the gift of the Roman suffrage to the people of Italy.

Before the Romans began their career of foreign conquest they possessed an army of 770,000 men; and from that time the consumption of citizens in war was incessant. Regions once crowded with the small freeholds of four or five acres, which were the ideal unit of Roman society and the sinew of the army and the State, were covered with herds of cattle and herds of slaves, and the substance of the governing democracy was drained. The policy of the agrarian reform was to reconstitute this peasant class out of the public domains, that is, out of lands which the ruling families had possessed for generations, which they had bought and sold, inherited, divided, cultivated, and improved. The conflict of interests that had so long slumbered revived with a fury unknown in the controversy between the patricians and the plebs. For it was now a question not of equal rights but of subjugation. The social restoration of democratic elements could not be accomplished without demolishing the senate; and this crisis at last exposed the defect of the machinery and the peril of divided powers that were not to be controlled or reconciled. The popular assembly, led by Gracchus, had the power of making laws; and the only constitutional check was, that one of the tribunes should be induced to bar the proceedings. Accordingly, the tribune Octavius interposed his veto. The tribunician power, the most sacred of powers, which could not be questioned because it was founded on a covenant between the two parts of the community and formed the keystone of their union, was employed, in opposition to the will of the people, to prevent a reform on which the preservation of the democracy depended. Gracchus caused Octavius to be deposed. Though not illegal, this was a thing unheard of, and it seemed to the Romans a sacrilegious act that shook the pillars of the State, for it was the first significant revelation of democratic sovereignty. A tribune might burn the arsenal and betray the city, yet he could not be called to account until his year of office had expired. But when he employed against the people the authority with which they had invested him, the spell was dissolved. The tribunes had been instituted as the champions of the oppressed, when the plebs feared oppression. It was resolved that they should not interfere on the weaker side when the democracy were the strongest. They were chosen by the people as their defence against the aristocracy. It was not to be borne that they should become the agents of the aristocracy to make them once more supreme. Against a popular tribune, whom no colleague was suffered to oppose, the wealthy classes were defenceless. It is true that he held office, and was inviolable, only for a year. But the younger Gracchus was re-elected. The nobles accused him of aiming at the crown. A tribune who should be practically irremovable, as well as legally irresistible, was little less than an emperor. The senate carried on the conflict as men do who fight, not for public interests but for their own existence. They rescinded the agrarian laws. They murdered the popular leaders. They abandoned the constitution to save themselves, and invested Sylla with a power beyond all monarchs, to exterminate their foes. The ghastly conception of a magistrate legally proclaimed superior to all the laws was familiar to the stern spirit of the Romans. The decemvirs had enjoyed that arbitrary authority; but practically they were restrained by the two provisions which alone were deemed efficacious in Rome, the short duration of office, and its distribution among several colleagues. But the appointment of Sylla was neither limited nor divided. It was to last as long as he chose. Whatever he might do was right; and he was empowered to put whomsoever he pleased to death, without trial or accusation. All the victims who were butchered by his satellites suffered with the full sanction of the law.

When at last the democracy conquered, the Augustan monarchy, by which they perpetuated their triumph, was moderate in comparison with the licensed tyranny of the aristocratic chief. The Emperor was the constitutional head of the Republic, armed with all the powers requisite to master the senate. The instrument which had served to cast down the patricians was efficient against the new aristocracy of wealth and office. The tribunician power, conferred in perpetuity, made it unnecessary to create a king or a dictator. Thrice the senate proposed to Augustus the supreme power of making laws. He declared that the power of the tribunes already supplied him with all that he required. It enabled him to preserve the forms of a simulated republic. The most popular of all the magistracies of Rome furnished the marrow of Imperialism. For the Empire was created, not by usurpation, but by the legal act of a jubilant people, eager to close the era of bloodshed and to secure the largess of grain and coin, which amounted, at last, to 900,000 pounds a year. The people transferred to the Emperor the plenitude of their own sovereignty. To limit his delegated power was to challenge their omnipotence, to renew the issue between the many and the few which had been decided at Pharsalus and Philippi. The Romans upheld the absolutism of the Empire because it was their own. The elementary antagonism between liberty and democracy, between the welfare of minorities and the supremacy of masses, became manifest. The friend of the one was a traitor to the other. The dogma, that absolute power may, by the hypothesis of a popular origin, be as legitimate as constitutional freedom, began, by the combined support of the people and the throne, to darken the air.

Legitimate, in the technical sense of modern politics, the Empire was not meant to be. It had no right or claim to subsist apart from the will of the people. To limit the Emperor's authority was to renounce their own; but to take it away was to assert their own. They gave the Empire as they chose. They took it away as they chose. The Revolution was as lawful and as irresponsible as the Empire. Democratic institutions continued to develop. The provinces were no longer subject to an assembly meeting in a distant capital. They obtained the privileges of Roman citizens. Long after Tiberius had stripped the inhabitants of Rome of their electoral function, the provincials continued in undisturbed enjoyment of the right of choosing their own magistrates. They governed themselves like a vast confederation of municipal republics; and, even after Diocletian had brought in the forms as well as the reality of despotism, provincial assemblies, the obscure germ of representative institutions, exercised some control over the Imperial officers.

But the Empire owed the intensity of its force to the popular fiction. The principle, that the Emperor is not subject to laws from which he can dispense others, *princeps legibus solutus,* was interpreted to imply that he was above all legal restraint. There was no appeal from his sentence. He was the living law. The Roman jurists, whilst they adorned their writings with the exalted philosophy of the Stoics, consecrated every excess of Imperial prerogative with those famous maxims which have been balm to so many consciences and have sanctioned so much wrong; and the code of Justinian became the greatest obstacle, next to feudalism, with which liberty had to contend.

Ancient democracy, as it was in Athens in the best days of Pericles, or in Rome when Polybius described it, or even as it is idealised by Aristotle in the Sixth Book of his *Politics*, and by Cicero in the beginning of the Republic, was never more than a partial and insincere solution of the problem of popular government. The ancient politicians aimed no higher than to diffuse power among a numerous class. Their liberty was bound up with slavery. They never attempted to found a free State on the thrift and energy of free labour. They never divined the harder but more grateful task that constitutes the political life of Christian nations.

By humbling the supremacy of rank and wealth; by forbidding the State to encroach on the domain which belongs to God; by teaching man to love his neighbour as himself; by promoting the sense of equality; by condemning the pride of race, which was a stimulus of conquest, and the doctrine of separate descent, which formed the philosopher's defence of slavery; and by addressing not the rulers but the masses of mankind, and making opinion superior to authority, the Church that preached the Gospel to the poor had visible points of contact with democracy. And yet Christianity did not directly influence political progress. The ancient watchword of the Republic was translated by Papinian into the language of the Church: "Summa est ratio quae pro religione fiat:" and for eleven hundred years, from the first to the last of the Constantines, the Christian Empire was as despotic as the pagan.

Meanwhile Western Europe was overrun by men who in their early home had been Republicans. The primitive constitution of the German communities was based on association rather than on subordination. They were accustomed to govern their affairs by common deliberation, and to obey authorities that were temporary and defined. It is one of the desperate enterprises of historical science to trace the free institutions of Europe and America, and Australia, to the life that was led in the forests of Germany. But the new States were founded on conquest, and in war the Germans were commanded by kings. The doctrine of self-government, applied to Gaul and Spain, would have made Frank and Goth disappear in the mass of the conquered people. It needed all the resources of a vigorous monarchy, of a military aristocracy, and of a territorial clergy, to construct States that were able to last. The result was the feudal system, the most absolute contradiction of democracy that has coexisted with civilisation.

The revival of democracy was due neither to the Christian Church nor to the Teutonic State, but to the quarrel between them. The effect followed the cause instantaneously. As soon as Gregory VII made the Papacy independent of the Empire, the great conflict began; and the same pontificate gave birth to the theory of the sovereignty of the people. The Gregorian party argued that the Emperor derived his crown from the nation, and that the nation could take away what it had bestowed. The Imperialists replied that nobody could take away what the nation had given. It is idle to look for the spark either in flint or steel. The object of both parties was unqualified supremacy. Fitznigel has no more idea of ecclesiastical liberty than John of Salisbury of political. Innocent IV is as perfect an absolutist as Peter de Vineis. But each party encouraged democracy in turn, by seeking the aid of the towns; each party in turn appealed to the people, and gave strength to the constitutional theory. In the fourteenth century English Parliaments judged and deposed their kings, as a matter of right; the Estates governed France without king or noble; and the wealth and liberties of the towns, which had worked out their independence from the centre of Italy to the North Sea, promised for a moment to transform European society. Even in the capitals of great princes, in Rome, in Paris, and, for two terrible days, in London, the commons obtained sway. But the curse of instability was on the municipal republics. Strasburg, according to Erasmus and Bodin, the best governed of all, suffered from perpetual commotions. An ingenious historian has reckoned seven thousand revolutions in the Italian cities. The democracies succeeded no better than feudalism in regulating the balance between rich and poor. The atrocities of the Jacquerie, and of Wat Tyler's rebellion, hardened the hearts of men against the common people. Church and State combined to put them down. And the last memorable struggles of medieval liberty—the insurrection of the Comuneros in Castile, the Peasants' War in Germany, the Republic of Florence, and the Revolt of Ghent—were suppressed by Charles V in the early years of the Reformation.

The Middle Ages had forged a complete arsenal of constitutional maxims: trial by jury, taxation by representation, local self-government, ecclesiastical independence, responsible authority. But they were not secured by institutions, and the

Reformation began by making the dry bones more dry. Luther claimed to be the first divine who did justice to the civil power. He made the Lutheran Church the bulwark of political stability, and bequeathed to his disciples the doctrine of divine right and passive obedience. Zwingli, who was a staunch republican, desired that all magistrates should be elected, and should be liable to be dismissed by their electors; but he died too soon for his influence, and the permanent action of the Reformation on democracy was exercised through the Presbyterian constitution of Calvin.

It was long before the democratic element in Presbyterianism began to tell. The Netherlands resisted Philip II for fifteen years before they took courage to depose him, and the scheme of the ultra-Calvinist Deventer, to subvert the ascendency of the leading States by the sovereign action of the whole people, was foiled by Leicester's incapacity, and by the consummate policy of Barnevelt. The Huguenots, having lost their leaders in 1572, reconstituted themselves on a democratic footing, and learned to think that a king who murders his subjects forfeits his divine right to be obeyed. But Junius Brutus and Buchanan damaged their credit by advocating regicide; and Hotoman, whose *Franco-Gallia* is the most serious work of the group, deserted his liberal opinions when the chief of his own party became king. The most violent explosion of democracy in that age proceeded from the opposite quarter. When Henry of Navarre became the next heir to the throne of France, the theory of the deposing power, which had proved ineffectual for more than a century, awoke with a new and more vigorous life. One-half of the nation accepted the view, that they were not bound to submit to a king they would not have chosen. A Committee of Sixteen made itself master of Paris, and, with the aid of Spain, succeeded for years in excluding Henry from his capital. The impulse thus given endured in literature for a whole generation, and produced a library of treatises on the right of Catholics to choose, to control, and to cashier their magistrates. They were on the losing side. Most of them were bloodthirsty, and were soon forgotten. But the greater part of the political ideas of Milton, Locke, and Rousseau, may be found in the ponderous Latin of Jesuits who were subjects of the Spanish Crown, of Lessius, Molina, Mariana, and Suarez.

The ideas were there, and were taken up when it suited them by extreme adherents of Rome and of Geneva; but they produced no lasting fruit until, a century after the Reformation, they became incorporated in new religious systems. Five years of civil war could not exhaust the royalism of the Presbyterians, and it required the expulsion of the majority to make the Long Parliament abandon monarchy. It had defended the constitution against the crown with legal arts, defending precedent against innovation, and setting up an ideal in the past which, with all the learning of Selden and of Prynne, was less certain than the Puritan statesmen supposed. The Independants brought in a new principle. Tradition had no authority for them, and the past no virtue. Liberty of conscience, a thing not to be found in the constitution, was more prized by many of them than all the statutes of the Plantagenets. Their idea that each congregation should govern itself abolished the force which is needed to preserve unity, and deprived monarchy of the weapon which made it injurious to freedom. An immense revolutionary energy resided in their doctrine, and it took root in America, and deeply coloured political thought in later times. But in England the sectarian democracy was strong only to destroy. Cromwell refused to be bound by it; and John Lilburne, the boldest thinker among English democrats, declared that it would be better for liberty to bring back Charles Stuart than to live under the sword of the Protector.

Lilburne was among the first to understand the real conditions of democracy, and the obstacle to its success in England. Equality of power could not be preserved, except by violence, together with an extreme inequality of possessions. There would always be danger, if power was not made to wait on property, that property would go to those who had the power. This idea of the necessary balance of property, developed by Harrington, and adopted by Milton in his later pamphlets, appeared to Toland, and even to John Adams, as important as the invention of printing, or the discovery of the circulation of the blood. At least it indicates the true explanation of the strange completeness with which the Republican party had vanished, a dozen years after the solemn trial and execution of the King. No extremity of misgovernment was able to revive it. When the treason of Charles II against the constitution was divulged, and the Whigs plotted to expel the incorrigible dynasty, their aspirations went no farther than a Venetian oligarchy, with Monmouth for Doge. The Revolution of 1688 confined power to the aristocracy of freeholders. The conservatism of the age was unconquerable. Republicanism was distorted even in Switzerland, and became in the eighteenth century as oppressive and as intolerant as its neighbours.

In 1769, when Paoli fled from Corsica, it seemed that, in Europe at least, democracy was dead. It had, indeed, lately been defended in books by a man of bad reputation, whom the leaders of public opinion treated with contumely, and whose declamations excited so little alarm that George III offered him a pension. What gave to Rousseau a power far exceeding that which any political writer had ever attained was the progress of events in America. The Stuarts had been willing that the colonies should serve as a refuge from their system of Church and State, and of all their colonies the one most favoured was the territory granted to William Penn. By the principles of the Society to which he belonged, it was necessary that the new State should be founded on liberty and equality. But Penn was further noted among Quakers as a follower of the new doctrine of Toleration. Thus it came to pass that Pennsylvania enjoyed the most democratic constitution in the world, and held up to the admiration of the eighteenth century an almost solitary example of freedom. It was principally through Franklin and the Quaker State that America influenced political opinion in Europe, and that the fanaticism of one revolutionary epoch was converted into the rationalism of another. American independence was the beginning of a new era, not merely as a revival of Revolution, but because no other Revolution ever proceeded from so slight a cause, or was ever conducted with so much moderation. The European monarchies supported it. The greatest statesmen in England averred that it was just. It established a pure democracy; but it was democracy in its highest perfection, armed and vigilant, less against aristocracy and monarchy than against its own weakness and excess. Whilst England was admired for the safeguards with which, in the course of many centuries, it had fortified liberty against the power of the crown, America appeared still more worthy of admiration for the safeguards which, in the deliberations of a single memorable year, it had set up against the power of its own sovereign people. It resembled no other known democracy, for it respected freedom, authority, and law. It resembled no other constitution, for it was contained in half a dozen intelligible articles. Ancient Europe opened its mind to two new ideas—that Revolution with very little provocation may be just; and that democracy in very large dimensions may be safe.

Whilst America was making itself independent, the spirit of reform had been abroad in Europe. Intelligent ministers, like Campomanes and Struensee, and well-meaning monarchs, of whom the most liberal was Leopold of Tuscany, were trying what could be done to make men happy by command. Centuries of absolute and intolerant rule had bequeathed abuses which nothing but the most vigorous use of power could remove. The age preferred the reign of intellect to the reign of liberty. Turgot, the ablest and most far-seeing reformer then living, attempted to do for France what less gifted men were doing with success in Lombardy, and Tuscany, and Parma. He attempted to employ the royal power for the good of the people, at the expense of the higher classes. The higher classes proved too strong for the crown alone; and Louis XVI abandoned internal reforms in despair, and turned for compensation to a war with England for the deliverance of her American Colonies. When the increasing debt obliged him to seek heroic remedies, and he was again repulsed by the privileged orders, he appealed at last to the nation. When the States-General met, the power had already passed to the middle class, for it was by them alone that the country could be saved. They were strong enough to triumph by waiting. Neither the Court, nor the nobles, nor the army, could do anything against them. During the six months from January 1789 to the fall of the Bastille in July, France travelled as far as England in the six hundred years between the Earl of

Leicester and Lord Beaconsfield. Ten years after the American alliance, the Rights of Man, which had been proclaimed at Philadelphia, were repeated at Versailles. The alliance had borne fruit on both sides of the Atlantic, and for France, the fruit was the triumph of American ideas over English. They were more popular, more simple, more effective against privilege, and, strange to say, more acceptable to the King. The new French constitution allowed no privileged orders, no parliamentary ministry, no power of dissolution, and only a suspensive veto. But the characteristic safeguards of the American Government were rejected: Federalism, separation of Church and State, the Second Chamber, the political arbitration of the supreme judicial body. That which weakened the Executive was taken: that which restrained the Legislature was left. Checks on the crown abounded; but should the crown be vacant, the powers that remained would be without a check. The precautions were all in one direction. Nobody would contemplate the contingency that there might be no king. The constitution was inspired by a profound disbelief in Louis XVI and a pertinacious belief in monarchy. The assembly voted without debate, by acclamation, a Civil List three times as large as that of Queen Victoria. When Louis fled, and the throne was actually vacant, they brought him back to it, preferring the phantom of a king who was a prisoner to the reality of no king at all.

Next to this misapplication of American examples, which was the fault of nearly all the leading statesmen, excepting Mounier, Mirabeau, and Sieyès, the cause of the Revolution was injured by its religious policy. The most novel and impressive lesson taught by the fathers of the American Republic was that the people, and not the administration, should govern. Men in office were salaried agents, by whom the nation wrought its will. Authority submitted to public opinion, and left to it not only the control, but the initiative of government. Patience in waiting for a wind, alacrity in catching it, the dread of exerting unnecessary influence, characterise the early presidents. Some of the French politicians shared this view, though with less exaggeration than Washington. They wished to decentralise the government, and to obtain, for good or evil, the genuine expression of popular sentiment. Necker himself, and Buzot, the most thoughtful of the Girondins, dreamed of federalising France. In the United States there was no current of opinion, and no combination of forces, to be seriously feared. The government needed no security against being propelled in a wrong direction. But the French Revolution was accomplished at the expense of powerful classes. Besides the nobles, the Assembly, which had been made supreme by the accession of the clergy, and had been led at first by popular ecclesiastics, by Sieyès, Talleyrand, Cicé, La Luzerne, made an enemy of the clergy. The prerogative could not be destroyed without touching the Church. Ecclesiastical patronage had helped to make the crown absolute. To leave it in the hands of Louis and his ministers was to renounce the entire policy of the constitution. To disestablish, was to make it over to the Pope. It was consistent with the democratic principle to introduce election into the Church. It involved a breach with Rome; but so, indeed, did the laws of Joseph II, Charles III, and Leopold. The Pope was not likely to cast away the friendship of France, if he could help it; and the French clergy were not likely to give trouble by their attachment to Rome. Therefore, amid the indifference of many, and against the urgent, and probably sincere, remonstrances of Robespierre and Marat, the Jansenists, who had a century of persecution to avenge, carried the Civil Constitution. The coercive measures which enforced it led to the breach with the King, and the fall of the monarchy; to the revolt of the provinces, and the fall of liberty. The Jacobins determined that public opinion should not reign, that the State should not remain at the mercy of powerful combinations. They held the representatives of the people under control, by the people itself. They attributed higher authority to the direct than to the indirect voice of the democratic oracle. They armed themselves with power to crush every adverse, every independent force, and especially to put down the Church, in whose cause the provinces had risen against the capital. They met the centrifugal federalism of the friends of the Gironde by the most resolute centralisation. France was governed by Paris; and Paris by its municipality and its mob. Obeying Rousseau's maxim, that the people cannot delegate its power, they raised

83

the elementary constituency above its representatives. As the greatest constituent body, the most numerous accumulation of primary electors, the largest portion of sovereignty, was in the people of Paris, they designed that the people of Paris should rule over France, as the people of Rome, the mob as well as the senate, had ruled, not ingloriously, over Italy, and over half the nations that surround the Mediterranean. Although the Jacobins were scarcely more irreligious than the Abbé Sieyès or Madame Roland, although Robespierre wanted to force men to believe in God, although Danton went to confession and Barère was a professing Christian, they imparted to modern democracy that implacable hatred of religion which contrasts so strangely with the example of its Puritan prototype.

The deepest cause which made the French Revolution so disastrous to liberty was its theory of equality. Liberty was the watchword of the middle class, equality of the lower. It was the lower class that won the battles of the third estate; that took the Bastille, and made France a constitutional monarchy; that took the Tuileries, and made France a Republic. They claimed their reward. The middle class, having cast down the upper orders with the aid of the lower, instituted a new inequality and a privilege for itself. By means of a taxpaying qualification it deprived its confederates of their vote. To those, therefore, who had accomplished the Revolution, its promise was not fulfilled. Equality did nothing for them. The opinion, at that time, was almost universal, that society is founded on an agreement which is voluntary and conditional, and that the links which bind men to it are terminable, for sufficient reason, like those which subject them to authority. From these popular premises the logic of Marat drew his sanguinary conclusions. He told the famished people that the conditions on which they had consented to bear their evil lot, and had refrained from violence, had not been kept to them. It was suicide, it was murder, to submit to starve and to see one's children starving, by the fault of the rich. The bonds of society were dissolved by the wrong it inflicted. The state of nature had come back, in which every man had a right to what he could take. The time had come for the rich to make way for the poor. With this theory of equality, liberty was quenched in blood, and Frenchmen became ready to sacrifice all other things to save life and fortune.

Twenty years after the splendid opportunity that opened in 1789, the reaction had triumphed everywhere in Europe; ancient constitutions had perished as well as new; and even England afforded them neither protection nor sympathy. The liberal, at least the democratic revival, came from Spain. The Spaniards fought against the French for a king, who was a prisoner in France. They gave themselves a constitution, and placed his name at the head of it. They had a monarchy, without a king. It required to be so contrived that it would work in the absence, possibly the permanent absence, of the monarch. It became, therefore, a monarchy only in name, composed, in fact, of democratic forces. The constitution of 1812 was the attempt of inexperienced men to accomplish the most difficult task in politics. It was smitten with sterility. For many years it was the standard of abortive revolutions among the so-called Latin nations. It promulgated the notion of a king who should flourish only in name, and should not even discharge the humble function which Hegel assigns to royalty, of dotting I's for the people.

The overthrow of the Cadiz constitution, in 1823, was the supreme triumph of the restored monarchy of France. Five years later, under a wise and liberal minister, the Restoration was advancing fairly on the constitutional paths, when the incurable distrust of the Liberal party defeated Martignac, and brought in the ministry of extreme royalists that ruined the monarchy. In labouring to transfer power from the class which the Revolution had enfranchised to those which it had overthrown, Polignac and La Bourdonnaie would gladly have made terms with the working men. To break the influence of intellect and capital by means of universal suffrage, was an idea long and zealously advocated by some of their supporters. They had not foresight or ability to divide their adversaries, and they were vanquished in 1830 by the united democracy.

The promise of the Revolution of July was to reconcile royalists and democrats. The King assured Lafayette that he was a republican at heart; and Lafayette assured France that Louis Philippe was the best of republics. The shock of the great event was felt in Poland, and Belgium, and even in England. It gave a direct impulse to democratic movements in Switzerland.

Swiss democracy had been in abeyance since 1815. The national will had no organ. The cantons were supreme; and governed as inefficiently as other governments under the protecting shade of the Holy Alliance. There was no dispute that Switzerland called for extensive reforms, and no doubt of the direction they would take. The number of the cantons was the great obstacle to all improvement. It was useless to have twenty-five governments in a country equal to one American State, and inferior in population to one great city. It was impossible that they should be good governments. A central power was the manifest need of the country. In the absence of an efficient federal power, seven cantons formed a separate league for the protection of their own interests. Whilst democratic ideas were making way in Switzerland, the Papacy was travelling in the opposite direction, and showing an inflexible hostility for ideas which are the breath of democratic life. The growing democracy and the growing Ultramontanism came into collision. The Sonderbund could aver with truth that there was no safety for its rights under the Federal Constitution. The others could reply, with equal truth, that there was no safety for the constitution with the Sonderbund. In 1847, it came to a war between national sovereignty and cantonal sovereignty. The Sonderbund was dissolved, and a new Federal Constitution was adopted, avowedly and ostensibly charged with the duty of carrying out democracy, and repressing the adverse influence of Rome. It was a delusive imitation of the American system. The President was powerless. The Senate was powerless. The Supreme Court was powerless. The sovereignty of the cantons was undermined, and their power centred in the House of Representatives. The Constitution of 1848 was a first step towards the destruction of Federalism. Another and almost a final step in the direction of centralisation was taken in 1874. The railways, and the vast interests they created, made the position of the cantonal governments untenable. The conflict with the Ultramontanes increased the demand for vigorous action; and the destruction of State Rights in the American war strengthened the hands of the Centralists.

The Constitution of 1874 is one of the most significant works of modern democracy. It is the triumph of democratic force over democratic freedom. It overrules not only the Federal principle, but the representative principle. It carries important measures away from the Federal Legislature to submit them to the votes of the entire people, separating decision from deliberation. The operation is so cumbrous as to be generally ineffective. But it constitutes a power such as exists, we believe, under the laws of no other country. A Swiss jurist has frankly expressed the spirit of the reigning system by saying, that the State is the appointed conscience of the nation.

The moving force in Switzerland has been democracy relieved of all constraint, the principle of putting in action the greatest force of the greatest number. The prosperity of the country has prevented complications such as arose in France. The ministers of Louis Philippe, able and enlightened men, believed that they would make the people prosper if they could have their own way, and could shut out public opinion. They acted as if the intelligent middle class was destined by heaven to govern. The upper class had proved its unfitness before 1789; the lower class, since 1789. Government by professional men, by manufacturers and scholars, was sure to be safe, and almost sure to be reasonable and practical. Money became the object of a political superstition, such as had formerly attached to land, and afterwards attached to labour. The masses of the people, who had fought against Marmont, became aware that they had not fought for their own benefit. They were still governed by their employers.

When the King parted with Lafayette, and it was found that he would not only reign but govern, the indignation of the republicans found a vent in street fighting. In 1836, when the horrors of the infernal machine had armed the crown with ampler powers, and had silenced the republican party, the term Socialism made its appearance in literature. Tocqueville, who was writing the philosophic chapters that conclude his work, failed to discover the power which the new system was destined to exercise on democracy. Until then, democrats and communists had stood apart. Although the socialist doctrines were defended by the best intellects of France, by Thierry, Comte, Chevalier, and Georges

Sand, they excited more attention as a literary curiosity than as the cause of future revolutions. Towards 1840, in the recesses of secret societies, republicans and socialists coalesced. Whilst the Liberal leaders, Lamartine and Barrot, discoursed on the surface concerning reform, Ledru Rollin and Louis Blanc were quietly digging a grave for the monarchy, the Liberal party, and the reign of wealth. They worked so well, and the vanquished republicans recovered so thoroughly, by this coalition, the influence they had lost by a long series of crimes and follies, that, in 1848, they were able to conquer without fighting. The fruit of their victory was universal suffrage.

From that time the promises of socialism have supplied the best energy of democracy. Their coalition has been the ruling fact in French politics. It created the "saviour of society," and the Commune; and it still entangles the footsteps of the Republic. It is the only shape in which democracy has found an entrance into Germany. Liberty has lost its spell; and democracy maintains itself by the promise of substantial gifts to the masses of the people.

Since the Revolution of July and the Presidency of Jackson gave the impulse which has made democracy preponderate, the ablest political writers, Tocqueville, Calhoun, Mill, and Laboulaye, have drawn, in the name of freedom, a formidable indictment against it. They have shown democracy without respect for the past or care for the future, regardless of public faith and of national honour, extravagant and inconstant, jealous of talent and of knowledge, indifferent to justice but servile towards opinion, incapable of organisation, impatient of authority, averse from obedience, hostile to religion and to established law. Evidence indeed abounds, even if the true cause be not proved. But it is not to these symptoms that we must impute the permanent danger and the irrepressible conflict. As much might be made good against monarchy, and an unsympathising reasoner might in the same way argue that religion is intolerant, that conscience makes cowards, that piety rejoices in fraud. Recent experience has added little to the observations of those who witnessed the decline after Pericles, of Thucydides, Aristophanes, Plato, and of the writer whose brilliant tract against the Athenian Republic is printed among the works of Xenophon. The manifest, the avowed difficulty is that democracy, no less than monarchy or aristocracy, sacrifices everything to maintain itself, and strives, with an energy and a plausibility that kings and nobles cannot attain, to override representation, to annul all the forces of resistance and deviation, and to secure, by Plebiscite, Referendum, or Caucus, free play for the will of the majority. The true democratic principle, that none shall have power over the people, is taken to mean that none shall be able to restrain or to elude its power. The true democratic principle, that the people shall not be made to do what it does not like, is taken to mean that it shall never be required to tolerate what it does not like. The true democratic principle, that every man's free will shall be as unfettered as possible, is taken to mean that the free will of the collective people shall be fettered in nothing. Religious toleration, judicial independence, dread of centralisation, jealousy of State interference, become obstacles to freedom instead of safeguards, when the centralised force of the State is wielded by the hands of the people. Democracy claims to be not only supreme, without authority above, but absolute, without independence below; to be its own master, not a trustee. The old sovereigns of the world are exchanged for a new one, who may be flattered and deceived, but whom it is impossible to corrupt or to resist, and to whom must be rendered the things that are Caesar's and also the things that are God's. The enemy to be overcome is no longer the absolutism of the State, but the liberty of the subject. Nothing is more significant than the relish with which Ferrari, the most powerful democratic writer since Rousseau, enumerates the merits of tyrants, and prefers devils to saints in the interest of the community.

For the old notions of civil liberty and of social order did not benefit the masses of the people. Wealth increased, without relieving their wants. The progress of knowledge left them in abject ignorance. Religion flourished, but failed to reach them. Society, whose laws were made by the upper class alone, announced that the best thing for the poor is not to be born, and the next best, to die in childhood, and suffered them to live in misery and crime and pain. As surely as the long reign of the rich has been employed in promoting the accumulation of wealth, the advent of the poor to power will be followed by schemes for diffusing it. Seeing how little was done by the wisdom of former times for education and public health, for insurance, association, and savings, for the protection of labour against the law of self-interest, and how much has been accomplished in this generation, there is reason in the fixed belief that a great change was needed, and that democracy has not striven in vain. Liberty, for the mass, is not happiness; and institutions are not an end but a means. The thing they seek is a force sufficient to sweep away scruples and the obstacle of rival interests, and, in some degree, to better their condition. They mean that the strong hand that heretofore has formed great States, protected religions, and defended the independence of nations, shall help them by preserving life, and endowing it for them with some, at least, of the things men live for. That is the notorious danger of modern democracy. That is also its purpose and its strength. And against this threatening power the weapons that struck down other despots do not avail. The greatest happiness principle positively confirms it. The principle of equality, besides being as easily applied to property as to power, opposes the existence of persons or groups of persons exempt from the common law, and independent of the common will; and the principle, that authority is a matter of contract, may hold good against kings, but not against the sovereign people, because a contract implies two parties.

If we have not done more than the ancients to develop and to examine the disease, we have far surpassed them in studying the remedy. Besides the French Constitution of the year III, and that of the American Confederates,—the most remarkable attempts that have been made since the archonship of Euclides to meet democratic evils with the antidotes which democracy itself supplies,—our age has been prolific in this branch of experimental politics.

Many expedients have been tried, that have been evaded or defeated. A divided executive, which was an important phase in the transformation of ancient monarchies into republics, and which, through the advocacy of Condorcet, took root in France, has proved to be weakness itself.

The constitution of 1795, the work of a learned priest, confined the franchise to those who should know how to read and write; and in 1849 this provision was rejected by men who intended that the ignorant voter should help them to overturn the Republic. In our time no democracy could long subsist without educating the masses; and the scheme of Daunou is simply an indirect encouragement to elementary instruction.

In 1799 Sieyès suggested to Bonaparte the idea of a great Council, whose function it should be to keep the acts of the Legislature in harmony with the constitution—a function which the *Nomophylakes* discharged at Athens, and the Supreme Court in the United States, and which produced the Sénat Conservateur, one of the favourite implements of Imperialism. Sieyès meant that his Council should also serve the purpose of a gilded ostracism, having power to absorb any obnoxious politician, and to silence him with a thousand a year.

Napoleon the Third's plan of depriving unmarried men of their votes would have disfranchised the two greatest Conservative classes in France, the priest and the soldier.

In the American constitution it was intended that the chief of the executive should be chosen by a body of carefully selected electors. But since, in 1825, the popular candidate succumbed to one who had only a minority of votes, it has become the practice to elect the President by the pledged delegates of universal suffrage.

The exclusion of ministers from Congress has been one of the severest strains on the American system; and the law which required a majority of three to one enabled Louis Napoleon to make himself Emperor. Large constituencies make independent deputies; but experience proves that small assemblies, the consequence of large constituencies, can be managed by Government.

The composite vote and the cumulative vote have been almost universally rejected as schemes for baffling the majority. But the principle of dividing the representatives equally between population and property has never had fair play. It was introduced by Thouret into the constitution of 1791. The Revolution made it inoperative; and it was so manipulated from 1817 to 1848 by the fatal dexterity of Guizot as to make opinion ripe for universal suffrage.

Constitutions which forbid the payment of deputies and the system of imperative instructions, which deny the power of dissolution, and make the Legislature last for a fixed term, or renew it by partial re-elections, and which require an interval between the several debates on the same measure, evidently strengthen the independence of the representative assembly. The Swiss veto has the same effect, as it suspends legislation only when opposed by a majority of the whole electoral body, not by a majority of those who actually vote upon it.

Indirect elections are scarcely anywhere in use out of Germany, but they have been a favourite corrective of democracy with many thoughtful politicians. Where the extent of the electoral district obliges constituents to vote for candidates who are unknown to them, the election is not free. It is managed by wire-pullers, and by party machinery, beyond the control of the electors. Indirect election puts the choice of the managers into their hands. The objection is that the intermediate electors are generally too few to span the interval between voters and candidates, and that they choose representatives not of better quality, but of different politics. If the intermediate body consisted of one in ten of the whole constituency, the contact would be preserved, the people would be really represented, and the ticket system would be broken down.

The one pervading evil of democracy is the tyranny of the majority, or rather of that party, not always the majority, that succeeds, by force or fraud, in carrying elections. To break off that point is to avert the danger. The common system of representation perpetuates the danger. Unequal electorates afford no security to majorities. Equal electorates give none to minorities. Thirty-five years ago it was pointed out that the remedy is proportional representation. It is profoundly democratic, for it increases the influence of thousands who would otherwise have no voice in the government; and it brings men more near an equality by so contriving that no vote shall be wasted, and that every voter shall contribute to bring into Parliament a member of his own opinions. The origin of the idea is variously claimed for Lord Grey and for Considérant. The successful example of Denmark and the earnest advocacy of Mill gave it prominence in the world of politics. It has gained popularity with the growth of democracy, and we are informed by M. Naville that in Switzerland Conservatives and Radicals combined to promote it.

Of all checks on democracy, federalism has been the most efficacious and the most congenial; but, becoming associated with the Red Republic, with feudalism, with the Jesuits, and with slavery, it has fallen into disrepute, and is giving way to centralism. The federal system limits and restrains the sovereign power by dividing it, and by assigning to Government only certain defined rights. It is the only method of curbing not only the majority but the power of the whole people, and it affords the strongest basis for a second chamber, which has been found the essential security for freedom in every genuine democracy.

The fall of Guizot discredited the famous maxim of the Doctrinaires, that Reason is sovereign, and not king or people; and it was further exposed to the scoffer by the promise of Comte that Positivist philosophers shall manufacture political ideas, which no man shall be permitted to dispute. But putting aside international and criminal law, in which there is some approach to uniformity, the domain of political economy seems destined to admit the rigorous certainty of science. Whenever that shall be attained, when the battle between Economists and Socialists is ended, the evil force which Socialism imparts to democracy will be spent. The battle is raging more violently than ever, but it has entered into a new phase, by the rise of a middle party. Whether that remarkable movement, which is promoted by some of the first economists in Europe, is destined to shake the authority of their science, or to conquer socialism, by robbing it of that which is the secret of its strength, it must be recorded here as the latest and the most serious effort that has been made to disprove the weighty sentence of Rousseau, that democracy is a government for gods, but unfit for man.

We have been able to touch on only a few of the topics that crowd Sir Erskine May's volumes. Although he has perceived more clearly than Tocqueville the contact of democracy with socialism, his judgment is untinged with Tocqueville's despondency, and he contemplates the direction of progress with a confidence that approaches optimism. The notion of an inflexible logic in history does not depress him, for he concerns himself with facts and with men more than with doctrines, and his book is a history of several democracies, not of democracy. There are links in the argument, there are phases of development which he leaves unnoticed, because his object has not been to trace out the properties and the connection of ideas, but to explain the results of experience. We should consult his pages, probably, without effect, if we wished to follow the origin and sequence of the democratic dogmas, that all men are equal; that speech and thought are free; that each generation is a law to itself only; that there shall be no endowments, no entails, no primogeniture; that the people are sovereign; that the people can do no wrong. The great mass of those who, of necessity, are interested in practical politics have no such antiquarian curiosity. They want to know what can be learned from the countries where the democratic experiments have been tried; but they do not care to be told how M. Waddington has emended the *Monumentum Ancyranum*, what connection there was between Mariana and Milton, or between Penn and Rousseau, or who invented the proverb *Vox Populi Vox Dei*. Sir Erskine May's reluctance to deal with matters speculative and doctrinal, and to devote his space to the mere literary history of politics, has made his touch somewhat uncertain in treating of the political action of Christianity, perhaps the most complex and comprehensive question that can embarrass a historian. He disparages the influence of the medieval Church on nations just emerging from a barbarous paganism, and he exalts it when it had become associated with despotism and persecution. He insists on the liberating action of the Reformation in the sixteenth century, when it gave a stimulus to absolutism; and he is slow to recognise, in the enthusiasm and violence of the sects in the seventeenth, the most potent agency ever brought to bear on democratic history. The omission of America creates a void between 1660 and 1789, and leaves much unexplained in the revolutionary movement of the last hundred years, which is the central problem of the book. But if some things are missed from the design, if the execution is not equal in every part, the praise remains to Sir Erskine May, that he is the only writer who has ever brought together the materials for a comparative study of democracy, that he has avoided the temper of party, that has shown a hearty sympathy for the progress and improvement of mankind, and a steadfast faith in the wisdom and the power that guide it.

4

NATIONALITY*

W henever great intellectual cultivation has been combined with that suffering which is inseparable from extensive changes in the condition of the people, men of speculative or imaginative genius have sought in the contemplation of an ideal society a remedy, or at least a consolation, for evils which they were practically unable to remove. Poetry has always preserved the idea, that at some distant time or place, in the Western islands or the Arcadian region, an innocent and contented people, free from the corruption and restraint of civilised life, have realised the legends of the golden age. The office of the poets is always nearly the same, and there is little variation in the features of their ideal world; but when philosophers attempt to admonish or reform mankind by devising an imaginary state, their motive is more definite and immediate, and their commonwealth is a satire as well as a model. Plato and Plotinus, More and Campanella, constructed their fanciful societies with those materials which

---

*Published as "Nationality," *Home and Foreign Review* 1 (July 1862): 1–25. Reprinted in Lord Acton, *The History of Freedom and Other Essays*, ed. John Neville Figgis and Reginald Vere Laurence (London: Macmillan, 1907), 270–300; *Selected Writings of Lord Acton*, ed. J. Rufus Fears, 3 vols. (Indianapolis: Liberty Fund, 1985–88), 1:409–33.

were omitted from the fabric of the actual communities, by the defects of which they were inspired. The Republic, the Utopia, and the City of the Sun were protests against a state of things which the experience of their authors taught them to condemn, and from the faults of which they took refuge in the opposite extremes. They remained without influence, and have never passed from literary into political history, because something more than discontent and speculative ingenuity is needed in order to invest a political idea with power over the masses of mankind. The scheme of a philosopher can command the practical allegiance of fanatics only, not of nations; and though oppression may give rise to violent and repeated outbreaks, like the convulsions of a man in pain, it cannot mature a settled purpose and plan of regeneration, unless a new notion of happiness is joined to the sense of present evil.

The history of religion furnishes a complete illustration. Between the later medieval sects and Protestantism there is an essential difference, that outweighs the points of analogy found in those systems which are regarded as heralds of the Reformation, and is enough to explain the vitality of the last in comparison with the others. Whilst Wycliffe and Hus contradicted certain particulars of the Catholic teaching, Luther rejected the authority of the Church, and gave to the individual conscience an independence which was sure to lead to an incessant resistance. There is a similar difference between the Revolt of the Netherlands, the Great Rebellion, the War of Independence, or the rising of Brabant, on the one hand, and the French Revolution on the other. Before 1789, insurrections were provoked by particular wrongs, and were justified by definite complaints and by an appeal to principles which all men acknowledged. New theories were sometimes advanced in the cause of controversy, but they were accidental, and the great argument against tyranny was fidelity to the ancient laws. Since the change produced by the French Revolution, those aspirations which are awakened by the evils and defects of the social state have come to act as permanent and energetic forces throughout the civilised world. They are spontaneous and aggressive, needing no prophet to proclaim, no champion to defend them, but popular, unreasoning, and almost irresistible. The Revolution effected this change, partly by its doctrines, partly by the indirect influence of events. It taught the people to regard their wishes and wants as the supreme criterion of right. The rapid vicissitudes of power, in which each party successively appealed to the favour of the masses as the arbiter of success, accustomed the masses to be arbitrary as well as insubordinate. The fall of many governments, and the frequent redistribution of territory, deprived all settlements of the dignity of permanence. Tradition and prescription ceased to be guardians of authority; and the arrangements which proceeded from revolutions, from the triumphs of war, and from treaties of peace, were equally regardless of established rights. Duty cannot be dissociated from right, and nations refuse to be controlled by laws which are no protection.

In this condition of the world, theory and action follow close upon each other, and practical evils easily give birth to opposite systems. In the realms of free-will, the regularity of natural progress is preserved by the conflict of extremes. The impulse of the reaction carries men from one extremity towards another. The pursuit of a remote and ideal object, which captivates the imagination by its splendour and the reason by its simplicity, evokes an energy which would not be inspired by a rational, possible end, limited by many antagonistic claims, and confined to what is reasonable, practicable, and just. One excess or exaggeration is the corrective of the other, and error promotes truth, where the masses are concerned, by counterbalancing a contrary error. The few have not strength to achieve great changes unaided; the many have not wisdom to be moved by truth unmixed. Where the disease is various, no particular definite remedy can meet the wants of all. Only the attraction of an abstract idea, or of an ideal state, can unite in a common action multitudes who seek a universal cure for many special evils, and a common restorative applicable to many different conditions. And hence false principles, which correspond with the bad as well as with the just aspirations of mankind, are a normal and necessary element in the social life of nations.

Theories of this kind are just, inasmuch as they are provoked by definite ascertained evils, and undertake their removal. They are useful in opposition, as a warning or a threat, to modify existing things, and keep awake the consciousness of wrong. They cannot serve as a basis for the reconstruction of civil society, as medicine cannot serve for food; but they may influence it with advantage, because they point out the direction, though not the measure, in which reform is needed. They oppose an order of things which is the result of a selfish and violent abuse of power by the ruling classes, and of artificial restriction on the natural progress of the world, destitute of an ideal element or a moral purpose. Practical extremes differ from the theoretical extremes they provoke, because the first are both arbitrary and violent, whilst the last, though also revolutionary, are at the same time remedial. In one case the wrong is voluntary, in the other it is inevitable. This is the general character of the contest between the existing order and the subversive theories that deny its legitimacy. There are three principal theories of this kind, impugning the present distribution of power, of property, and of territory, and attacking respectively the aristocracy, the middle class, and the sovereignty. They are the theories of equality, communism, and nationality. Though sprung from a common origin, opposing cognate evils, and connected by many links, they did not appear simultaneously. Rousseau proclaimed the first, Baboeuf the second, Mazzini the third; and the third is the most recent in its appearance, the most attractive at the present time, and the richest in promise of future power.

In the old European system, the rights of nationalities were neither recognised by governments nor asserted by the people. The interest of the reigning families, not those of the nations, regulated the frontiers; and the administration was conducted generally without any reference to popular desires. Where all liberties were suppressed, the claims of national independence were necessarily ignored, and a princess, in the words of Fénelon, carried a monarchy in her wedding portion. The eighteenth century acquiesced in this oblivion of corporate rights on the Continent, for the absolutists cared only for the State, and the liberals only for the individual. The Church, the nobles, and the nation had no place in the popular theories of the age; and they devised none in their own defence, for they were not openly attacked. The aristocracy retained its privileges, and the Church her property; and the dynastic interest, which overruled the natural inclination of the nations and destroyed their independence, nevertheless maintained their integrity. The national sentiment was not wounded in its most sensitive part. To dispossess a sovereign of his hereditary crown, and to annex his dominions, would have been held to inflict an injury upon all monarchies, and to furnish their subjects with a dangerous example, by depriving royalty of its inviolable character. In time of war, as there was no national cause at stake, there was no attempt to rouse national feeling. The courtesy of the rulers towards each other was proportionate to the contempt for the lower orders. Compliments passed between the commanders of hostile armies; there was no bitterness, and no excitement; battles were fought with the pomp and pride of a parade. The art of war became a slow and learned game. The monarchies were united not only by a natural community of interests, but by family alliances. A marriage contract sometimes became the signal for an interminable war, whilst family connections often set a barrier to ambition. After the wars of religion came to an end in 1648, the only wars were those which were waged for an inheritance or a dependency, or against countries whose system of government exempted them from the common law of dynastic States, and made them not only unprotected but obnoxious. These countries were England and Holland, until Holland ceased to be a republic, and until, in England, the defeat of the Jacobites in the forty-five terminated the struggle for the Crown. There was one country, however, which still continued to be an exception; one monarch whose place was not admitted in the comity of kings.

Poland did not possess those securities for stability which were supplied by dynastic connections and the theory of legitimacy, wherever a crown could be obtained by marriage or inheritance. A monarch without royal blood, a crown bestowed by the nation, were an anomaly and an outrage in that age of dynastic absolutism. The country was excluded from the European system by the nature of its institutions. It excited a cupidity which could not be satisfied. It gave the reigning families of Europe no hope of permanently strengthening themselves by intermarriage with its rulers, or of obtaining it by bequest or by inheritance. The Habsburgs had contested the possession of Spain and the Indies with the French Bourbons, of Italy with the Spanish Bourbons, of the empire with the house of Wittelsbach, of Silesia with the house of Hohenzollern. There had been wars between rival houses for half the territories of Italy and Germany. But none could hope to redeem their losses or increase their power in a country to which marriage and descent gave no claim. Where they could not permanently inherit they endeavoured, by intrigues, to prevail at each election, and after contending in support of candidates who were their partisans, the neighbours at last appointed an instrument for the final demolition of the Polish State. Till then no nation had been deprived of its political existence by the Christian Powers, and whatever disregard had been shown for national interests and sympathies, some care had been taken to conceal the wrong by a hypocritical perversion of law. But the partition of Poland was an act of wanton violence, committed in open defiance not only of popular feeling but of public law. For the first time in modern history a great State was suppressed, and a whole nation divided among its enemies.

This famous measure, the most revolutionary act of the old absolutism, awakened the theory of nationality in Europe, converting a dormant right into an aspiration, and a sentiment into a political claim. "No wise or honest man," wrote Edmund Burke, "can approve of that partition, or can contemplate it without prognosticating great mischief from it to all countries at some future time."[1] Thenceforward there was a nation demanding to be united in a State,—a soul, as it were, wandering in search of a body in which to begin life over again; and, for the first time, a cry was heard that the arrangement of States was unjust—that their limits were unnatural, and that a whole people was deprived of its right to constitute an independent community. Before that claim could be efficiently asserted against the overwhelming power of its opponents,—before it gained energy, after the last partition, to overcome the influence of long habits

---

[1] "Observations on the Conduct of the Minority," *Works*, v. 112.

of submission, and of the contempt which previous disorders had brought upon Poland,—the ancient European system was in ruins, and a new world was rising in its place.

The old despotic policy which made the Poles its prey had two adversaries,—the spirit of English liberty, and the doctrines of that revolution which destroyed the French monarchy with its own weapons; and these two contradicted in contrary ways the theory that nations have no collective rights. At the present day, the theory of nationality is not only the most powerful auxiliary of revolution, but its actual substance in the movements of the last three years. This, however, is a recent alliance, unknown to the first French Revolution. The modern theory of nationality arose partly as a legitimate consequence, partly as a reaction against it. As the system which overlooked national division was opposed by liberalism in two forms, the French and the English, so the system which insists upon them proceeds from two distinct sources, and exhibits the character either of 1688 or of 1789. When the French people abolished the authorities under which it lived, and became its own master, France was in danger of dissolution: for the common will is difficult to ascertain, and does not readily agree. "The laws," said Vergniaud, in the debate on the sentence of the king, "are obligatory only as the presumptive will of the people, which retains the right of approving or condemning them. The instant it manifests its wish the work of the national representation, the law, must disappear." This doctrine resolved society into its natural elements, and threatened to break up the country into as many republics as there were communes. For true republicanism is the principle of self-government in the whole and in all the parts. In an extensive country, it can prevail only by the union of several independent communities in a single confederacy, as in Greece, in Switzerland, in the Netherlands, and in America; so that a large republic not founded on the federal principle must result in the government of a single city, like Rome and Paris, and, in a less degree, Athens, Berne, and Amsterdam; or, in other words, a great democracy must either sacrifice self-government to unity, or preserve it by federalism.

The France of history fell together with the French State, which was the growth of centuries. The old sovereignty was destroyed. The local authorities were looked upon with aversion and alarm. The new central authority needed to be established on a new principle of unity. The state of nature, which was the ideal of society, was made the basis of the nation; descent was put in the place of tradition, and the French people was regarded as a physical product: an ethnological, not historic, unit. It was assumed that a unity existed separate from the representation and the government, wholly independent of the past, and capable at any moment of expressing or of changing its mind. In the words of Sieyès, it was no longer France, but some unknown country to which the nation was transported. The central power possessed authority, inasmuch as it obeyed the whole, and no divergence was permitted from the universal sentiment. This power, endowed with volition, was personified in the Republic One and Indivisible. The title signified that a part could not speak or act for the whole,—that there was a power supreme over the State, distinct from, and independent of, its members; and it expressed, for the first time in history, the notion of an abstract nationality. In this manner the idea of the sovereignty of the people, uncontrolled by the past, gave birth to the idea of nationality independent of the political influence of history. It sprang from the rejection of the two authorities,—of the State and of the past. The kingdom of France was, geographically as well as politically, the product of a long series of events, and the same influences which built up the State formed the territory. The Revolution repudiated alike the agencies to which France owed her boundaries and those to which she owed her government. Every effaceable trace and relic of national history was carefully wiped away,—the system of administration, the physical divisions of the country, the classes of society, the corporations, the weights and measures, the calendar. France was no longer bounded by the limits she had received from the condemned influence of her history; she could recognise only those which were set by nature. The definition of the nation was borrowed from the material world, and, in order to avoid a loss of territory, it became not only an abstraction but a fiction.

There was a principle of nationality in the ethnological character of the movement, which is the source of the common observation that revolution is more frequent in Catholic than in Protestant countries. It is, in fact, more frequent in the Latin than in the Teutonic world, because it depends partly on a national impulse, which is only awakened where there is an alien element, the vestige of a foreign dominion, to expel. Western Europe has undergone two conquests—one by the Romans and one by the Germans, and twice received laws from the invaders. Each time it rose again against the victorious race; and the two great reactions, while they differ according to the different characters of the two conquests, have the phenomenon of imperialism in common. The Roman republic laboured to crush the subjugated nations into a homogeneous and obedient mass; but the increase which the proconsular authority obtained in the process subverted the republican government, and the reaction of the provinces against Rome assisted in establishing the empire. The Caesarean system gave an unprecedented freedom to the dependencies, and raised them to a civil equality which put an end to the dominion of race over race and of class over class. The monarchy was hailed as a refuge from the pride and cupidity of the Roman people; and the love of equality, the hatred of nobility, and the tolerance of despotism implanted by Rome became, at least in Gaul, the chief feature of the national character. But among the nations whose vitality had been broken down by the stern republic, not one retained the materials necessary to enjoy independence, or to develop a new history. The political faculty which organises states and finds society in a moral order was exhausted, and the Christian doctors looked in vain over the waste of ruins for a people by whose aid the Church might survive the decay of Rome. A new element of national life was brought to that declining world by the enemies who destroyed it. The flood of barbarians settled over it for a season, and then subsided; and when the landmarks of civilisation appeared once more, it was found that the soil had been impregnated with a fertilising and regenerating influence, and that the inundation had laid the germs of future states and of a new society. The political sense and energy came with the new blood, and was exhibited in the power exercised by the younger race upon the old, and in the establishment of a graduated freedom. Instead of universal equal rights, the actual enjoyment of which is necessarily contingent on, and commensurate with, power, the rights of the people were made dependent on a variety of conditions, the first of which was the distribution of property. Civil society became a classified organism instead of a formless combination of atoms, and the feudal system gradually arose.

Roman Gaul had so thoroughly adopted the ideas of absolute authority and undistinguished equality during the five centuries between Caesar and Clovis, that the people could never be reconciled to the new system. Feudalism remained a foreign importation, and the feudal aristocracy an alien race, and the common people of France sought protection against both in the Roman jurisprudence and the power of the crown. The development of absolute monarchy by the help of democracy is the one constant character of French history. The royal power, feudal at first, and limited by the immunities and the great vassals, became more popular as it grew more absolute; while the suppression of aristocracy, the removal of the intermediate authorities, was so particularly the object of the nation, that it was more energetically accomplished after the fall of the throne. The monarchy which had been engaged from the thirteenth century in curbing the nobles, was at last thrust aside by the democracy, because it was too dilatory in the work, and was unable to deny its own origin and effectually ruin the class from which it sprang. All those things which constitute the peculiar character of the French Revolution,—the demand for equality, the hatred of nobility and feudalism, and of the Church which was connected with them, the constant reference to pagan examples, the suppression of monarchy, the new code of law, the breach with tradition, and the substitution of an ideal system for everything that had proceeded from the mixture and mutual action of the races,— all these exhibit the common type of a reaction against the effects of the Frankish invasion. The hatred of royalty was less than the hatred of aristocracy; privileges were more detested than tyranny; and the king perished because of the origin of his authority rather than because of its abuse. Monarchy unconnected with aristocracy became popular in France, even when most uncontrolled; whilst the attempt to reconstitute the throne, and to limit and fence it with its peers, broke down, because the old Teutonic elements on which it relied—hereditary nobility, primogeniture, and privilege—were no longer tolerated. The substance of the ideas of 1789 is not the limitation of the sovereign power, but the abrogation of inter-mediate powers. These powers, and the classes which enjoyed them, come in Latin Europe from a barbarian origin; and the movement which calls itself liberal is essentially national. If liberty were its object, its means would be the establishment of great independent authorities not derived from the State, and its model would be England. But its object is equality; and it seeks, like France in 1789, to cast out the elements of inequality which were introduced by the Teutonic race. This is the object which Italy and Spain have had in common with France, and herein consists the natural league of the Latin nations.

This national element in the movement was not understood by the revolutionary leaders. At first, their doctrine appeared entirely contrary to the idea of nationality. They taught that certain general principles of government were absolutely right in all States; and they asserted in theory the unrestricted freedom of the individual, and the supremacy of the will over every external necessity or obligation. This is in apparent contradiction to the national theory, that certain natural forces ought to determine the character, the form, and the policy of the State, by which a kind of fate is put in the place of freedom. Accordingly the national sentiment was not developed directly out of the revolution in which it was involved, but was exhibited first in resistance to it, when the attempt to emancipate had been absorbed in the desire to subjugate, and the republic had been succeeded by the empire. Napoleon called a new power into existence by attacking nationality in Russia, by delivering it in Italy, by governing in defiance of it in Germany and Spain. The sovereigns of these countries were deposed or degraded; and a system of administration was introduced which was French in its origin, its spirit, and its instruments. The people resisted the change. The movement against it was popular and spontaneous, because

107

the rulers were absent or helpless; and it was national, because it was directed against foreign institutions. In Tyrol, in Spain, and afterwards in Prussia, the people did not receive the impulse from the government, but undertook of their own accord to cast out the armies and the ideas of revolutionised France. Men were made conscious of the national element of the revolution by its conquests, not in its rise. The three things which the Empire most openly oppressed—religion, national independence, and political liberty—united in a short-lived league to animate the great uprising by which Napoleon fell. Under the influence of that memorable alliance a political spirit was called forth on the Continent, which clung to freedom and abhorred revolution, and sought to restore, to develop, and to reform the decayed national institutions. The men who proclaimed these ideas, Stein and Görres, Humboldt, Müller, and De Maistre,[2] were

---

[2] There are some remarkable thoughts on nationality in the State Papers of the Count de Maistre:

> En premier lieu les nations sont quelque chose dans le monde, il n'est pas permis de les compter pour rien, de les affliger dans leurs convenances, dans leurs affections, dans leurs intérêts les plus chers.... Or le traité du 30 mai anéantit complétement la Savoie; il divise l'indivisible; il partage en trois portions une malheureuse nation de 400,000 hommes, une par la langue, une par la religion, une par le caractère, une par l'habitude invétérée, une enfin par les limites naturelles.... L'union des nations ne souffre pas de difficultés sur la carte géographique; mais dans la réalité, c'est autre chose; il y a des nations *immiscibles*.... Je lui parlai par occasion de l'esprit italien qui s'agite dans ce moment; il (Count Nesselrode) me répondit: "Oui, Monsieur; mais cet esprit est un grand mal, car il peut gêner les arrangements de l'Italie." (*Correspondance Diplomatique de J. de Maistre*, ii. 7, 8, 21, 25)

In the same year, 1815, Görres wrote:

> In Italien wie allerwarts ist das Volk gewecht; es will etwas grossartiges, es will Ideen haben, die, wenn es sie auch nicht ganz begreift, doch einen freien unendlichen Gesichtskreis seiner Einbildung eröffnen.... Es ist reiner Naturtrieb, dass ein Volk, also scharf und deutlich in seine natürlichen Gränzen eingeschlossen, aus der Zerstreuung in die Einheit sich zu sammeln sucht. (*Werke*, ii. 20)

as hostile to Bonapartism as to the absolutism of the old governments, and insisted on the national rights, which had been invaded equally by both, and which they hoped to restore by the destruction of the French supremacy. With the cause that triumphed at Waterloo the friends of the Revolution had no sympathy, for they had learned to identify their doctrine with the cause of France. The Holland House Whigs in England, the Afrancesados in Spain, the Muratists in Italy, and the partisans of the Confederation of the Rhine, merging patriotism in their revolutionary affections, regretted the fall of the French power, and looked with alarm at those new and unknown forces which the War of Deliverance had evoked, and which were as menacing to French liberalism as to French supremacy.

But the new aspirations for national and popular rights were crushed at the restoration. The liberals of those days cared for freedom, not in the shape of national independence, but of French institutions; and they combined against the nations with the ambition of the governments. They were as ready to sacrifice nationality to their ideal as the Holy Alliance was to the interests of absolutism. Talleyrand indeed declared at Vienna that the Polish question ought to have precedence over all other questions, because the partition of Poland had been one of the first and greatest causes of the evils which Europe had suffered; but dynastic interests prevailed. All the sovereigns represented at Vienna recovered their dominions, except the King of Saxony, who was punished for his fidelity to Napoleon; but the States that were unrepresented in the reigning families—Poland, Venice, and Genoa—were not revived, and even the Pope had great difficulty in recovering the Legations from the grasp of Austria. Nationality, which the old *régime* had ignored, which had been outraged by the revolution and the empire, received, after its first open demonstration, the hardest blow at the Congress of Vienna. The principle which the first partition had generated, to which the revolution had given a basis of theory, which had been lashed by the empire into a momentary convulsive effort, was matured by the long error of the restoration into a consistent doctrine, nourished and justified by the situation of Europe.

The governments of the Holy Alliance devoted themselves to suppress with equal care the revolutionary spirit by which they had been threatened, and the national spirit by which they had been restored. Austria, which owed nothing to the national movement, and had prevented its revival after 1809, naturally took the lead in repressing it. Every disturbance of the final settlements of 1815, every aspiration for changes or reforms, was condemned as sedition. This system repressed the good with the evil tendencies of the age; and the resistance which it provoked, during the generation that passed away from the restoration to the fall of Metternich, and again under the reaction which commenced with Schwarzenberg and ended with the administrations of Bach and Manteuffel, proceeded from various combinations of the opposite forms of liberalism. In the successive phases of that struggle, the idea that national claims are above all other rights gradually rose to the supremacy which it now possesses among the revolutionary agencies.

The first liberal movement, that of the Carbonari in the south of Europe, had no specific national character, but was supported by the Bonapartists both in Spain and Italy. In the following years the opposite ideas of 1813 came to the front, and a revolutionary movement, in many respects hostile to the principles of revolution, began in defence of liberty, religion, and nationality. All these causes were united in the Irish agitation, and in the Greek, Belgian, and Polish revolutions. Those sentiments which had been insulted by Napoleon, and had risen against him, rose against the governments of the restoration. They had been oppressed by the sword, and then by the treaties. The national principle added force, but not justice, to this movement, which, in every case but Poland, was successful. A period followed in which it degenerated into a purely national idea, as the agitation for repeal succeeded emancipation, and Panslavism and Panhellenism arose under the auspices of the Eastern Church. This was the third phase of the resistance to the settlement of Vienna, which was weak, because it failed to satisfy national or constitutional aspirations, either of which would have been a safeguard against the other, by a moral if not by a popular justification. At first, in 1813, the people rose against their conquerors, in defence of their legitimate rulers. They refused to be governed by usurpers. In the period between 1825 and 1831, they resolved that they would not be misgoverned by strangers. The French administration was often better than that which it displaced, but there were prior claimants for the authority exercised by the French, and at first the national contest was a contest for legitimacy. In the second period this element was wanting. No dispossessed princes led the Greeks, the Belgians, or the Poles. The Turks, the Dutch, and the Russians were attacked, not as usurpers, but as oppressors,—because they misgoverned, not because they were of a different race. Then began a time when the text simply was, that nations would not be governed by foreigners. Power legitimately obtained, and exercised with moderation, was declared invalid. National rights, like religion, had borne part in the previous combinations, and had been auxiliaries in the struggles for freedom, but now nationality became a paramount claim, which was to assert itself alone, which might put forward as pretexts the rights of rulers, the liberties of the people, the safety of religion, but which, if no such union could be formed, was to prevail at the expense of every other cause for which nations make sacrifices.

Matternich is, next to Napoleon, the chief promoter of this theory; for the anti-national character of the restoration was most distinct in Austria, and it is in opposition to the Austrian Government that nationality grew into a system. Napoleon, who, trusting to his armies, despised moral forces in politics, was overthrown by their rising. Austria committed the same fault in the government of her Italian provinces. The kingdom of Italy had united all the northern part of the Peninsula in a single State; and the national feelings, which the French repressed elsewhere, were encouraged as a safeguard of their power in Italy and in Poland. When the tide of victory turned, Austria invoked against the French the aid of the new sentiment they had fostered. Nugent announced, in his proclamation to the Italians, that they should become an independent nation. The same spirit served different masters, and contributed first to the destruction of the old States, then to the expulsion of the French, and again, under Charles Albert, to a new revolution. It was appealed to in the name of the most contradictory principles of government, and served all parties in succession, because it was one in which all could unite. Beginning by a protest against the dominion of race over race, its mildest and least-developed form, it grew into a condemnation of every State that included different races, and finally became the complete and consistent theory, that the State and the nation must be co-extensive. "It is," says Mr. Mill, "in general a necessary condition of free institutions, that the boundaries of governments should coincide in the main with those of nationalities."[3]

The outward historical progress of this idea from an indefinite aspiration to be the keystone of a political system, may be traced in the life of the man who gave to it the element in which its strength resides,—Giuseppe Mazzini. He found Carbonarism impotent against the measures of the governments, and resolved to give new life to the liberal movement by transferring it to the ground of nationality. Exile is the nursery of nationality, as oppression is the school of liberalism; and Mazzini conceived the idea of Young Italy when he was a refugee at Marseilles. In the same way, the Polish exiles are the champions of every national movement; for to them all political rights are absorbed in the idea of independence, which, however they may differ with each other, is the one aspiration common to them all. Towards the year 1830 literature also contributed to the national idea. "It was the time," says Mazzini, "of the great conflict between the romantic and the classical school, which might with equal truth be called a conflict between the partisans of freedom and of authority." The romantic school was infidel in Italy, and Catholic in Germany; but in both it had the common effect of encouraging national history and literature, and Dante was as great an authority with the Italian democrats as with the leaders of the medieval revival at Vienna, Munich, and Berlin. But neither the influence of the exiles, nor that of the poets and critics of the new party, extended over the masses. It was a sect without popular sympathy or encouragement, a conspiracy founded not on a grievance, but on a doctrine; and when the attempt to

---

[3] *Considerations on Representative Government*, p. 298.

rise was made in Savoy, in 1834, under a banner with the motto "Unity, Independence, God and Humanity," the people were puzzled at its object, and indifferent to its failure. But Mazzini continued his propaganda, developed his *Giovine Italia* into a *Giovine Europa*, and established in 1847 the international league of nations. "The people," he said, in his opening address, "is penetrated with only one idea, that of unity and nationality.... There is no international question as to forms of government, but only a national question."

The revolution of 1848, unsuccessful in its national purpose, prepared the subsequent victories of nationality in two ways. The first of these was the restoration of the Austrian power in Italy, with a new and more energetic centralisation, which gave no promise of freedom. Whilst that system prevailed, the right was on the side of the national aspirations, and they were revived in a more complete and cultivated form by Manin. The policy of the Austrian Government, which failed during the ten years of the reaction to convert the tenure by force into a tenure by right, and to establish with free institutions the condition of allegiance, gave a negative encouragement to the theory. It deprived Francis Joseph of all active support and sympathy in 1859, for he was more clearly wrong in his conduct than his enemies in their doctrines. The real cause of the energy which the national theory has acquired is, however, the triumph of the democratic principle in France, and its recognition by the European Powers. The theory of nationality is involved in the democratic theory of the sovereignty of the general will. "One hardly knows what any division of the human race should be free to do, if not to determine with which of the various collective bodies of human beings they choose to associate themselves."[4] It is by this act that a nation constitutes itself. To have a collective will, unity is necessary, and independence is requisite in order to assert it. Unity and nationality are still more essential to the notion of the sovereignty of the people than the cashiering of monarchs, or the revocation of laws. Arbitrary acts of this kind may be prevented by the happiness of the people or the

---

[4] Mill's *Considerations*, p. 296.

popularity of the king, but a nation inspired by the democratic idea cannot with consistency allow a part of itself to belong to a foreign State, or the whole to be divided into several native States. The theory of nationality therefore proceeds from both the principles which divide the political world,—from legitimacy, which ignores its claims, and from the revolution, which assumes them; and for the same reason it is the chief weapon of the last against the first.

In pursuing the outward and visible growth of the national theory we are prepared for an examination of its political character and value. The absolutism which has created it denies equally that absolute right of national unity which is a product of democracy, and that claim of national liberty which belongs to the theory of freedom. These two views of nationality, corresponding to the French and to the English systems, are connected in name only, and are in reality the opposite extremes of political thought. In one case, nationality is founded on the perpetual supremacy of the collective will, of which the unity of the nation is the necessary condition, to which every other influence must defer, and against which no obligation enjoys authority, and all resistance is tyrannical. The nation is here an ideal unit founded on the race, in defiance of the modifying action of external causes, of tradition, and of existing rights. It overrules the rights and wishes of the inhabitants, absorbing their divergent interests in a fictitious unity; sacrifices their several inclinations and duties to the higher claim of nationality, and crushes all natural rights and all established liberties for the purpose of vindicating itself.[5] Whenever a single definite object is made the supreme end of the State, be it the advantage of a class, the safety or the power of the country, the greatest happiness of the greatest number, or the support of any speculative

---

[5] "Le sentiment d'indépendance nationale est encore plus général et plus profondément gravé dans le cœur des peuples que l'amour d'une liberté constitutionnelle. Les nations les plus soumises au despotisme éprouvent ce sentiment avec autant de vivacité que les nations libres; les peuples les plus barbares le sentent même encore plus vivement que les nations policées." (*L'Italie au Dixneuvième Siècle*, p. 148, Paris, 1821)

idea, the State becomes for the time inevitably absolute. Liberty alone demands for its realisation the limitation of the public authority, for liberty is the only object which benefits all alike, and provokes no sincere opposition. In supporting the claims of national unity, governments must be subverted in whose title there is no flaw, and whose policy is beneficent and equitable, and subjects must be compelled to transfer their allegiance to an authority for which they have no attachment, and which may be practically a foreign domination. Connected with this theory in nothing except in the common enmity of the absolute state, is the theory which represents nationality as an essential, but not a supreme element in determining the forms of the State. It is distinguished from the other, because it tends to diversity and not to uniformity, to harmony and not to unity; because it aims not at an arbitrary change, but at careful respect for the existing conditions of political life, and because it obeys the laws and results of history, not the aspirations of an ideal future. While the theory of unity makes the nation a source of despotism and revolution, the theory of liberty regards it as the bulwark of self-government, and the foremost limit to the excessive power of the State. Private rights, which are sacrificed to the unity, are preserved by the union of nations. No power can so efficiently resist the tendencies of centralisation, of corruption, and of absolutism, as that community which is the vastest that can be included in a State, which imposes on its members a consistent similarity of character, interest, and opinion, and which arrests the action of the sovereign by the influence of a divided patriotism. The presence of different nations under the same sovereignty is similar in its effect to the independence of the Church in the State. It provides against the servility which flourishes under the shadow of a single authority, by balancing interests, multiplying associations, and giving to the subject the restraint and support of a combined opinion. In the same way it promotes independence by forming definite groups of public opinion, and by affording a great source and centre of political sentiments, and of notions of duty not derived from the sovereign will. Liberty provokes diversity, and diversity preserves liberty by supplying the means of organisation. All those portions

115

of law which govern the relations of men with each other, and regulate social life, are the varying result of national custom and the creation of private society. In these things, therefore, the several nations will differ from each other; for they themselves have produced them, and they do not owe them to the State which rules them all. This diversity in the same State is a firm barrier against the intrusion of the government beyond the political sphere which is common to all into the social department which escapes legislation and is ruled by spontaneous laws. This sort of interference is characteristic of an absolute government, and is sure to provoke a reaction, and finally a remedy. That intolerance of social freedom which is natural to absolutism is sure to find a corrective in the national diversities, which no other force could so efficiently provide. The co-existence of several nations under the same State is a test, as well as the best security of its freedom. It is also one of the chief instruments of civilisation; and, as such, it is in the natural and providential order, and indicates a state of greater advancement than the national unity which is the ideal of modern liberalism.

The combination of different nations in one State is as necessary a condition of civilised life as the combination of men in society. Inferior races are raised by living in political union with races intellectually superior. Exhausted and decaying nations are revived by the contact of a younger vitality. Nations in which the elements of organisation and the capacity for government have been lost, either through the demoralising influence of despotism, or the disintegrating action of democracy, are restored and educated anew under the discipline of a stronger and less corrupted race. This fertilising and regenerating process can only be obtained by living under one government. It is in the cauldron of the State that the fusion takes place by which the vigour, the knowledge, and the capacity of one portion of mankind may be communicated to another. Where political and national boundaries coincide, society ceases to advance, and nations relapse into a condition corresponding to that of men who renounce intercourse with their fellow-men. The difference between the two unites mankind not only by the benefits it confers on those who live together, but because it connects society either by a political or a national bond, gives to every people an interest in its neighbours, either because they are under the same government or because they are of the same race, and thus promotes the interests of humanity, of civilisation, and of religion.

Christianity rejoices at the mixture of races, as paganism identifies itself with their differences, because truth is universal, and errors various and particular. In the ancient world idolatry and nationality went together, and the same term is applied in Scripture to both. It was the mission of the Church to overcome national differences. The period of her undisputed supremacy was that in which all Western Europe obeyed the same laws, all literature was contained in one language, and the political unity of Christendom was personified in a single potentate, while its intellectual unity was represented in one university. As the ancient Romans concluded their conquests by carrying away the gods of the conquered people, Charlemagne overcame the national resistance of the Saxons only by the forcible destruction of their pagan rites. Out of the medieval period, and the combined action of the German race and the Church, came forth a new system of nations and a new conception of nationality. Nature was overcome in the nation as well as in the individual. In pagan and uncultivated times, nations were distinguished from each other by the widest diversity, not only in religion, but in customs, language, and character. Under the new law they had many things in common; the old barriers which separated them were removed, and the new principle of self-government, which Christianity imposed, enabled them to live together under the same authority, without necessarily losing their cherished habits, their customs, or their laws. The new idea of freedom made room for different races in one State. A nation was no longer what it had been to the ancient world,—the progeny of a common ancestor, or the aboriginal product of a particular region,—a result of merely physical and material causes,—but a moral and political being; not the creation of geographical or physiological unity, but developed in the course of history by the action of the State. It is derived from the State, not supreme over it. A State may in course of time produce a nationality; but

117

that a nationality should constitute a State is contrary to the nature of modern civilisation. The nation derives its rights and its power from the memory of a former independence.

The Church has agreed in this respect with the tendency of political progress, and discouraged wherever she could the isolation of nations; admonishing them of their duties to each other, and regarding conquest and feudal investiture as the natural means of raising barbarous or sunken nations to a higher level. But though she has never attributed to national independence an immunity from the accidental consequences of feudal law, of hereditary claims, or of testamentary arrangements, she defends national liberty against uniformity and centralisation with an energy inspired by perfect community of interests. For the same enemy threatens both; and the State which is reluctant to tolerate differences, and to do justice to the peculiar character of various races, must from the same cause interfere in the internal government of religion. The connection of religious liberty with the emancipation of Poland or Ireland is not merely the accidental result of local causes; and the failure of the Concordat to unite the subjects of Austria is the natural consequence of a policy which did not desire to protect the provinces in their diversity and autonomy, and sought to bribe the Church by favours instead of strengthening her by independence. From this influence of religion in modern history has proceeded a new definition of patriotism.

The difference between nationality and the State is exhibited in the nature of patriotic attachment. Our connection with the race is merely natural or physical, whilst our duties to the political nation are ethical. One is a community of affections and instincts infinitely important and powerful in savage life, but pertaining more to the animal than to the civilised man; the other is an authority governing by laws, imposing obligations, and giving a moral sanction and character to the natural relations of society. Patriotism is in political life what faith is in religion, and it stands to the domestic feelings and to home-sickness as faith to fanaticism and to superstition. It has one aspect derived from private life and nature, for it is an extension of the family affections, as the tribe is an extension of the family. But in its real political character, patriotism consists in the development of the instinct of self-preservation into a moral duty which may involve self-sacrifice. Self-preservation is both an instinct and a duty, natural and involuntary in one respect, and at the same time a moral obligation. By the first it produces the family; by the last the State. If the nation could exist without the State, subject only to the instinct of self-preservation, it would be incapable of denying, controlling, or sacrificing itself; it would be an end and a rule to itself. But in the political order moral purposes are realised and public ends are pursued to which private interests and even existence must be sacrificed. The great sign of true patriotism, the development of selfishness into sacrifice, is the product of political life. That sense of duty which is supplied by race is not entirely separated from its selfish and instinctive basis; and the love of country, like married love, stands at the same time on a material and a moral foundation. The patriot must distinguish between the two causes or objects of his devotion. The attachment which is given only to the country is like obedience given only to the State—a submission to physical influences. The man who prefers his country before every other duty shows the same spirit as the man who surrenders every right to the State. They both deny that right is superior to authority.

There is a moral and political country, in the language of Burke, distinct from the geographical, which may be possibly in collision with it. The Frenchmen who bore arms against the Convention were as patriotic as the Englishmen who bore arms against King Charles, for they recognised a higher duty than that of obedience to the actual sovereign. "In an address to France," said Burke,

> in an attempt to treat with it, or in considering any scheme at all relative to it, it is impossible we should mean the geographical, we must always mean the moral and political, country.... The truth is, that France is out of itself—the moral France is separated from the geographical. The master of the house is expelled, and the robbers are in possession. If we look for the corporate people of France, existing as corporate in the eye and

intention of public law (that corporate people, I mean, who are free to deliberate and to decide, and who have a capacity to treat and conclude), they are in Flanders and Germany, in Switzerland, Spain, Italy, and England. There are all the princes of the blood, there are all the orders of the State, there are all the parliaments of the kingdom.... I am sure that if half that number of the same description were taken out of this country, it would leave hardly anything that I should call the people of England.[6]

Rousseau draws nearly the same distinction between the country to which we happen to belong and that which fulfils towards us the political functions of the State. In the Emile he has a sentence of which it is not easy in a translation to convey the point: "Qui n'a pas une patrie a du moins un pays." And in his tract on Political Economy he writes: "How shall men love their country if it is nothing more for them than for strangers, and bestows on them only that which it can refuse to none?" It is in the same sense he says, further on, "La patrie ne peut subsister sans la liberté."[7]

The nationality formed by the State, then, is the only one to which we owe political duties, and it is, therefore, the only one which has political rights. The Swiss are ethnologically either French, Italian, or German; but no nationality has the slightest claim upon them, except the purely political nationality of Switzerland. The Tuscan or the Neapolitan State has formed a nationality, but the citizens of Florence and of Naples have no

---

[6] Burke's "Remarks on the Policy of the Allies" (β, v. 26, 29, 30).

[7] *Œuvres*, i. 593, 595, ii. 717. Bossuet, in a passage of great beauty on the love of country, does not attain to the political definition of the word:

> La société humaine demande qu'on aime la terre où l'on habite ensemble, ou la regarde comme une mère et une nourrice commune.... Les hommes en effet se sentent liés par quelque chose de fort, lorsqu'ils songent, que la même terre qui les a portés et nourris étant vivants, les recevra dans son sein quand ils seront morts. ("Politique tirée de l'Ecriture Sainte," *Œuvres*, x. 317)

political community with each other. There are other States which have neither succeeded in absorbing distinct races in a political nationality, nor in separating a particular district from a larger nation. Austria and Mexico are instances on the one hand, Parma and Baden on the other. The progress of civilisation deals hardly with the last description of States. In order to maintain their integrity they must attach themselves by confederations, or family alliances, to greater Powers, and thus lose something of their independence. Their tendency is to isolate and shut off their inhabitants, to narrow the horizon of their views, and to dwarf in some degree the proportions of their ideas. Public opinion cannot maintain its liberty and purity in such small dimensions, and the currents that come from larger communities sweep over a contracted territory. In a small and homogeneous population there is hardly room for a natural classification of society, or for inner groups of interests that set bounds to sovereign power. The government and the subjects contend with borrowed weapons. The resources of the one and the aspirations of the other are derived from some external source, and the consequence is that the country becomes the instrument and the scene of contests in which it is not interested. These States, like the minuter communities of the Middle Ages, serve a purpose, by constituting partitions and securities of self-government in the larger States; but they are impediments to the progress of society, which depends on the mixture of races under the same governments.

The vanity and peril of national claims founded on no political tradition, but on race alone, appear in Mexico. There the races are divided by blood, without being grouped together in different regions. It is, therefore, neither possible to unite them nor to convert them into the elements of an organised State. They are fluid, shapeless, and unconnected, and cannot be precipitated, or formed into the basis of political institutions. As they cannot be used by the State, they cannot be recognised by it; and their peculiar qualities, capabilities, passions, and attachments are of no service, and therefore obtain no regard. They are necessarily ignored, and are therefore perpetually outraged. From this difficulty of races with political pretensions, but without political position, the Eastern world escaped by the institution of castes. Where there are only two races there is the resource of slavery; but when different races inhabit the different territories of one Empire composed of several smaller States, it is of all possible combinations the most favourable to the establishment of a highly developed system of freedom. In Austria there are two circumstances which add to the difficulty of the problem, but also increase its importance. The several nationalities are at very unequal degrees of advancement, and there is no single nation which is so predominant as to overwhelm or absorb the others. These are the conditions necessary for the very highest degree of organisation which government is capable of receiving. They supply the greatest variety of intellectual resource; the perpetual incentive to progress, which is afforded not merely by competition, but by the spectacle of a more advanced people; the most abundant elements of self-government, combined with the impossibility for the State to rule all by its own will; and the fullest security for the preservation of local customs and ancient rights. In such a country as this, liberty would achieve its most glorious results, while centralisation and absolutism would be destruction.

The problem presented to the government of Austria is higher than that which is solved in England, because of the necessity of admitting the national claims. The parliamentary system fails to provide for them, as it presupposes the unity of the people. Hence in those countries in which different races dwell together, it has not satisfied their desires, and is regarded as an imperfect form of freedom. It brings out more clearly than before the differences it does not recognise, and thus continues the work of the old absolutism, and appears as a new phase of centralisation. In those countries, therefore, the power of the imperial parliament must be limited as jealously as the power of the crown, and many of its functions must be discharged by provincial diets, and a descending series of local authorities.

The great importance of nationality in the State consists in the fact that it is the basis of political capacity. The character of a nation determines in great measure the form and vitality of the State. Certain political habits and ideas belong to particular nations, and they vary with the course of the national history. A people just emerging from barbarism, a people effete from the excesses of a luxurious civilisation, cannot possess the means of governing itself; a people devoted to equality, or to absolute monarchy, is incapable of producing an aristocracy; a people averse to the institution of private property is without the first element of freedom. Each of these can be converted into efficient members of a free community only by the contact of a superior race, in whose power will lie the future prospects of the State. A system which ignores these things, and does not rely for its support on the character and aptitude of the people, does not intend that they should administer their own affairs, but that they should simply be obedient to the supreme command. The denial of nationality, therefore, implies the denial of political liberty.

The greatest adversary of the rights of nationality is the modern theory of nationality. By making the State and the nation commensurate with each other in theory, it reduces practically to a subject condition all other nationalities that may be within the boundary. It cannot admit them to an equality with the ruling nation which constitutes the State, because the State would then cease to be national, which would be a contradiction of the principle of its existence. According, therefore, to the degree of humanity and civilisation in that dominant body which claims all the rights of the community, the inferior races are exterminated, or reduced to servitude, or outlawed, or put in a condition of dependence.

If we take the establishment of liberty for the realisation of moral duties to be the end of civil society, we must conclude that those states are substantially the most perfect which, like the British and Austrian Empires, include various distinct nationalities without oppressing them. Those in which no mixture of races has occurred are imperfect; and those in which its effects have disappeared are decrepit. A State which is incompetent to satisfy different races condemns itself; a State which labours to neutralise, to absorb, or to expel them, destroys its own vitality; a State which does not include them is destitute of the chief basis of self-government. The theory of nationality, therefore, is a retrograde step in history. It is the most advanced form of the revolution, and must retain its power to the end of the revolutionary period, of which it announces the approach. Its great historical importance depends on two chief causes.

First, it is a chimera. The settlement at which it aims is impossible. As it can never be satisfied and exhausted, and always continues to assert itself, it prevents the government from ever relapsing into the condition which provoked its rise. The danger is too threatening, and the power over men's minds too great, to allow any system to endure which justifies the resistance of nationality. It must contribute, therefore, to obtain that which in theory it condemns,—the liberty of different nationalities as members of one sovereign community. This is a service which no other force could accomplish; for it is a corrective alike of absolute monarchy, of democracy, and of constitutionalism, as well as of the centralisation which is common to all three. Neither the monarchical, nor the revolutionary, nor the parliamentary system can do this; and all the ideas which have excited enthusiasm in past times are impotent for the purpose except nationality alone.

And secondly, the national theory marks the end of the revolutionary doctrine and its logical exhaustion. In proclaiming the supremacy of the rights of nationality, the system of democratic equality goes beyond its own extreme boundary, and falls into contradiction with itself. Between the democratic and the national phase of the revolution, socialism had intervened, and had already carried the consequences of the principle to an absurdity. But that phase was passed. The revolution survived its offspring, and produced another further result. Nationality is more advanced than socialism, because it is a more arbitrary system. The social theory endeavours to provide for the existence of the individual beneath the terrible burdens which modern society heaps upon labour. It is not merely a development of the notion of equality, but a refuge from real misery and starvation. However false the solution, it was a reasonable demand that the poor should be saved from destruction; and if the freedom of the State was sacrificed to the safety of the individual, the more immediate object was, at least in theory, attained. But nationality does not aim either at liberty or prosperity, both of which it sacrifices to the imperative necessity of making the nation the mould and measure of the State. Its course will be marked with material as well as moral ruin, in order that a new invention may prevail over the works of God and the interests of mankind. There is no principle of change, no phase of political speculation conceivable, more comprehensive, more subversive, or more arbitrary than this. It is a confutation of democracy, because it sets limits to the exercise of the popular will, and substitutes for it a higher principle. It prevents not only the division, but the extension of the State, and forbids to terminate war by conquest, and to obtain a security for peace. Thus, after surrendering the individual to the collective will, the revolutionary system makes the collective will subject to conditions which are independent of it, and rejects all law, only to be controlled by an accident.

Although, therefore, the theory of nationality is more absurd and more criminal than the theory of socialism, it has an important mission in the world, and marks the final conflict, and therefore the end, of two forces which are the worst enemies of civil freedom,—the absolute monarchy and the revolution.

5

INAUGURAL LECTURE
ON THE STUDY OF HISTORY[*]

Fellow students—I look back today to a time before the middle of the century, when I was reading at Edinburgh and fervently wishing to come to this University. At three colleges I applied for admission, and, as things then were, I was refused by all. Here, from the first, I vainly fixed my hopes, and here, in a happier hour, after five-and-forty years, they are at last fulfilled.

I desire, first, to speak to you of that which I may reasonably call the Unity of Modern History, as an easy approach to questions necessary to be met on the threshold by any one occupying this place, which my predecessor has made so formidable to me by the reflected lustre of his name.

You have often heard it said that Modern History is a subject to which neither beginning nor end can be assigned. No beginning, because the dense web of the fortunes of man is woven without a void; because, in society as in nature, the structure is continuous, and we can trace things back uninterruptedly, until we dimly descry the Declaration of Independence in the

---

*Published as *A Lecture on the Study of History* (London: Macmillan, 1895). Reprinted in Lord Acton, *Lectures on Modern History*, ed. John Neville Figgis and Reginald Vere Laurence (London: Macmillan, 1906), 1–28; *Selected Writings of Lord Acton*, ed. J. Rufus Fears, 3 vols. (Indianapolis: Liberty Fund, 1985–88), 2:504–52.

forests of Germany. No end, because, on the same principle, history made and history making are scientifically inseparable and separately unmeaning.

"Politics," said Sir John Seeley, "are vulgar when they are not liberalised by history, and history fades into mere literature when it loses sight of its relation to practical politics." Everybody perceives the sense in which this is true. For the science of politics is the one science that is deposited by the stream of history, like grains of gold in the sand of a river; and the knowledge of the past, the record of truths revealed by experience, is eminently practical, as an instrument of action and a power that goes to the making of the future.[1] In France, such is the weight attached to the study of our own time, that there is an appointed course of contemporary history, with appropriate text-books.[2] That is a chair which, in the progressive division of labour by which both science and government prosper,[3] may some day be founded in this country. Meantime, we do well to acknowledge the points at which the two epochs diverge. For the contemporary differs from the modern in this, that many of its facts cannot by us be definitely ascertained. The living do not give up their secrets with the candour of the dead; one key is always excepted, and a generation passes before we can ensure accuracy. Common

---

[1] No political conclusions of any value for practice can be arrived at by direct experience. All true political science is, in one sense of the phrase, a priori, being deduced from the tendencies of things, tendencies known either through our general experience of human nature, or as the result of an analysis of the course of history, considered as a progressive evolution.—Mill, *Inaugural Address*, 51.

[2] Contemporary history is, in Dr. Arnold's opinion, more important than either ancient or modern; and in fact superior to it by all the superiority of the end to the means.—Seeley, *Lectures and Essays*, 306.

[3] The law of all progress is one and the same, the evolution of the simple into the complex by successive differentiations.—*Edinburgh Review*, clvii. 428. Die Entwickelung der Völker vollzieht sich nach zwei Gesetzen. Das erste Gesetz ist das der Differenzierung. Die primitiven Einrichtungen sind einfach und einheitlich, die der Civilisation zusammengesetzt und geteilt, und die Arbeitsteilung nimmt beständig zu.—Sickel, *Goettingen Gelehrte Anzeigen*, 1890, 563.

report and outward seeming are bad copies of the reality, as the initiated know it. Even of a thing so memorable as the war of 1870, the true cause is still obscure; much that we believed has been scattered to the winds in the last six months, and further revelations by important witnesses are about to appear. The use of history turns far more on certainty than on abundance of acquired information.

Beyond the question of certainty is the question of detachment. The process by which principles are discovered and appropriated is other than that by which, in practice, they are applied; and our most sacred and disinterested convictions ought to take shape in the tranquil regions of the air, above the tumult and the tempest of active life.[4] For a man is justly despised who has one opinion in history and another in politics, one for abroad and another at home, one for opposition and another for office. History compels us to fasten on abiding issues, and rescues us from the temporary and transient. Politics and history are interwoven, but are not commensurate. Ours is a domain that reaches farther than affairs of state, and is not subject to the jurisdiction of governments. It is our function to keep in view and to command the movement of ideas, which are not the effect but the cause of public events;[5] and even to allow some priority to ecclesiastical history over civil, since, by reason of the graver issues concerned, and the vital consequences of error, it opened the way in research, and was the first to be treated by close reasoners and scholars of the higher rank.[6]

---

[4] Nous risquons toujours d'être influencés par les préjugés de notre époque; mais nous sommes libres des préjugés particuliers aux époques antérieures.—E. NAVILLE, *Christianisme de Fénelon*, 9.

[5] La nature n'est qu'un écho de l'esprit. L'idée est la mère du fait, elle façonne graduellement le monde à son image.—FEUCHTERSLEBEN, in Caro, *Nouvelles Études Morales*, 132. Il n'est pas d'étude morale qui vaille l'histoire d'une idée.—LABOULAYE, *Liberté Religieuse*, 25.

[6] Il y a des savants qui raillent le sentiment religieux. Ils ne savent pas que c'est à ce sentiment, et par son moyen, que la science historique doit d'avoir pu sortir de l'enfance.… Depuis des siècles les âmes indépendantes discutaient les textes et les traditions de l'église, quand

In the same manner, there is wisdom and depth in the philosophy which always considers the origin and the germ, and glories in history as one consistent epic.[7] Yet every student ought to know that mastery is acquired by resolved limitation. And confusion ensues from the theory of Montesquieu and of his school, who, adapting the same term to things unlike, insist that freedom is the primitive condition of the race from which we are sprung.[8] If we are to account mind not matter, ideas not force, the spiritual property that gives dignity and grace and intellectual value to history, and its action on the ascending life of man, then we shall not be prone to explain the universal by the national, and civilisation by custom.[9] A speech of Antigone,

---

les lettrés n'avaient pas encore eu l'idée de porter un regard critique sur les textes de l'antiquité mondaine.—*La France Protestante*, ii. 17.

[7] In our own history, above all, every step in advance has been at the same time a step backwards. It has often been shown how our latest constitution is, amidst all external differences, essentially the same as our earliest, how every struggle for right and freedom, from the thirteenth century onwards, has simply been a struggle for recovering something old.—FREEMAN, *Historical Essays*, iv. 253. Nothing but a thorough knowledge of the social system, based upon a regular study of its growth, can give us the power we require to affect it.—HARRISON, *Meaning of History*, 19. Eine Sache wird nur völlig auf dem Wege verstanden, wie sie selbst entsteht.—In dem genetischen Verfahren sind die Gründe der Sache, auch die Gründe des Erkennens.—TRENDELENBURG, *Logische Untersuchungen*, ii. 395, 388.

[8] Une telle liberté ... n'a rien de commun avec le savant système de garanties qui fait libres les peuples modernes—BOUTMY, *Annales des Sciences Politiques*, i. 157. Les trois grandes réformes qui ont renouvelé l'Angleterre, la liberté religieuse, la réforme parlementaire, et la liberté économique, ont été obtenues sous la pression des organisations extra-constitutionnelles.—OSTROGORSKI, *Revue Historique*, lii. 272.

[9] The question which is at the bottom of all constitutional struggles, the question between the national will and the national law.—GARDINER, *Documents*, xviii. Religion, considered simply as the principle which balances the power of human opinion, which takes man out of the grasp of custom and fashion, and teaches him to refer himself to a higher tribunal, is an infinite aid to moral strength and elevation.—CHANNING, *Works*, iv. 83. Je tiens que le passé ne suffit jamais au présent. Personne

a single sentence of Socrates, a few lines that were inscribed on an Indian rock before the Second Punic War, the footsteps of a silent yet prophetic people who dwelt by the Dead Sea, and perished in the fall of Jerusalem, come nearer to our lives than the ancestral wisdom of barbarians who fed their swine on the Hercynian acorns.

For our present purpose, then, I describe as Modern History that which begins four hundred years ago, which is marked off by an evident and intelligible line from the time immediately preceding, and displays in its course specific and distinctive characteristics of its own.[10] The modern age did not proceed from the medieval by normal succession, with outward tokens of legitimate descent. Unheralded, it founded a new order of things, under a law of innovation, sapping the ancient reign of continuity. In those days Columbus subverted the notions of the world, and reversed the conditions of production, wealth, and power; in those days Machiavelli released government from the restraint of law; Erasmus diverted the current of ancient learning from profane into Christian channels; Luther broke the chain of authority and tradition at the strongest link; and Copernicus erected an invincible power that set forever the mark of progress upon the time that was to come. There is the same unbound originality and disregard for inherited sanctions in the rare philosophers as in the discovery of Divine Right, and the intruding Imperialism of Rome. The like effects are visible everywhere, and one generation beheld them all. It was an awakening of new life; the world revolved in a different orbit,

---

n'est plus disposé que moi à profiter de ses leçons; mais en même temps, je le demande, le présent ne fournit-il pas toujours les indications qui lui sont propres?—MOLÉ, in FALLOUX, Études et Souvenirs, 130. Admirons la sagesse de nos pères, et tachons de l'imiter, en faisant ce qui convient à notre siècle.—GALIANI, *Dialogues*, 40.

[10] Ceterum in legendis Historiis malim te ductum animi, quam anxias leges sequi. Nullae sunt, quae non magnas habeant utilitates; et melius haerent, quae libenter legimus. In universum tamen, non incipere ab antiquissimis, sed ab his, quae nostris temporibus nostraeque notitiae propius cohaerent, ac paulatim deinde in remotiora eniti, magis è re arbitror.—GROTIUS, *Epistolae*, 18.

determined by influences unknown before. After many ages persuaded of the headlong decline and impending dissolution of society,[11] and governed by usage and the will of masters who were in their graves, the sixteenth century went forth armed for untried experience, and ready to watch with hopefulness a prospect of incalculable change.

That forward movement divides it broadly from the older world; and the unity of the new is manifest in the universal spirit of investigation and discovery which did not cease to operate, and withstood the recurring efforts of reaction, until, by the advent of the reign of general ideas which we call the Revolution, it at length prevailed.[12] This successive deliverance and gradual pas-

---

[11] The older idea of a law of degeneracy, of a "fatal drift towards the worse," is as obsolete as astrology or the belief in witchcraft. The human race has become hopeful, sanguine.—SEELEY, *Rede Lecture*, 1887. *Fortnightly Review*, July 1887, 124.

[12] Formuler des idées générales, c'est changer le salpêtre en poudre.— A. DE MUSSET, *Confessions d'un Enfant du Siècle*, 15. Les révolutions c'est l'avènement des idées libérales. C'est presque toujours par les révolutions qu'elles prévalent et se fondent, et quand les idées libérales en sont véritablement le principe et le but, quand elles leur ont donné naissance, et quand elles les couronnent à leur dernier jour, alors ces révolutions sont légitimes.—RÉMUSAT, 1839, in *Revue des Deux Mondes*, 1875, vi. 335. Il y a même des personnes de piété qui prouvent par raison qu'il faut renoncer à la raison; que ce n'est point la lumière, mais la foi seule qui doit nous conduire, et que l'obéissance aveugle est la principale vertu des chrétiens. La paresse des inférieurs et leur esprit flatteur s'accommode souvent de cette vertu prétendue, et l'orgueil de ceux qui commandent en est toujours très content. De sorte qu'il se trouvera peut-être des gens qui seront scandalisés que je fasse cet honneur à la raison, de l'élever au-dessus de toutes les puissances, et qui s'imagineront que je me révolte contre les autorités légitimes à cause que je prends son parti et que je soutiens que c'est à elle à décider et à regner.—MALEBRANCHE, *Morale*, i. 2, 13. That great statesman (Mr. Pitt) distinctly avowed that the application of philosophy to politics was at that time an innovation, and that it was an innovation worthy to be adopted. He was ready to make the same avowal in the present day which Mr. Pitt had made in 1792.—CANNING, 1st June 1827. *Parliamentary Review*, 1828, 71. American history knows but one avenue of success in

sage, for good and evil, from subordination to independence is a phenomenon of primary import to us, because historical science has been one of its instruments.[13] If the Past has been an obstacle and a burden, knowledge of the Past is the safest and the surest emancipation. And the earnest search for it is one of the signs that distinguish the four centuries of which I speak from those that went before. The Middle Ages, which possessed good writers of contemporary narrative, were careless and impatient of older fact. They became content to be deceived, to live in a twilight of fiction, under clouds of false witness, inventing according to convenience, and glad to welcome the forger and the cheat.[14] As time went on, the atmosphere of accredited mendacity thickened, until, in the Renaissance, the art of exposing falsehood dawned upon keen Italian minds. It was then that History as we understand it began to be understood, and the illustrious dynasty of scholars arose to whom we

---

American legislation, freedom from ancient prejudice. The best lawgivers in our colonies first became as little children.—BANCROFT, *History of the United States*, i. 494. Every American, from Jefferson and Gallatin down to the poorest squatter, seemed to nourish an idea that he was doing what he could to overthrow the tyranny which the past had fastened on the human mind.—ADAMS, *History of the United States*, i. 175.

[13] The greatest changes of which we have had experience as yet are due to our increasing knowledge of history and nature. They have been produced by a few minds appearing in three or four favoured nations, in comparatively a short period of time. May we be allowed to imagine the minds of men everywhere working together during many ages for the completion of our knowledge? May not the increase of knowledge transfigure the world?—JOWETT, *Plato*, i. 414. Nothing, I believe, is so likely to beget in us a spirit of enlightened liberality, of Christian forbearance, of large-hearted moderation, as the careful study of the history of doctrine and the history of interpretation.—PEROWNE, *Psalms*, i. p. xxxi.

[14] Ce n'est guère avant la seconde moitié du XVIIᵉ siècle qu'il devint impossible de soutenir l'authenticité des fausses décrétales, des Constitutions apostoliques, des Récognitions Clémentines, du faux Ignace, du pseudo-Dionys, et de l'immense fatras d'œuvres anonymes ou pseudonymes qui grossissait souvent du tiers ou de la moitié l'héritage littéraire des auteurs les plus considérables.—DUCHESNE, *Témoins anténicéens de la Trinité*, 1883, 36.

still look both for method and material. Unlike the dreaming prehistoric world, ours knows the need and the duty to make itself master of the earlier times, and to forfeit nothing of their wisdom or their warnings,[15] and has devoted its best energy and treasure to the sovereign purpose of detecting error and vindicating entrusted truth.[16]

In this epoch of full-grown history men have not acquiesced in the given conditions of their lives. Taking little for granted they have sought to know the ground they stand on, and the road they travel, and the reason why. Over them, therefore, the historian has obtained an increasing ascendency.[17] The law of stability was overcome by the power of ideas, constantly varied and rapidly renewed;[18] ideas that give life and motion, that take wing and traverse seas and frontiers, making it futile to pursue the consecutive order of events in the seclusion of a separate nationality.[19] They compel us to share the existence of societ-

---

[15] A man who does not know what has been thought by those who have gone before him is sure to set an undue value upon his own ideas.—M. PATTISON, *Memoirs*, 78.

[16] Travailler à discerner, dans cette discipline, le solide d'avec le frivole, le vrai d'avec le vraisemblable, la science d'avec l'opinion, ce qui forme le jugement d'avec ce qui ne fait que charger la mémoire.—LAMY, *Connoissance de soi-même*, v. 459.

[17] All our hopes of the future depend on a sound understanding of the past.—HARRISON, *The Meaning of History*, 6.

[18] The real history of mankind is that of the slow advance of resolved deed following laboriously just thought; and all the greatest men live in their purpose and effort more than it is possible for them to live in reality.—The things that actually happened were of small consequence—the thoughts that were developed are of infinite consequence.—RUSKIN. Facts are the mere dross of history. It is from the abstract truth which interpenetrates them, and lies latent among them like gold in the ore, that the mass derives its value.—MACAULAY, *Works*, v. 131.

[19] Die Gesetze der Geschichte sind eben die Gesetze der ganzen Menschheit, gehen nicht in die Geschicke eines Volkes, einer Generation oder gar eines Einzelnen auf. Individuen und Geschlechter, Staaten und Nationen, können zerstäuben, die Menschheit bleibt.—A. SCHMIDT, *Züricher Monatsschrift*, i. 45.

ies wider than our own, to be familiar with distant and exotic types, to hold our march upon the loftier summits, along the central range, to live in the company of heroes, and saints, and men of genius, that no single country could produce. We cannot afford wantonly to lose sight of great men and memorable lives, and are bound to store up objects for admiration as far as may be;[20] for the effect of implacable research is constantly to reduce their number. No intellectual exercise, for instance, can be more invigorating than to watch the working of the mind of Napoleon, the most entirely known as well as the ablest of historic men. In another sphere, it is the vision of a higher world to be intimate with the character of Fénelon, the cherished model of politicians, ecclesiastics, and men of letters, the witness against one century and precursor of another, the advocate of the poor against oppression, of liberty in an age of arbitrary power, of tolerance in an age of persecution, of the humane virtues among men accustomed to sacrifice them to authority, the

----

[20] Le grand péril des âges démocratiques, soyez-en sûr, c'est la destruction ou l'affaiblissement excessif des parties du corps social en présence du tout. Tout ce qui relève de nos jours l'idée de l'individu est sain.—TOCQUEVILLE, 3rd January 1840, Œuvres, vii. 97. En France, il n'y a plus d'hommes. On a systématiquement tué l'homme au profit du peuple, des masses, comme disent nos législateurs écervelés. Puis un beau jour, on s'est aperçu que ce peuple n'avait jamais existé qu'en projet, que ces masses étaient un troupeau mi-partie de moutons et de tigres. C'est une triste histoire. Nous avons à relever l'âme humaine contre l'aveugle et brutale tyrannie des multitudes.—LANFREY, 23rd March 1855. M. DU CAMP, Souvenirs Littéraires, ii. 273. C'est le propre de la vertu d'être invisible, même dans l'histoire, à tout autre œil que celui de la conscience.—VACHEROT, Comptes Rendus de l'Institut, lxix. 319. Dans l'histoire où la bonté est la perle rare, qui a été bon passe presque avant qui a été grand.—V. HUGO, Les Misérables, vii. 46. Grosser Maenner Leben und Tod der Wahrheit gemaess mit Liebe zu schildern, ist zu allen Zeiten herzerhebend; am meisten aber dann, wenn im Kreislauf der irdischen Dinge die Sterne wieder aehnlich stehen wie damals als sie unter uns lebten.—LASAULX, Sokrates, 3. Instead of saying that the history of mankind is the history of the masses, it would be much more true to say that the history of mankind is the history of its great men.— KINGSLEY, Lectures, 329.

man of whom one enemy says that his cleverness was enough to strike terror, and another, that genius poured in torrents from his eyes. For the minds that are greatest and best alone furnish the instructive examples. A man of ordinary proportion or inferior metal knows not how to think out the rounded circle of his thought, how to divest his will of its surroundings and to rise above the pressure of time and race and circumstance,[21] to choose the star that guides his course, to correct, and test, and assay his convictions by the light within,[22] and, with a resolute conscience and ideal courage, to remodel and reconstitute the character which birth and education gave him.[23]

For ourselves, if it were not the quest of the higher level and the extended horizon, international history would be imposed by the exclusive and insular reason that parliamentary reporting is younger than parliaments. The foreigner has no mystic fabric in his government, and no *arcanum imperii.* For him the foundations have been laid bare; every motive and function of the mechanism is accounted for as distinctly as the works of a

---

[21] Le génie n'est que la plus complète émancipation de toutes les influences de temps, de mœurs et de pays.—NISARD, *Souvenirs,* ii. 43.

[22] Meine kritische Richtung zieht mich in der Wissenschaft durchaus zur Kritik meiner eigenen Gedanken hin, nicht zu der der Gedanken Anderer.—ROTHE, *Ethik,* i. p. xi.

[23] When you are in young years the whole mind is, as it were, fluid, and is capable of forming itself into any shape that the owner of the mind pleases to order it to form itself into.—CARLYLE, *On the Choice of Books,* 131. Nach allem erscheint es somit unzweifelhaft als eine der psychologischen Voraussetzungen des Strafrechts, ohne welche der Zurechnungsbegriff nicht haltbar wäre, dass der Mensch für seinen Charakter verantwortlich ist und ihn muss abändern können.—RÜMELIN, *Reden und Aufsätze,* ii. 60. An der tiefen und verborgenen Quelle, woraus der Wille entspringt, an diesem Punkt, nur hier steht die Freiheit, und führt das Steuer und lenkt den Willen. Wer nicht bis zu dieser Tiefe in sich einkehren und seinen natürlichen Charakter von hier aus bemeistern kann, der hat nicht den Gebrauch seiner Freiheit, der ist nicht frei, sondern unterworfen dem Triebwerk seiner Interessen, und dadurch in der Gewalt des Weltlaufs, worin jede Begebenheit und jede Handlung eine nothwendige Folge ist aller vorhergehenden.—FISCHER, *Problem der Freiheit,* 27.

watch. But with our indigenous constitution, not made with hands or written upon paper, but claiming to develop by a law of organic growth; with our disbelief in the virtue of definitions and general principles and our reliance on relative truths, we can have nothing equivalent to the vivid and prolonged debates in which other communities have displayed the inmost secrets of political science to every man who can read. And the discussions of constituent assemblies, at Philadelphia, Versailles and Paris, at Cadiz and Brussels, at Geneva, Frankfort and Berlin, above nearly all, those of the most enlightened States in the American Union, when they have recast their institutions, are paramount in the literature of politics, and proffer treasures which at home we have never enjoyed.

To historians the later part of their enormous subject is precious because it is inexhaustible. It is the best to know because it is the best known and the most explicit. Earlier scenes stand out from a background of obscurity. We soon reach the sphere of hopeless ignorance and unprofitable doubt. But hundreds and even thousands of the moderns have borne testimony against themselves, and may be studied in their private correspondence and sentenced on their own confession. Their deeds are done in the daylight. Every country opens its archives and invites us to penetrate the mysteries of State. When Hallam wrote his chapter on James II, France was the only Power whose reports were available. Rome followed, and the Hague; and then came the stores of the Italian States, and at last the Prussian and the Austrian papers, and partly those of Spain. Where Hallam and Lingard were dependent on Barillon, their successors consult the diplomacy of ten governments. The topics indeed are few on which the resources have been so employed that we can be content with the work done for us and never wish it to be done over again. Part of the lives of Luther and Frederic, a little of the Thirty Years' War, much of the American Revolution and the French Restoration, the early years of Richelieu and Mazarin, and a few volumes of Mr. Gardiner, show here and there like Pacific islands in the ocean. I should not even venture to claim for Ranke, the real originator of the heroic study of records, and the most prompt and fortunate of European pathfinders, that

137

there is one of his seventy volumes that has not been overtaken and in part surpassed. It is through his accelerating influence mainly that our branch of study has become progressive, so that the best master is quickly distanced by the better pupil.[24] The Vatican archives alone, now made accessible to the world, filled 3239 cases when they were sent to France; and they are not the richest. We are still at the beginning of the documentary age, which will tend to make history independent of historians, to develop learning at the expense of writing, and to accomplish a revolution in other sciences as well.[25]

To men in general I would justify the stress I am laying on Modern History, neither by urging its varied wealth, nor the rupture with precedent, nor the perpetuity of change and increase of pace, nor the growing predominance of opinion over belief, and of knowledge over opinion, but by the argument that it is a narrative told of ourselves, the record of a life which is our own, of efforts not yet abandoned to repose, of problems that still entangle the feet and vex the hearts of men. Every part of it is weighty with inestimable lessons that we must learn by experience and at a great price, if we know not how to profit by the

---

[24] I must regard the main duty of a Professor to consist, not simply in communicating information, but in doing this in such a manner, and with such an accompaniment of subsidiary means, that the information he conveys may be the occasion of awakening his pupils to a vigorous and varied exertion of their faculties.—Sir W. Hamilton, *Lectures*, i. 14. No great man really does his work by imposing his maxims on his disciples, he evokes their life. The pupil may become much wiser than his instructor, he may not accept his conclusions, but he will own, "You awakened me to be myself; for that I thank you."—Maurice, *The Conscience*, 7, 8.

[25] Ich sehe die Zeit kommen, wo wir die neuere Geschichte nicht mehr auf die Berichte selbst nicht der gleichzeitigen Historiker, ausser in so weit ihnen neue originale Kenntniss beiwohnte, geschweige denn auf die weiter abgeleiteten Bearbeitungen zu gründen haben, sondern aus den Relationen der Augenzeugen und der ächten und unmittelbarsten Urkunden aufbauen werden.—Ranke, *Reformation*, Preface, 1838. Ce qu'on a trouvé et mis en œuvre est considérable en soi: c'est peu de chose au prix de ce qui reste à trouver et à mettre en œuvre.—Aulard, Études sur la Révolution, 21.

example and teaching of those who have gone before us, in a society largely resembling the one we live in.[26] Its study fulfils its purpose even if it only makes us wiser, without producing books, and gives us the gift of historical thinking, which is better than historical learning.[27] It is a most powerful ingredient in the formation of character and the training of talent, and our historical judgments have as much to do with hopes of heaven as public or private conduct. Convictions that have been strained through the instances and the comparisons of modern times differ immeasurably in solidity and force from those which every new fact perturbs, and which are often little better than illusions or unsifted prejudice.[28]

---

[26] N'attendez donc pas les leçons de l'expérience; elles coûtent trop cher aux nations.—O. BARROT, *Mémoires*, ii. 435. Il y a des leçons dans tous les temps, pour tous les temps; et celles qu'on emprunte à des ennemis ne sont pas les moins précieuses.—LANFREY, *Napoléon*, v. p. ii. Old facts may always be fresh, and may give out a fresh meaning for each generation.—MAURICE, *Lectures*, 62. The object is to lead the student to attend to them; to make him take interest in history not as a mere narrative, but as a chain of causes and effects still unwinding itself before our eyes, and full of momentous consequences to himself and his descendants—an unremitting conflict between good and evil powers, of which every act done by any one of us, insignificant as we are, forms one of the incidents; a conflict in which even the smallest of us cannot escape from taking part, in which whoever does not help the right side is helping the wrong.—MILL, *Inaugural Address*, 59.

[27] I hold that the degree in which Poets dwell in sympathy with the Past, marks exactly the degree of their poetical faculty.—WORDSWORTH, in C. FOX, *Memoirs*, June 1842. In all political, all social, all human questions whatever, history is the main resource of the inquirer.—HARRISON, *Meaning of History*, 15. There are no truths which more readily gain the assent of mankind, or are more firmly retained by them, than those of an historical nature, depending upon the testimony of others.—PRIESTLEY, *Letters to French Philosophers*, 9. Improvement consists in bringing our opinions into nearer agreement with facts; and we shall not be likely to do this while we look at facts only through glasses coloured by those very opinions.—MILL, *Inaugural Address*, 25.

[28] He who has learnt to understand the true character and tendency of many succeeding ages is not likely to go very far wrong in estimating

The first of human concerns is religion, and it is the salient feature of the modern centuries. They are signalised as the scene of Protestant developments. Starting from a time of extreme indifference, ignorance, and decline, they were at once occupied with that conflict which was to rage so long, and of which no man could imagine the infinite consequences. Dogmatic conviction—for I shun to speak of faith in connection with many characters of those days—dogmatic conviction rose to be the centre of universal interest, and remained down to Cromwell the supreme influence and motive of public policy. A time came when the intensity of prolonged conflict, when even the energy of antagonistic assurance abated somewhat, and the controversial spirit began to make room for the scientific; and as the storm subsided, and the area of settled questions emerged, much of the dispute was abandoned to the serene and soothing touch of historians, invested as they are with the prerogative of redeeming the cause of religion from many unjust reproaches, and

---

his own.—LECKY, *Value of History*, 21. C'est à l'histoire qu'il faut se prendre, c'est le fait que nous devons interroger, quand l'idée vacille et fuit à nos yeux.—MICHELET, *Disc. d'Ouverture*, 263. C'est la loi des faits telle qu'elle se manifeste dans leur succession. C'est la règle de conduite donnée par la nature humaine et indiquée par l'histoire. C'est la logique, mais cette logique qui ne fait qu'un avec l'enchaînement des choses. C'est l'enseignement de l'expérience.—SCHERER, *Mélanges*, 558. Wer seine Vergangenheit nicht als seine Geschichte hat und weiss wird und ist characterlos Wem ein Ereigniss sein Sonst plötzlich abreisst von seinem Jetzt wird leicht wurzellos.—KLIEFOTH, *Rheinwalds Repertorium*, xliv. 20. La politique est une des meilleures écoles pour l'esprit. Elle force à chercher la raison de toutes choses, et ne permet pas cependant de la chercher hors des faits.—Rémusat, *Le Temps Passé*, i. 31. It is an unsafe partition that divides opinions without principle from unprincipled opinions.—COLERIDGE, *Lay Sermons*, 373.

Wer nicht von drei tausend Jahren sich weiss Rechenschaft
    zu geben,
Bleib' im Dunkeln unerfahren, mag von Tag zu Tage leben!
        —GOETHE

What can be rationally required of the student of philosophy is not a preliminary and absolute, but a gradual and progressive, abrogation of prejudices.—SIR W. HAMILTON, *Lectures*, iv. 92.

from the graver evil of reproaches that are just. Ranke used to say that Church interests prevailed in politics until the Seven Years' War, and marked a phase of society that ended when the hosts of Brandenburg went into action at Leuthen, chaunting their Lutheran hymns.[29] That bold proposition would be disputed even if applied to the present age. After Sir Robert Peel had broken up his party, the leaders who followed him declared that no popery was the only basis on which it could be reconstructed.[30] On the other side may be urged that, in July 1870, at the outbreak of the French war, the only government that insisted on the abolition of the temporal power was Austria; and since then we have witnessed the fall of Castelar, because he attempted to reconcile Spain with Rome.

Soon after 1850 several of the most intelligent men in France, struck by the arrested increase of their own population and by the telling statistics from Further Britain, foretold the coming preponderance of the English race. They did not foretell, what none could then foresee, the still more sudden growth of Prussia, or that the three most important countries of the globe would, by the end of the century, be those that chiefly belonged to the conquests of the Reformation. So that in Religion, as in so many things, the product of these centuries has favoured the new elements; and the centre of gravity, moving from the Mediterranean nations to the Oceanic, from the Latin to the Teuton, has also passed from the Catholic to the Protestant.[31]

---

[29] Die Schlacht bei Leuthen ist wohl die letzte, in welcher diese religiösen Gegensätze entscheidend eingewirkt haben.—RANKE, *Allgemeine Deutsche Biographie*, vii. 70.

[30] The only real cry in the country is the proper and just old No Popery cry.—*Major Beresford*, July 1847. Unfortunately the strongest bond of union amongst them is an apprehension of Popery.—*Stanley*, 12th September 1847. The great Protectionist party having degenerated into a No Popery, No Jew Party, I am still more unfit now than I was in 1846 to lead it.—*G. Bentinck*, 26th December 1847; *Croker's Memoirs*, iii. 116, 132, 157.

[31] In the case of Protestantism, this constitutional instability is now a simple matter of fact, which has become too plain to be denied. The system is not fixed, but in motion; and the motion is for the time in

Out of these controversies proceeded political as well as historical science. It was in the Puritan phase, before the restoration of the Stuarts, that theology, blending with politics, effected a fundamental change. The essentially English reformation of the seventeenth century was less a struggle between churches than between sects, often subdivided by questions of discipline and self-regulation rather than by dogma. The sectaries cherished no purpose or prospect of prevailing over the nations; and they were concerned with the individual more than with the congregation, with conventicles, not with State churches. Their view was narrowed, but their sight was sharpened. It appeared to them that governments and institutions are made to pass away, like things of earth, whilst souls are immortal; that there is no more proportion between liberty and power than between eternity and time; that, therefore, the sphere of enforced command ought to be restricted within fixed limits, and that which had been done by authority, and outward discipline, and organised violence, should be attempted by division of power, and committed to the intellect and the conscience of free men.[32] Thus

---

the direction of complete self-dissolution.—We take it for a transitory scheme, whose breaking up is to make room in due time for another and far more perfect state of the Church.—The new order in which Protestantism is to become thus complete cannot be reached without the co-operation and help of Romanism.—Nevin, *Mercersburg Review*, iv. 48.

[32] Diese Heiligen waren es, die aus dem unmittelbaren Glaubensleben und den Grundgedanken der christlichen Freiheit zuerst die Idee allgemeiner Menschenrechte abgeleitet und rein von Selbstsucht vertheidigt haben.—Weingarten, *Revolutionskirchen*, 447. Wie selbst die Idee allgemeiner Menschenrechte, die in dem gemeinsamen Character der Ebenbildlichkeit Gottes gegründet sind, erst durch das Christenthum zum Bewusstsein gebracht werden, während jeder andere Eifer für politische Freiheit als ein mehr oder weniger selbstsüchtiger und beschränkter sich erwiesen hat.—Neander, *Pref. to Uhden's Wilberforce*, p. v. The rights of individuals and the justice due to them are as dear and precious as those of states; indeed the latter are founded on the former, and the great end and object of them must be to secure and support the rights of individuals, or else vain is government.—Cushing, in Conway, *Life of Paine*, i. 217. As it is owned the whole scheme of Scripture is not yet understood; so, if it ever comes to be understood, before the restitu-

was exchanged the dominion of will over will for the dominion of reason over reason. The true apostles of toleration are not those who sought protection for their own beliefs, or who had none to protect; but men to whom, irrespective of their cause, it was a political, a moral, and a theological dogma, a question of conscience involving both religion and policy.[33] Such a man was Socinus; and others arose in the smaller sects,—the Independent founder of the colony of Rhode Island, and the Quaker patriarch of Pennsylvania. Much of the energy and zeal which had laboured for authority of doctrine was employed for liberty of prophesying. The air was filled with the enthusiasm of a new cry; but the cause was still the same. It became a boast that religion was the mother of freedom, that freedom was the lawful offspring of religion; and this transmutation, this subversion of established forms of political life by the development of religious thought, brings us to the heart of my subject, to the significant and central feature of the historic cycles before us. Beginning with the strongest religious movement and the most refined despotism ever known, it has led to the superiority of politics over divinity in the life of nations, and terminates in the equal claim of every man to be unhindered by man in the fulfillment of duty to God[34]—a doctrine laden with storm and

---

tion of all things, and without miraculous interpositions, it must be in the same way as natural knowledge is come at—by the continuance and progress of learning and liberty.—BUTLER, *Analogy*, ii. 3.

[33] Comme les lois elles-mêmes sont faillibles, et qu'il peut y avoir une autre justice que la justice écrite, les sociétés modernes ont voulu garantir les droits de la conscience à la poursuite d'une justice meilleure que celle qui existe; et là est le fondement de ce qu'on appelle liberté de conscience, liberté d'écrire, liberté de pensée.—JANET, *Philosophie Contemporaine*, 308. Si la force matérielle a toujours fini par céder à l'opinion, combien plus ne sera-t-elle pas contrainte de céder à la conscience? Car la conscience, c'est l'opinion renforcée par le sentiment de l'obligation.—VINET, *Liberté Religieuse*, 3.

[34] Après la volonté d'un homme, la raison d'état; après la raison d'état, la religion; après la religion, la liberté. Voilà toute la philosophie de l'histoire.—FLOTTES, *La Souveraineté du Peuple*, 1851, 192. La répartition plus égale des biens et des droits dans ce monde est le plus grand

havoc, which is the secret essence of the Rights of Man, and the indestructible soul of Revolution.

When we consider what the adverse forces were, their sustained resistance, their frequent recovery, the critical moments when the struggle seemed forever desperate, in 1685, in 1772, in 1808, it is no hyperbole to say that the progress of the world towards self-government would have been arrested but for the strength afforded by the religious motive in the seventeenth century. And this constancy of progress, of progress in the direction of organised and assured freedom, is the characteristic fact of Modern History, and its tribute to the theory of Providence.[35]

---

objet que doivent se proposer ceux qui mènent les affaires humaines. Je veux seulement que l'égalité en politique consiste à être également libre.—TOCQUEVILLE, 10th September 1856. *Mme. Swetchine*, i. 455. On peut concevoir une législation très simple, lorsqu'on voudra en écarter tout ce qui est arbitraire, ne consulter que les deux premières lois de la liberté et de la propriété, et ne point admettre de lois positives qui ne tirent leur raison de ces deux lois souveraines de la justice essentielle et absolue.—LETROSNE, *Vues sur la Justice Criminelle*, 16. Summa enim libertas est, ad optimum recta ratione cogi.—Nemo optat sibi hanc libertatem, volendi quae velit, sed potius volendi optima.—LEIBNIZ, *De Fato*. TRENDELENBURG, *Beiträge zur Philosophie*, ii. 190.

[35] All the world is, by the very law of its creation, in eternal progress; and the cause of all the evils of the world may be traced to that natural, but most deadly error of human indolence and corruption, that our business is to preserve and not to improve.—ARNOLD, *Life*, i. 259. In whatever state of knowledge we may conceive man to be placed, his progress towards a yet higher state need never fear a check, but must continue till the last existence of society.—HERSCHEL, *Prel. Dis.* 360. It is in the development of thought as in every other development; the present suffers from the past, and the future struggles hard in escaping from the present.—MAX MÜLLER, *Science of Thought*, 617. Most of the great positive evils of the world are in themselves removable, and will, if human affairs continue to improve, be in the end reduced within narrow limits. Poverty in any sense implying suffering may be completely extinguished by the wisdom of society combined with the good sense and providence of individuals.—All the grand sources, in short, of human suffering are in a great degree, many of them almost entirely, conquerable by human care and effort.—J. S. MILL, *Utilitarianism*, 21, 22. The ultimate standard of worth is personal worth, and the only

Many persons, I am well assured, would detect that this is a very

---

progress that is worth striving after, the only acquisition that is truly good and enduring, is the growth of the soul.—BIXBY, *Crisis of Morals*, 210. La science, et l'industrie qu'elle produit, ont, parmi tous les autres enfants du génie de l'homme, ce privilège particulier, que leur vol non-seulement ne peut pas s'interrompre, mais qu'il s'accélère sans cesse.—CUVIER, *Discours sur la Marche des Sciences*, 24 Avril 1816. Aucune idée parmi celles qui se réfèrent à l'ordre des faits naturels, ne tient de plus près à la famille des idées religieuses que l'idée du progrès, et n'est plus propre à devenir le principe d'une sorte de foi religieuse pour ceux qui n'en ont pas d'autres. Elle a, comme la foi religieuse, la vertu de relever les âmes et les caractères.—COURNOT, *Marche des Idées*, ii. 425. Dans le spectacle de l'humanité errante, souffrante et travaillant toujours à mieux voir, à mieux penser, à mieux agir, à diminuer l'infirmité de l'être humain, à apaiser l'inquiétude de son cœur, la science découvre une direction et un progrès.—A SOREL, *Discours de Réception*, 14. Le jeune homme qui commence son éducation quinze ans après son père, à une époque où celui-ci, engagé dans une profession spéciale et active, ne peut que suivre les anciens principes, acquiert une supériorité théorique dont on doit tenir compte dans la hiérarchie sociale. Le plus souvent le père n'est-il pas pénétré de l'esprit de routine, tandis que le fils représente et défend la science progressive? En diminuant l'écart qui existait entre l'influence des jeunes générations et celle de la vieillesse ou de l'âge mûr, les peuples modernes n'auraient donc fait que reproduire dans leur ordre social un changement de rapports qui s'était déjà accompli dans la nature intime des choses.—BOUTMY, *Revue Nationale*, xxi. 393. Il y a dans l'homme individuel des principes de progrès viager; il y a, en toute société, des causes constantes qui transforment ce progrès viager en progrès héréditaire. Une société quelconque tend à progresser tant que les circonstances ne touchent pas aux causes de progrès que nous avons reconnues, l'imitation des dévanciers par les successeurs, des étrangers par les indigènes.—LACOMBE, *L'Histoire comme Science*, 292. Veram creatae mentis beatitudinem consistere in non impedito progressu ad bona majora.—LEIBNIZ to WOLF, 21st February 1705. In cumulum etiam pulchritudinis perfectionisque universalis operum divinorum progressus quidam perpetuus liberrimusque totius universi est agnoscendus, ita ut ad majorem semper cultum procedat.—LEIBNIZ ed. Erdmann, 150*a*. Der Creaturen und also auch unsere Vollkommenheit bestehen in einem ungehinderten starken Forttrieb zu neuen und neuen Vollkommenheiten.—LEIBNIZ, *Deutsche Schriften*, ii. 36. Hegel, welcher annahm, der Fortschritt der Neuzeit

old story, and a trivial commonplace, and would challenge proof

gegen das Mittelalter sei dieser, dass die Principien der Tugend und des Christenthums, welche im Mittelalter sich allein im Privatleben und der Kirche zur Geltung gebracht hätten, nun auch anfingen, das politische Leben zu durchdringen.—FORTLAGE, *Allg. Monatsschrift*, 1853, 777. Wir Slawen wissen, dass die Geister einzelner Menschen und ganzer Völker sich nur durch die Stufe ihrer Entwicklung unterscheiden.— MICKIEWICZ, *Slawische Literatur*, ii. 436. Le progrès ne disparait jamais, mais il se déplace souvent. Il va des gouvernants aux gouvernés. La tendance des révolutions est de le ramener toujours parmi les gouvernants. Lorsqu'il est à la tête des sociétés, il marche hardiment, car il conduit. Lorsqu'il est dans la masse, il marche à pas lents, car il lutte.— NAPOLEON III, *Des Idées Napoléoniennes*. La loi du progrès avait jadis l'inexorable rigueur du destin; elle prend maintenant de jour en jour la douce puissance de la Providence. C'est l'erreur, c'est l'iniquité, c'est le vice, que la civilisation tend à emporter dans sa marche irrésistible; mais la vie des individus et des peuples est devenue pour elle une chose sacrée. Elle transforme plutôt qu'elle ne détruit les choses qui s'opposent à son développement; elle procède par absorption graduelle plutôt que par brusque exécution; elle aime à conquérir par l'influence des idées plutôt que par la force des armes, un peuple, une classe, une institution qui résiste au progrès.—VACHEROT, *Essais de Philosophie Critique*, 443. Peu à peu l'homme intellectuel finit par effacer l'homme physique.—QUETELET, *De l'Homme*, ii. 285, In dem Fortschritt der ethischen Anschauungen liegt daher der Kern des geschichtlichen Fortschritts überhaupt.—SCHÄFER, *Arbeitsgebiet der Geschichte*, 24. Si l'homme a plus de devoirs à mesure qu'il avance en âge, ce qui est mélancolique, mais ce qui est vrai, de même aussi l'humanité est tenue d'avoir une morale plus sévère à mesure qu'elle prend plus de siècles.—FAGUET, *Revue des Deux Mondes*, 1894, iii. 871. Si donc il y a une loi de progrès, elle se confond avec la loi morale, et la condition fondamentale du progrès, c'est la pratique de cette loi.—CARRAU, *Ib.* 1875, v. 585. L'idée du progrès, du développement, me paraît être l'idée fondamentale contenue sous le mot de civilisation.—GUIZOT, *Cours d'Histoire*, 1828, 15. Le progrès n'est sous un autre nom, que la liberté en action.—BROGLIE, *Journal des Débats*, 28th January 1869. Le progrès social est continu. Il a ses périodes de fièvre ou d'atonie, de surexcitation ou de léthargie; il a ses soubresauts et ses haltes, mais il avance toujours.—DE DECKER, *La Providence*, 174. Ce n'est pas au bonheur seul, c'est au perfectionnement que notre destin nous appelle; et la liberté politique est le plus puissant, le plus énergique moyen de perfectionnement que le ciel nous

that the world is making progress in aught but intellect, that it is gaining in freedom, or that increase in freedom is either a progress or a gain. Ranke, who was my own master, rejected the view that I have stated;[36] Comte, the master of better men, believed that we drag a lengthening chain under the gathered

---

ait donné.—B. CONSTANT, *Cours de Politique*, il. 559. To explode error, on whichever side it lies, is certainly to secure progress.—MARTINEAU, *Essays*, i. 114. Die sämmtlichen Freiheitsrechte, welche der heutigen Menschheit so theuer sind, sind im Grunde nur Anwendungen des Rechts der Entwickelung.—BLUNTSCHLI, *Kleine Schriften*, i. 51. Geistiges Leben ist auf Freiheit beruhende Entwicklung, mit Freiheit vollzogene That und geschichtlicher Fortschritt.—*Münchner Gel. Anzeigen*, 1849, ii. 83. Wie das Denken erst nach und nach reift, so wird auch der freie Wille nicht fertig geboren, sondern in der Entwickelung erworben.— TRENDELENBURG, *Logische Untersuchungen*, ii. 94. Das Liberum Arbitrium im vollen Sinne (die vollständig aktuelle Macht der Selbstbestimmung) lässt sich seinem Begriff zufolge schlechterdings nicht unmittelbar geben; es kann nur erworben werden durch das Subjekt selbst, in sich moralisch hervorgebracht werden kraft seiner eigenen Entwickelung.— ROTHE, *Ethik*, 1. 360. So gewaltig sei der Andrang der Erfindungen und Entdeckungen, dass "Entwicklungsperioden, die in früheren Zeiten erst in Jahrhunderten durchlaufen wurden, die im Beginn unserer Zeitperiode noch der Jahrzehnte bedurften, sich heute in Jahren vollenden, häufig schon in voller Ausbildung ins Dasein treten."— PHILIPPOVICH, *Fortschritt und Kulturentwicklung*, 1892, i., quoting SIEMENS, 1886. Wir erkennen dass dem Menschen die schwere körperliche Arbeit, von der er in seinem Kampfe um's Dasein stets schwer niedergedrückt war und grossenteils noch ist, mehr und mehr durch die wachsende Benutzung der Naturkräfte zur mechanischen Arbeitsleistung abgenommen wird, dass die ihm zufallende Arbeit immer mehr eine intellektuelle wird.—SIEMENS, 1886, *Ib.* 6.

[36] Once, however, he wrote:—Darin könnte man den idealen Kern der Geschichte des menschlichen Geschlechtes überhaupt sehen, dass in den Kämpfen, die sich in den gegenseitigen Interessen der Staaten und Völker vollziehen, doch immer höhere Potenzen emporkommen, die das Allgemeine demgemäss umgestalten und ihm wieder einen anderen Charakter verleihen.—RANKE, *Weltgeschichte*, iii. 1, 6.

weight of the dead hand;[37] and many of our recent classics—
Carlyle, Newman, Froude—were persuaded that there is no
progress justifying the ways of God to man, and that the mere
consolidation of liberty is like the motion of creatures whose
advance is in the direction of their tails. They deem that anxious precaution against bad government is an obstruction to
good, and degrades morality and mind by placing the capable
at the mercy of the incapable, dethroning enlightened virtue
for the benefit of the average man. They hold that great and
salutary things are done for mankind by power concentrated,
not by power balanced and cancelled and dispersed, and that
the whig theory, sprung from decomposing sects, the theory
that authority is legitimate only by virtue of its checks, and that
the sovereign is dependent on the subject, is rebellion against
the divine will manifested all down the stream of time.

I state the objection not that we may plunge into the crucial
controversy of a science that is not identical with ours, but in
order to make my drift clear by the defining aid of express contradiction. No political dogma is as serviceable to my purpose
here as the historian's maxim to do the best he can for the other
side, and to avoid pertinacity or emphasis on his own. Like the
economic precept *laissez faire*,[38] which the eighteenth century
derived from Colbert, it has been an important, if not a final
step in the making of method. The strongest and most impressive personalities, it is true, like Macaulay, Thiers, and the two
greatest of living writers, Mommsen and Treitschke, project their
own broad shadow upon their pages. This is a practice proper
to great men, and a great man may be worth several immaculate
historians. Otherwise there is virtue in the saying that a histo-

---

[37] Toujours et partout, les hommes furent de plus en plus dominés
par l'ensemble de leurs prédécesseurs, dont ils purent seulement modi-
fier l'empire nécessaire.—COMTE, *Politique Positive*, iii. 621.

[38] La liberté est l'âme du commerce.—Il faut laisser faire les hommes qui s'appliquent sans peine à ce qui convient le mieux; c'est ce qui
apporte le plus d'avantage.—COLBERT, in *Comptes Rendus de l'Institut*,
xxxix. 93.

rian is seen at his best when he does not appear.[39] Better for us is the example of the Bishop of Oxford, who never lets us know what he thinks of anything but the matter before him; and of his illustrious French rival, Fustel de Coulanges, who said to an excited audience: "Do not imagine you are listening to me; it is history itself that speaks."[40] We can found no philosophy on the observation of four hundred years, excluding three thousand. It would be an imperfect and a fallacious induction. But I hope that even this narrow and disedifying section of history will aid you to see that the action of Christ who is risen on mankind whom he redeemed fails not, but increases;[41] that

---

[39] Il n'y a que les choses humaines exposées dans leur vérité, c'est-à-dire avec leur grandeur, leur variété, leur inépuisable fécondité, qui aient le droit de retenir le lecteur et qui le retiennent en effet. Si l'écrivain parait une fois, il ennuie ou fait sourire de pitié les lecteurs sérieux.—THIERS to STE. BEUVE, *Lundis*, iii. 195. Comme l'a dit Taine, la disparition du style, c'est la perfection du style.—FAGUET, *Revue Politique*, lii. 67.

[40] Ne m'applaudissez pas; ce n'est pas moi qui vous parle; c'est l'histoire qui parle par ma bouche.—*Revue Historique*, xli. 278.

[41] Das Evangelium trat als Geschichte in die Welt, nicht als Dogma—wurde als Geschichte in der christlichen Kirche deponirt.—ROTHE, *Kirchengeschichte*, ii. p. x. Das Christenthum ist nicht der Herr Christus, sondern dieser macht es. Es ist sein Werk, und zwar ein Werk, das er stets unter der Arbeit hat.—Er selbst, Christus der Herr, bleibt, der er ist in alle Zukunft, dagegen liegt es ausdrücklich im Begriffe seines Werks, des Christenthums, dass es nicht so bleibt, wie es anhebt.—ROTHE, *Allgemeine kirchliche Zeitschrift*, 1864, 299. Diess Werk, weil es dem Wesen der Geschichte zufolge eine Entwickelung ist, muss über Stufen hinweggehen, die einander ablösen, und von denen jede folgende neue immer nur unter der Zertrümmerung der ihr vorangehenden Platz greifen kann.—ROTHE, *Ib.* 19th April 1865. Je grösser ein geschichtliches Princip ist, desto langsamer und über mehr Stufen hinweg entfaltet es seinen Gehalt; desto langlebiger ist es aber ebendeshalb auch in diesen seinen unaufhörlichen Abwandelungen.—ROTHE, *Stille Stunden*, 301. Der christliche Glaube geht nicht von der Anerkennung abstracter Lehrwahrheiten aus, sondern von der Anerkennung einer Reihe von Thatsachen, die in der Erscheinung Jesu ihren Mittelpunkt haben.—NITZSCH, *Dogmengeschichte*, i. 17. Der Gedankengang der evangelischen Erzählung gibt darum auch eine vollständige Darstellung der

the wisdom of divine rule appears not in the perfection but in the improvement of the world;[42] and that achieved liberty

---

christlichen Lehre in ihren wesentlichen Grundzügen; aber er gibt sie im allseitigen lebendigen Zusammenhange mit der Geschichte der christlichen Offenbarung, und nicht in einer theoretisch zusammen-hängenden Folgenreihe von ethischen und dogmatischen Lehrsätzen.—DEUTINGER, *Reich Gottes*, i. p. v.

[42] L'Univers ne doit pas estre considéré seulement dans ce qu'il est; pour le bien connoître, il faut le voir aussi dans ce qu'il doit estre. C'est cet avenir surtout qui a été le grand objet de Dieu dans la création, et c'est pour cet avenir seul que le présent existe.—D'HOUTEVILLE, *Essai sur la Providence*, 273. La Providence emploie les siècles à élever toujours un plus grand nombre de familles et d'individus à ces biens de la liberté et de l'égalité légitimes que, dans l'enfance des sociétés, la force avait rendus le privilège de quelques-uns.—GUIZOT, *Gouvernement de la France*, 1820, 9. La marche de la Providence n'est pas assujettie à d'étroites limites; elle ne s'inquiète pas de tirer aujourd'hui la conséquence du principe qu'elle a posé hier; elle la tirera dans des siècles, quand l'heure sera venue; et pour raisonner lentement selon nous, sa logique n'est pas moins sûre.—GUIZOT, *Histoire de la Civilisation*, 20. Der Keim fortschreitender Entwicklung ist, auch auf göttlichem Geheisse, der Menschheit eingepflanzt. Die Weltgeschichte ist der blosse Ausdruck einer vorbestimmten Entwicklung.—A. HUMBOLDT, 2nd January 1842, *Im Neuen Reich*, 1872, i. 197. Das historisch grosse ist religiös gross; es ist die Gottheit selbst, die sich offenbart.—RAUMER, April 1807, *Erinnerungen*, i. 85.

is the one ethical result that rests on the converging and combined conditions of advancing civilisation.[43] Then you

---

[43] Je suis arrivé à l'âge où je suis, à travers bien des évènements différents, mais avec une seule cause, celle de la liberté régulière.— TOCQUEVILLE, 1st May 1852, *Œuvres Inédites*, ii. 185. Me trouvant dans un pays où la religion et le libéralisme sont d'accord, j'avais respiré.— J'exprimais ce sentiment, il y a plus de vingt ans, dans l'avant-propos de la *Démocratie*. Je l'éprouve aujourd'hui aussi vivement que si j'étais encore jeune, et je ne sais s'il y a une seule pensée qui ait été plus constamment présente à mon esprit.—5th August 1857, *Œuvres*, vi. 395. Il n'y a que la liberté (j'entends la modérée et la régulière) et la religion, qui, par un effort combiné, puissent soulever les hommes au-dessus du bourbier où l'égalité démocratique les plonge naturellement.—1st December 1852, *Œuvres*, vii. 295. L un de mes rêves, le principal en entrant dans la vie politique, était de travailler à concilier l'esprit libéral et l'esprit de religion, la société nouvelle et l'église.—15th November 1843, *Œuvres Inédites*, ii. 121. La véritable grandeur de l'homme n'est que dans l'accord du sentiment libéral et du sentiment religieux.— 17th September 1853, *Œuvres Inédites*, ii. 228. Qui cherche dans la liberté autre chose qu'elle-même est fait pour servir.—*Ancien Régime*, 248. Je regarde, ainsi que je l'ai toujours fait, la liberté comme le premier des biens; je vois toujours en elle l'une des sources les plus fécondes des vertus mâles et des actions grandes. Il n'y a pas de tranquillité ni de bien-être qui puisse me tenir lieu d'elle.—7th January 1856, *Mme. Swetchine*, i. 452. La liberté a un faux air d'aristocratie; en donnant pleine carrière aux facultés humaines, en encourageant le travail et l'économie, elle fait ressortir les supériorités naturelles ou acquises.— LABOULAYE, *L'État et ses Limites*, 154. Dire que la liberté n'est point par elle-même, qu'elle dépend d'une situation, d'une opportunité, c'est lui assigner une valeur négative. La liberté n'est pas dès qu'on la subordonne. Elle n'est pas un principe purement négatif, un simple élément de contrôle et de critique. Elle est le principe actif, créateur organisateur par excellence. Elle est le moteur et la règle, la source de toute vie, et le principe de l'ordre. Elle est, en un mot, le nom que prend la conscience souveraine, lorsque, se posant en face du monde social et politique, elle émerge du moi pour modeler les sociétés sur les données de la raison.—BRISSON, *Revue Nationale*, xxiii. 214. Le droit, dans l'histoire, est le développement progressif de la liberté, sous la loi de la raison.—LERMINIER, *Philosophie du Droit*, i. 211. En prouvant par les leçons de l'histoire que la liberté fait vivre les peuples et que le despotisme les tue, en montrant que l'expiation suit la faute et que la fortune

will understand what a famous philosopher said, that History

---

finit d'ordinaire par se ranger du côté de la vertu, Montesquieu n'est ni moins moral ni moins religieux que Bossuet.—LABOULAYE, *Œuvres de Montesquieu*, ii. 109. Je ne comprendrais pas qu'une nation ne plaçât pas les libertés politiques au premier rang, parce que c'est des libertés politiques que doivent découler toutes les autres.—THIERS, *Discours*, x. 8, 28th March 1865. Nous sommes arrivés à une époque où la liberté est le but sérieux de tous, où le reste n'est plus qu'une question de moyens.—J. LEBEAU, *Observations sur le Pouvoir Royal*: Liège, 1830, p. 10. Le libéralisme, ayant la prétention de se fonder uniquement sur les principes de la raison, croit d'ordinaire n'avoir pas besoin de tradition. Là est son erreur. L'erreur de l'école libérale est d'avoir trop cru qu'il est facile de créer la liberté par la réflexion, et de n'avoir pas vu qu'un établissement n'est solide que quand il a des racines historiques.— RENAN, 1858, *Nouvelle Revue*, lxxix. 596. Le respect des individus et des droits existants est autant au-dessus du bonheur de tous, qu'un intérêt moral surpasse un intérêt purement temporel.—RENAN, 1858, *Ib.* lxxix. 597. Die Rechte gelten nichts, wo es sich handelt um das Recht, und das Recht der Freiheit kann nie verjähren, weil es die Quelle alles Rechtes selbst ist.—C. FRANTZ, *Ueber die Freiheit*, 110. Wir erfahren hienieden nie die ganze Wahrheit: wir geniessen nie die ganze Freiheit.—REUSS, *Reden*, 56. Le gouvernement constitutionnel, comme tout gouvernement libre, présente et doit présenter un état de lutte permanent. La liberté est la perpétuité de la lutte.—DE SERRE. BROGLIE, *Nouvelles Études*, 243. The experiment of free government is not one which can be tried once for all. Every generation must try it for itself. As each new generation starts up to the responsibilities of manhood, there is, as it were, a new launch of Liberty, and its voyage of experiment begins afresh.—WINTHROP, *Addresses*, 163. L'histoire perd son véritable caractère du moment que la liberté en a disparu; elle devient une sorte de physique sociale. C'est l'élément personnel de l'histoire qui en fait la réalité.—VACHEROT, *Revue des Deux Mondes*, 1869, iv. 215. Demander la liberté pour soi et la refuser aux autres, c'est la définition du despotisme.—LABOULAYE, 4th December 1874. Les causes justes profitent de tout, des bonnes intentions comme des mauvaises, des calculs personnels comme des dévouemens courageux, de la démence, enfin, comme de la raison. —B. CONSTANT, *Les Cent Jours*, ii. 29. Sie ist die Kunst, das Gute der schon weit gediehenen Civilisation zu sichern.—BALTISCH, *Politische Freiheit*, 9. In einem Volke, welches sich zur bürgerlichen Gesellschaft, überhaupt zum Bewusstseyn der Unendlichkeit des Freien—entwickelt hat, ist nur die constitutionelle Monarchie möglich.—HEGEL's *Philosophie des*

is the true demonstration of Religion.[44]

Rechts, § 137, *Hegel und Preussen*, 1841, 31. Freiheit ist das höchste Gut. Alles andere ist nur das Mittel dazu: gut falls es ein Mittel dazu ist, übel falls es dieselbe hemmt.—FICHTE, *Werke*, iv. 403. You are not to inquire how your trade may be increased, nor how you are to become a great and powerful people, but how your liberties can be secured. For liberty ought to be the direct end of your government.—PATRICK HENRY, 1788; WIRT, *Life of Henry*, 272.

[44] Historiae ipsius praeter delectationem utilitas nulla est, quam ut religionis Christianae veritas demonstretur, quod aliter quam per historiam fieri non potest.—LEIBNIZ, *Opera*, ed. Dutens, vi. 297. The study of Modern History is, next to Theology itself, and only next in so far as Theology rests on a divine revelation, the most thoroughly religious training that the mind can receive. It is no paradox to say that Modern History, including Medieval History in the term, is co-extensive in its field of view, in its habits of criticism, in the persons of its most famous students, with Ecclesiastical History.—STUBBS, *Lectures*, 9. Je regarde donc l'étude de l'histoire comme l'étude de la providence.—L'histoire est vraiment une seconde philosophie.—Si Dieu ne parle pas toujours, il agit toujours en Dieu.—D'AGUESSEAU, *Œuvres*, xv. 34, 31, 35. Für diejenigen, welche das Wesen der menschlichen Freiheit erkannt haben, bildet die denkende Betrachtung der Weltgeschichte, besonders des christlichen Weltalters, die höchste, und umfassendste Theodicee.—VATKE, *Die Menschliche Freiheit*, 1841, 516. La théologie, que l'on regarde volontiers comme la plus étroite et la plus stérile des sciences, en est, au contraire, la plus étendue et la plus féconde. Elle confine à toutes les études et touche à toutes les questions. Elle renferme tous les éléments d'une instruction libérale.—SCHERER, *Mélanges*, 522. The belief that the course of events and the agency of man are subject to the laws of a divine order, which it is alike impossible for any one either fully to comprehend or effectually to resist—this belief is the ground of all our hope for the future destinies of mankind.—THIRLWALL, *Remains*, iii. 282. A true religion must consist of ideas and facts both; not of ideas alone without facts, for then it would be mere philosophy; nor of facts alone without ideas, of which those facts are the symbols, or out of which they are grounded; for then it would be mere history.—COLERIDGE, *Table Talk*, 144. It certainly appears strange that the men most conversant with the order of the visible universe should soonest suspect it empty of directing mind; and, on the other hand, that humanistic, moral and historical studies—which first open the terrible problems of suffering and grief, and contain all the reputed provocatives of denial and despair—

But what do people mean who proclaim that liberty is the palm, and the prize, and the crown, seeing that it is an idea of which there are two hundred definitions, and that this wealth of interpretation has caused more bloodshed than anything, except theology? Is it Democracy as in France, or Federalism as in America, or the national independence which bounds the Italian view, or the reign of the fittest, which is the ideal of Germans?[45] I know not whether it will ever fall within my sphere of duty to trace the slow progress of that idea through the chequered scenes of our history, and to describe how subtle speculations touching the nature of conscience promoted a nobler and more spiritual conception of the liberty that protects it,[46] until the guardian of rights developed into the guardian of

---

should confirm, and enlarge rather than disturb, the prepossessions of natural piety.—MARTINEAU, *Essays*, i. 122. Die Religion hat nur dann eine Bedeutung für den Menschen, wenn er in der Geschichte einen Punkt findet, dem er sich völlig unbedingt hingeben kann.—STEFFENS, *Christliche Religionsphilosophie*, 440, 1839. Wir erkennen darin nur eine Thätigkeit des zu seinem ächten und wahren Leben, zu seinem verlornen, objectiven Selbstverständnisse sich zurücksehnenden christlichen Geistes unserer Zeit, einen Ausdruck für das Bedürfniss desselben, sich aus den unwahren und unächten Verkleidungen, womit ihn der moderne, subjective Geschmack der letzten Entwicklungsphase des theologischen Bewusstseyns umhüllt hat, zu seiner historischen allein wahren und ursprünglichen Gestalt wiederzugebären, zu derjenigen Bedeutung zurückzukehren, die ihm in dem Bewusstseyn der Geschichte allein zukommt und deren Verständniss in dem wogenden luxuriösen Leben der modernen Theologie längst untergegangen ist.—GEORGII, *Zeitschrift für Hist. Theologie*, ix. 5, 1839.

[45] Liberty, in fact, means just so far as it is realised, the right man in the right place.—SEELEY, *Lectures and Essays*, 109.

[46] In diesem Sinne ist Freiheit und sich entwickelnde moralische Vernunft und Gewissen gleichbedeutend. In diesem Sinne ist der Mensch frei, sobald sich das Gewissen in ihm entwickelt.—SCHEIDLER, *Ersch und Gruber*, xlix. 20. Aus der unendlichen und ewigen Geltung der menschlichen Persönlichkeit vor Gott, aus der Vorstellung von der in Gott freien Persönlichkeit, folgt auch der Anspruch auf das Recht derselben in der weltlichen Sphäre, auf bürgerliche und politische Freiheit, auf Gewissen und Religionsfreiheit, auf freie wissenschaftliche Forschung

duties which are the cause of rights,47 and that which had been prized as the material safeguard for treasures of earth became sacred as security for things that are divine. All that we require is a workday key to history, and our present need can be supplied without pausing to satisfy philosophers. Without inquiring how far Sarasa or Butler, Kant or Vinet, is right as to the infallible voice of God in man, we may easily agree in this, that where absolutism reigned, by irresistible arms, concentrated possessions, auxiliary churches, and inhuman laws, it reigns no more; that commerce having risen against land, labour against wealth, the State against the forces dominant in society,48 the division of power against the State, the thought of individuals against the practice of ages, neither authorities, nor minorities, nor majorities can command implicit obedience; and, where there has been long and arduous experience, a rampart of tried conviction and accumulated knowledge,49 where there is a fair level of general morality, education, courage, and self-restraint,

---

u.s.w., und namentlich die Forderung, dass niemand lediglich zum Mittel für andere diene.—MARTENSEN, *Christliche Ethik*, i. 50.

47 Es giebt angeborne Menschenrechte, weil es angeborne Menschenpflichten giebt.—WOLFF, *Naturrecht*; Loeper, *Einleitung zu Faust*, lvii.

48 La constitution de l'état reste jusqu'à un certain point à notre discrétion. La constitution de la société ne dépend pas de nous; elle est donnée par la force des choses, et si l'on veut élever le langage, elle est l'œuvre de la Providence.—RÉMUSAT, *Revue des Deux Mondes*, 1861, v. 795.

49 Die Freiheit ist bekanntlich kein Geschenk der Götter, sondern ein, Gut das jedes Volk sich selbst verdankt und das nur bei dem erforderlichen Mass moralischer Kraft und Würdigkeit gedeiht.—IHERING, *Geist des Römischen Rechts*, ii. 290. Liberty, in the very nature of it, absolutely requires, and even supposes, that people be able to govern themselves in those respects in which they are free; otherwise their wickedness will be in proportion to their liberty, and this greatest of blessings will become a curse.—BUTLER, *Sermons*, 331. In each degree and each variety of public development there are corresponding institutions, best answering the public needs; and what is meat to one is poison to another. Freedom is for those who are fit for it.—PARKMAN, *Canada*, 396. Die Freiheit ist die Wurzel einer neuen Schöpfung in der Schöpfung.—SEDERHOLM, *Die ewigen Thatsachen*, 86.

there, if there only, a society may be found that exhibits the condition of life towards which, by elimination of failures, the world has been moving through the allotted space.[50] You will know it by outward signs: Representation, the extinction of slavery, the reign of opinion, and the like; better still by less apparent evidences: the security of the weaker groups[51] and the liberty of conscience, which, effectually secured, secures the rest.

Here we reach a point at which my argument threatens to abut on a contradiction. If the supreme conquests of society are won more often by violence than by lenient arts, if the trend and drift of things is towards convulsions and catastrophes,[52] if the world owes religious liberty to the Dutch Revolution, constitutional government to the English, federal republicanism to the American, political equality to the French and its successors,[53]

---

[50] La liberté politique, qui n'est qu'une complexité plus grande, de plus en plus grande, dans le gouvernement d'un peuple, à mesure que le peuple lui-même contient un plus grand nombre de forces diverses ayant droit et de vivre et de participer à la chose publique, est un fait de civilisation qui s'impose lentement à une société organisée, mais qui n'apparait point comme un principe à une société qui s'organise.—FAGUET, *Revue des Deux Mondes*, 1889, ii. 942.

[51] Il y a bien un droit du plus sage, mais non pas un droit du plus fort.—La justice est le droit du plus faible.—JOUBERT, *Pensées*, i. 355, 358.

[52] Nicht durch ein pflanzenähnliches Wachsthum, nicht aus den dunklen Gründen der Volksempfindung, sondern durch den männlichen Willen, durch die Ueberzeugung, durch die That, durch den Kampf entsteht, behauptet, entwickelt sich das Recht. Sein historisches Werden ist ein bewusstes, im hellen Mittagslicht der Erkenntniss und der Gesetzgebung.—*Rundschau*, November 1893, 13. Nicht das Normale, Zahme, sondern das Abnorme, Wilde, bildet überall die Grundlage und den Anfang einer neuen Ordnung.—LASAULX, *Philosophie der Geschichte*, 143.

[53] Um den Sieg zu vervollständigen, erübrigte das zweite Stadium oder die Aufgabe: die Berechtigung der Mehrheit nach allen Seiten hin zur gleichen Berechtigung aller zu erweitern, d.h. bis zur Gleichstellung aller Bekenntnisse im Kirchenrecht, aller Völker im Völkerrecht, aller Staatsbürger im Staatsrecht und aller socialen Interessen im Gesellschaftsrecht fortzuführen.—A. SCHMIDT, *Züricher Monatschrift*, i. 68.

what is to become of us, docile and attentive students of the absorbing Past? The triumph of the Revolutionist annuls the historian.[54] By its authentic exponents, Jefferson and Sieyès, the Revolution of the last century repudiates history. Their followers renounced acquaintance with it, and were ready to destroy its records and to abolish its inoffensive professors. But the unexpected truth, stranger than fiction, is that this was not the ruin but the renovation of history. Directly and indirectly, by process of development and by process of reaction, an impulse was given which made it infinitely more effectual as a factor of civilisation than ever before, and a movement began in the world of minds which was deeper and more serious than the revival of ancient learning.[55] The dispensation under which we live and labour consists first in the recoil from the negative spirit that rejected the law of growth, and partly in the endeavour to classify and adjust the Revolution, and to account for it by the natural working of historic causes. The Conservative line of writers, under

---

[54] Notre histoire ne nous enseignait nullement la liberté. Le jour où la France voulut être libre, elle eut tout à créer, tout à inventer dans cet ordre de faits.—Cependant il faut marcher, l'avenir appelle les peuples. Quand on n'a point pour cela l'impulsion du passé, il faut bien se confier à la raison.—DUPONT WHITE, *Revue des Deux Mondes*, 1861, vi. 191. Le peuple français a peu de goût pour le développement graduel des institutions. Il ignore son histoire, il ne s'y reconnaît pas, elle n'a pas laissé de trace dans sa conscience.—SCHERER, *Études Critiques*, i. 100. Durch die Revolution befreiten sich die Franzosen von ihrer Geschichte.—ROSENKRANZ, *Aus einem Tagebuch*, 199.

[55] The discovery of the comparative method in philology, in mythology—let me add in politics and history and the whole range of human thought—marks a stage in the progress of the human mind at least as great and memorable as the revival of Greek and Latin learning.— FREEMAN, *Historical Essays*, iv. 301. The diffusion of a critical spirit in history and literature is affecting the criticism of the Bible in our own day in a manner not unlike the burst of intellectual life in the fifteenth and sixteenth centuries.—JOWETT, *Essays and Reviews*, 346. As the revival of literature in the sixteenth century produced the Reformation, so the growth of the critical spirit, and the change that has come over mental science, and the mere increase of knowledge of all kinds, threaten now a revolution less external but not less profound.—HADDAN, *Replies*, 348.

the name of the Romantic or Historical School, had its seat in Germany, looked upon the Revolution as an alien episode, the error of an age, a disease to be treated by the investigation of its origin, and strove to unite the broken threads and to restore the normal conditions of organic evolution. The Liberal School, whose home was France, explained and justified the Revolution as a true development, and the ripened fruit of all history.[56] These are the two main arguments of the generation to which

---

[56] In his just contempt and detestation of the crimes and follies of the Revolutionists, he suffers himself to forget that the revolution itself is a process of the Divine Providence, and that as the folly of men is the wisdom of God, so are their iniquities instruments of His goodness.—COLERIDGE, *Biographia Literaria*, ii. 240. In other parts of the world, the idea of revolutions in government is, by a mournful and indissoluble association, connected with the idea of wars, and all the calamities attendant on wars. But happy experience teaches us to view such revolutions in a very different light—to consider them only as progressive steps in improving the knowledge of government, and increasing the happiness of society and mankind.—J. WILSON, 26th November 1787, *Works*, iii. 293. La Révolution, c'est-à-dire l'œuvre des siècles, ou, si vous voulez, le renouvellement progressif de la société, ou encore, sa nouvelle constitution.—RÉMUSAT, *Correspondance*, 11th October 1818. A ses yeux loin d'avoir rompu le cours naturel des évènements, ni la Révolution d'Angleterre, ni la nôtre, n'ont rien dit, rien fait, qui n'eût été dit, souhaité, fait, ou tenté cent fois avant leur explosion. "Il faut en ceci," dit-il, "tout accorder à leurs adversaires, les surpasser même en sévérité, ne regarder à leurs accusations que pour y ajouter, s'ils en oublient; et puis les sommer de dresser, à leur tour, le compte des erreurs, des crimes, et des maux de ces temps et de ces pouvoirs qu'ils ont pris sous leur garde."—*Revue de Paris*, xvi. 303, on Guizot. Quant aux nouveautés mises en œuvre par la Révolution Française on les retrouve une à une, en remontant d'âge en âge, chez les philosophes du XVIIIᵉ siècle, chez les grands penseurs du XVIᵉ, chez certains Pères d'Église et jusque dans la République de Platon.—En présence de cette belle continuité de l'histoire, qui ne fait pas plus de sauts que la nature, devant cette solidarité nécessaire des révolutions avec le passé qu'elles brisent.—KRANTZ, *Revue Politique*, xxxiii. 264. L'esprit du XIXᵉ siècle est de comprendre et de juger les choses du passé. Notre œuvre est d'expliquer ce que le XVIIIᵉ siècle avait mission de nier.—VACHEROT, *De la Démocratie*, pref., 28.

we owe the notion and the scientific methods that make history so unlike what it was to the survivors of the last century. Severally, the innovators were not superior to the men of old. Muratori was as widely read, Tillemont as accurate, Leibniz as able, Fréret as acute, Gibbon as masterly in the craft of composite construction. Nevertheless, in the second quarter of this century, a new era began for historians.

I would point to three things in particular, out of many, which constitute the amended order. Of the incessant deluge of new and unsuspected matter I need say little. For some years, the secret archives of the papacy were accessible at Paris; but the time was not ripe, and almost the only man whom they availed was the archivist himself.[57] Towards 1830 the documentary studies began on a large scale, Austria leading the way. Michelet, who claims, towards 1836, to have been the pioneer,[58] was preceded by such rivals as Mackintosh, Bucholtz, and Mignet. A new and more productive period began thirty years later, when the war of 1859 laid open the spoils of Italy. Every country in succession has now allowed the exploration of its records, and there is more fear of drowning than of drought. The result has been that a lifetime spent in the largest collection of printed books would not suffice to train a real master of modern history. After he had turned from literature to sources, from Burnet to Pocock, from Macaulay to Madame Campana, from Thiers to the interminable correspondence of the Bonapartes, he would still feel

---

[57] La commission recherchera, dans toutes les parties des archives pontificales, les pièces relatives à l'abus que les papes ont fait de leur ministère spirituel contre l'autorité des souveraines et la tranquillité des peuples.—DAUNOU, *Instructions*, 3rd January 1811. LABORDE, *Inventaires*, p. cxii.

[58] Aucun des historiens remarquables de cette époque n'avait senti encore le besoin de chercher les faits hors des livres imprimés, aux sources primitives, la plupart inédites alors, aux manuscrits de nos bibliothèques, aux documents de nos archives.—MICHELET, *Histoire de France*, 1869, i. 2.

instant need of inquiry at Venice or Naples, in the Ossuna library or at the Hermitage.[59]

These matters do not now concern us. For our purpose, the main thing to learn is not the art of accumulating material, but the sublimer art of investigating it, of discerning truth from falsehood and certainty from doubt. It is by solidity of criticism more than by the plenitude of erudition, that the study of history strengthens, and straightens, and extends the mind.[60] And the

---

[59] Doch besteht eine Grenze, wo die Geschichte aufhört und das Archiv anfängt, und die von der Geschichtschreibung nicht überschritten werden sollte. *Unsere Zeit*, 1866, ii. 635. Il faut avertir nos jeunes historiens à la fois de la nécessité inéluctable du document et, d'autre part, du danger qu'il présente.—M. HANOTAUX.

[60] This process consists in determining with documentary proofs, and by minute investigations duly set forth, the literal, precise, and positive inferences to be drawn at the present day from every authentic statement, without regard to commonly received notions, to sweeping generalities, or to possible consequences.—HARRISSE, *Discovery of America*, 1892, p. vi. Perhaps the time has not yet come for synthetic labours in the sphere of History. It may be that the student of the Past must still content himself with critical inquiries.—*Ib.* p. v. Few scholars are critics, few critics are philosophers, and few philosophers look with equal care on both sides of a question.—W. S. LANDOR in HOLYOAKE's *Agitator's Life*, ii. 15. Introduire dans l'histoire, et sans tenir compte des passions politiques et religieuses, le doute méthodique que Descartes, le premier, appliqua à l'étude de la philosophie, n'est-ce pas là une excellente méthode? n'est-ce pas même la meilleure?—CHANTELAUZE, *Correspondant*, 1883, i. 129. La critique historique ne sera jamais populaire. Comme elle est de toutes les sciences la plus délicate, la plus déliée, elle n'a de crédit qu'auprès des esprits cultivés.—CHERBULIEZ, *Revue des Deux Mondes*, xcvii. 517. Nun liefert aber die Kritik, wenn sie rechter Art ist, immer nur einzelne Data, gleichsam die Atome des Thatbestandes, und jede Kombination, jede Zusammenfassung und Schlussfolgerung, ohne die es doch einmal nicht abgeht, ist ein subjektiver Akt des Forschers. Demnach blieb Waitz, bei des eigenen Arbeit wie bei jener des anderen, immer höchst mistrauisch gegen jedes Résumé, jede Definition, jedes abschliessende Wort.—SYBEL, *Historische Zeitschrift*, lvi. 484. Mit blosser Kritik wird darin nichts ausgerichtet, denn die ist nur eine Vorarbeit, welche da aufhört, wo die echte historische Kunst anfängt.—LASAULX, *Philosophie der Künste*, 212.

accession of the critic in the place of the indefatigable compiler, of the artist in coloured narrative, the skilled limner of character, the persuasive advocate of good, or other, causes, amounts to a transfer of government, to a change of dynasty, in the historic realm. For the critic is one who, when he lights on an interesting statement, begins by suspecting it. He remains in suspense until he has subjected his authority to three operations. First, he asks whether he has read the passage as the author wrote it. For the transcriber, and the editor, and the official or officious censor on the top of the editor, have played strange tricks, and have much to answer for. And if they are not to blame, it may turn out that the author wrote his book twice over, that you can discover the first jet, the progressive variations, things added, and things struck out. Next is the question where the writer got his information. If from a previous writer, it can be ascertained, and the inquiry has to be repeated. If from unpublished papers, they must be traced, and when the fountain-head is reached, or the track disappears, the question of veracity arises. The responsible writer's character, his position, antecedents, and probable motives have to be examined into; and this is what, in a different and adapted sense of the word, may be called the higher criticism, in comparison with the servile and often mechanical work of pursuing statements to their root. For a historian has to be treated as a witness, and not believed unless his sincerity is established.[61] The maxim that a man must be presumed to be innocent until his guilt is proved, was not made for him.

For us, then, the estimate of authorities, the weighing of testimony, is more meritorious than the potential discovery of new matter.[62] And modern history, which is the widest field of application, is not the best to learn our business in; for it is too wide,

---

[61] The only case in which such extraneous matters can be fairly called in is when facts are stated resting on testimony; then it is not only just, but it is necessary for the sake of truth, to inquire into the habits of mind of him by whom they are adduced.—BABBAGE, *Bridgewater Treatise*, p. xiv.

[62] There is no part of our knowledge which it is more useful to obtain at first hand—to go to the fountain-head for—than our knowledge of History.—J. S. MILL, *Inaugural Address*, 34. The only sound intellects are

and the harvest has not been winnowed as in antiquity, and further on to the Crusades. It is better to examine what has been done for questions that are compact and circumscribed, such as the sources of Plutarch's *Pericles*, the two tracts on Athenian government, the origin of the epistle to Diognetus, the date of the life of St. Antony; and to learn from Schwegler how this analytical work began. More satisfying because more decisive has been the critical treatment of the medieval writers, parallel with the new editions, on which incredible labour has been lavished, and of which we have no better examples than the prefaces of Bishop Stubbs. An important event in this series was the attack on Dino Compagni, which, for the sake of Dante, roused the best Italian scholars to a not unequal contest. When we are told that England is behind the Continent in critical faculty, we must admit that this is true as to quantity, not as to quality of work. As they are no longer living, I will say of two Cambridge professors, Lightfoot and Hort, that they were critical scholars whom neither Frenchman nor German has surpassed.

The third distinctive note of the generation of writers who dug so deep a trench between history as known to our grandfathers and as it appears to us, is their dogma of impartiality. To an ordinary man the word means no more than justice. He considers that he may proclaim the merits of his own religion, of his prosperous and enlightened country, of his political persuasion, whether democracy, or liberal monarchy, or historic conservatism, without transgression or offence, so long as he is fair to the relative, though inferior, merits of others, and never treats men as saints or as rogues for the side they take. There is no impartiality, he would say, like that of a hanging judge. The men who, with the compass of criticism in their hands, sailed the uncharted sea of original research proposed a different view. History, to be above evasion or dispute, must stand on documents, not on opinions. They had their own notion of truthfulness, based on the exceeding difficulty of finding truth, and the still greater difficulty of impressing it when found.

---

those which, in the first instance, set their standard of proof high.—J. S. MILL, *Examination of Hamilton's Philosophy*, 525.

They thought it possible to write, with so much scruple, and simplicity, and insight, as to carry along with them every man of good will, and, whatever his feelings, to compel his assent. Ideas which, in religion and in politics, are truths, in history are forces. They must be respected; they must not be affirmed. By dint of a supreme reserve, by much self-control, by a timely and discreet indifference, by secrecy in the matter of the black cap, history might be lifted above contention, and made an accepted tribunal, and the same for all.[63] If men were truly sincere, and delivered judgment by no canons but those of evident morality, then Julian would be described in the same terms by Christian and pagan, Luther by Catholic and Protestant, Washington by Whig and Tory, Napoleon by patriotic Frenchman and patriotic

---

[63] There are so few men mentally capable of seeing both sides of a question; so few with consciences sensitively alive to the obligation of seeing both sides; so few placed under conditions either of circumstance or temper, which admit of their seeing both sides.—GREG, *Political Problems*, 1870, 173. Il n'y a que les Allemands qui sachent être aussi complètement objectifs. Ils se dédoublent, pour ainsi dire, en deux hommes, l'un qui a des principes très arrêtés et des passions très vives, l'autre qui sait voir et observer comme s'il n'en avait point.—LAVELEYE, *Revue des Deux Mondes*, 1868, i. 431. L'écrivain qui penche trop dans le sens où il incline, et qui ne se défie pas de ses qualités presque autant que ses défauts, cet écrivain tourne à la manière.—SCHERER, *Mélanges*, 484. Il faut faire volteface, et vivement, franchement, tourner le dos au moyen âge, à ce passé morbide, qui, même quand il n'agit pas, influe terriblement par la contagion de la mort. Il ne faut ni combattre, ni critiquer, mais oublier. Oublions et marchons!—MICHELET, *La Bible de l'Humanité*, 483. It has excited surprise that Thucydides should speak of Antiphon, the traitor to the democracy, and the employer of assassins, as "a man inferior in virtue to none of his contemporaries." But neither here nor elsewhere does Thucydides pass moral judgments.—JOWETT, *Thucydides*, ii. 501.

German.[64] I speak of this school with reverence, for the good it

---

[64] Non theologi provinciam suscepimus; scimus enim quantum hoc ingenii nostri tenuitatem superet: ideo sufficit nobis τὸ ὅτι fideliter ex antiquis auctoribus retulisse.—MORINUS, *De Poenitentia*, ix. 10.—Il faut avouer que la religion chrétienne a quelque chose d'étonnant! C'est parce que vous y êtes né, dira-t-on. Tant s'en faut, je me roidis contre par cette raison-là même, de peur que cette prévention ne me suborne.—PASCAL, *Pensées*, xvi. 7.—I was fond of Fleury for a reason which I express in the advertisement; because it presented a sort of photograph of ecclesiastical history without any comment upon it. In the event, that simple representation of the early centuries had a good deal to do with unsettling me.—NEWMAN, *Apologia*, 152.—Nur was sich vor dem Richterstuhl einer ächten, unbefangenen, nicht durch die Brille einer philosophischen oder dogmatischen Schule stehenden Wissenschaft als wahr bewährt, kann zur Erbauung, Belehrung und Warnung tüchtig seyn.—NEANDER, *Kirchengeschichte*, i. p. vii. Wie weit bei katholischen Publicisten bei der Annahme der Ansicht von der Staatsanstalt apologetische Gesichtspunkte massgebend gewesen sind, mag dahingestellt bleiben. Der Historiker darf sich jedoch nie durch apologetische Zwecke leiten lassen; sein einziges Ziel soll die Ergründung der Wahrheit sein.—PASTOR, *Geschichte der Päbste*, ii. 545. Church history falsely written is a school of vainglory, hatred, and uncharitableness; truly written, it is a discipline of humility, of charity, of mutual love.—SIR W. HAMILTON, *Discussions*, 506. The more trophies and crowns of honour the Church of former ages can be shown to have won in the service of her adorable head, the more tokens her history can be brought to furnish of his powerful presence in her midst, the more will we be pleased and rejoice, Protestant though we be.—NEVIN, *Mercersburg Review*, 1851, 168. S'il est une chose à laquelle j'ai donné tous mes soins, c'est à ne pas laisser influencer mes jugements par les opinions politiques ou religieuses; que si j'ai quelquefois péché par quelque excès, c'est par la bienveillance pour les œuvres de ceux qui pensent autrement que moi.—MONOD, *R. Hist.* xvi. 184. Nous n'avons nul intérêt à faire parler l'histoire en faveur de nos propres opinions. C'est son droit imprescriptible que le narrateur reproduise tous les faits sans aucune réticence et range toutes les évolutions dans leur ordre naturel. Notre récit restera complètement en dehors des préoccupations de la dogmatique et des déclamations de la polémique. Plus les questions auxquelles nous aurons à toucher agitent et passionnent de nos jours les esprits, plus il est du devoir de l'historien de s'effacer devant les faits qu'il veut faire connaître.—REUSS, *Nouvelle Revue de Théologie*, vi. 193, 1860. To love

has done, by the assertion of historic truth and of its legitimate authority over the minds of men. It provides a discipline which every one of us does well to undergo, and perhaps also well to relinquish. For it is not the whole truth. Lanfrey's essay on Carnot, Chuquet's wars of the Revolution, Ropes's military histories, Roget's Geneva in the time of Calvin, will supply you with examples of a more robust impartiality than I have described. Renan calls it the luxury of an opulent and aristocratic society, doomed to vanish in an age of fierce and sordid striving. In our universities it has a magnificent and appointed refuge; and to serve its cause, which is sacred, because it is the cause of truth and honour, we may import a profitable lesson from the highly unscientific region of public life. There a man does not take long to find out that he is opposed by some who are abler and better than himself. And, in order to understand the cosmic force and the true connection of ideas, it is a source of power, and an excellent school of principle, not to rest until, by excluding the fallacies, the prejudices, the exaggerations which perpetual contention and the consequent precautions breed, we have made out for our opponents a stronger and more impressive

---

truth for truth's sake is the principal part of human perfection in this world, and the seed-plot of all other virtues.—LOCKE, *Letter to Collins*. Il n'est plus possible aujourd'hui à l'historien d'être national dans le sens étroit du mot. Son patriotisme à lui c'est l'amour de la vérité. Il n'est pas l'homme d'une race ou d'un pays, il est l'homme de tous les pays, il parle au nom de la civilisation générale.—LANFREY, *Hist. de Nap.* iii. 2, 1870. Juger avec les parties de soi-même qui sont le moins des formes du tempérament, et le plus des facultés pénétrées et modelées par l'expérience, par l'étude, par l'investigation, par le non-moi.—FAGUET, *R. de Paris*, i. 151. Aucun critique n'est aussi impersonnel que lui, aussi libre de partis pris et d'opinions préconçues, aussi objectif.—Il ne mêle ou paraît mêler à ses appréciations ni inclinations personnelles de goût ou d'humeur, ou théories d'aucune sorte. G. MONOD, of Faguet, *Revue Historique*, xlii. 417. On dirait qu'il a peur, et généralisant ses observations, en systématisant ses connaissances, de mêler de luimême aux choses.—Je lis tout un volume de M. Faguet, sans penser une fois à M. Faguet: je ne vois que les originaux qu'il montre.—J'envisage toujours une réalité objective, jamais l'idée de M. Faguet, jamais la doctrine de M. Faguet.—LANSON, *Revue Politique*, 1894, i. 98.

case than they present themselves.[65] Excepting one to which we are coming before I release you, there is no precept less faithfully observed by historians.

Ranke is the representative of the age which instituted the modern study of History. He taught it to be critical, to be colourless, and to be new. We meet him at every step, and he has done more for us than any other man. There are stronger books than any one of his, and some may have surpassed him in political, religious, philosophic insight, in vividness of the creative imagination, in originality, elevation, and depth of thought; but by the extent of important work well executed, by his influence on able men, and by the amount of knowledge which mankind receives and employs with the stamp of his mind upon it, he stands without a rival. I saw him last in 1877, when he was feeble, sunken, and almost blind, and scarcely able to read or write. He uttered his farewell with kindly emotion, and I feared that the next I should hear of him would be the news of his death. Two years later he began a Universal History, which is not without traces of weakness, but which, composed after the age of eighty-

---

[65] It should teach us to disentangle principles first from parties, and again from one another; first of all as showing how imperfectly all parties represent their own principles, and then how the principles themselves are a mingled tissue.—Arnold, *Modern History*, 184. I find it a good rule, when I am contemplating a person from whom I want to learn, always to look out for his strength, being confident that the weakness will discover itself.—Maurice, *Essays*, 305. We may seek for agreement somewhere with our neighbours, using that as a point of departure for the sake of argument. It is this latter course that I wish here to explain and defend. The method is simple enough, though not yet very familiar.—It aims at conciliation; it proceeds by making the best of our opponent's case, instead of taking him at his worst.—The most interesting part of every disputed question only begins to appear when the rival ideals admit each other's right to exist.—A. Sidgwick, *Distinction and the Criticism of Beliefs*, 1892, 211. That cruel reticence in the breasts of wise men which makes them always hide their deeper thought.—Ruskin, *Sesame and Lilies*, i. 16. Je offener wir die einzelnen Wahrheiten des Sozialismus anerkennen, desto erfolgreicher können wir seine fundamentalen Unwahrheiten widerlegen.—Roscher, *Deutsche Vierteljahrschrift*, 1849, i. 177.

three, and carried, in seventeen volumes, far into the Middle Ages, brings to a close the most astonishing career in literature.

His course had been determined, in early life, by *Quentin Durward*. The shock of the discovery that Scott's Louis the Eleventh was inconsistent with the original in Commynes made him resolve that his object thenceforth should be above all things to follow, without swerving, and in stern subordination and surrender, the lead of his authorities. He decided effectually to repress the poet, the patriot, the religious or political partisan, to sustain no cause, to banish himself from his books, and to write nothing that would gratify his own feelings or disclose his private convictions.[66] When a strenuous divine, who, like him, had written on the Reformation, hailed him as a comrade, Ranke repelled his advances. "You," he said, "are in the first place a Christian: I am in the first place a historian.

---

[66] Dann habe ihn die Wahrnehmung, dass manche Angaben in den historischen Romanen Walter Scott's, mit den gleichzeitigen Quellen im Widerspruch standen, "mit Erstaunen" erfüllt, und ihn zu dem Entschlusse gebracht, auf das Gewissenhafteste an der Ueberlieferung der Quellen festzuhalten.—SYBEL, *Gedächtnissrede auf Ranke. Akad. der Wissenschaften*, 1887, p. 6. Sich frei zu halten von allem Widerschein der Gegenwart, sogar, soweit das menschenmöglich, von dem der eignen subjectiven Meinung in den Dingen des Staates, der Kirche und der Gesellschaft.—A. DOVE, *Im Neuen Reich*, 1875, ii. 967. Wir sind durchaus nicht für die leblose und schemenartige Darstellungsweise der Ranke'schen Schule eingenommen; es wird uns immer kühl bis ans Herz heran, wenn wir derartige Schilderungen der Reformation und der Revolution lesen, welche so ganz im kühlen Element des Pragmatismus sich bewegen und dabei so ganz Undinenhaft sind und keine Seele haben.—Wir lassen es uns lieber gefallen, dass die Männer der Geschichte hier und dort gehofmeistert werden, als dass sie uns mit Glasaugen ansehen, so meisterhaft immer die Kunst sein mag, die sie ihnen eingesetzt hat.—GOTTSCHALL, *Unsere Zeit*, 1866, ii. 636, 637. A vivre avec des diplomates, il leur a pris des qualités qui sont un défaut chez un historien. L'historien n'est pas un témoin, c'est un juge; c'est à lui d'accuser et de condamner au nom du passé opprimé et dans l'intérêt de l'avenir.—LABOULAYE on RANKE; *Débats*, 12th January 1852.

There is a gulf between us."[67] He was the first eminent writer who exhibited what Michelet calls *le désintéressement des morts*. It was a moral triumph for him when he could refrain from judging, show that much might be said on both sides, and leave the rest to Providence.[68] He would have felt sympathy with the two famous London physicians of our day, of whom it is told that they could not make up their minds on a case and reported dubiously. The head of the family insisted on a positive opinion. They answered that they were unable to give one, but he might easily find fifty doctors who could.

Niebuhr had pointed out that chroniclers who wrote before the invention of printing generally copied one predecessor at a time, and knew little about sifting or combining authorities. The suggestion became luminous in Ranke's hands, and with his light and dexterous touch he scrutinised and dissected the principal historians, from Machiavelli to the *Mémoires d'un Homme d'État*, with a rigour never before applied to moderns. But whilst Niebuhr dismissed the traditional story, replacing it with a construction of his own, it was Ranke's mission to preserve, not to undermine, and to set up masters whom, in their proper sphere, he could obey. The many excellent dissertations in which he displayed this art, though his successors in the next generation matched his skill and did still more thorough work, are the best introduction from which we can learn the technical process by which within living memory the study of modern history has been renewed. Ranke's contemporaries, weary of his

---

[67] Un théologien qui a composé une éloquente histoire de la Réformation, rencontrant à Berlin un illustre historien qui, lui aussi, a raconté Luther et le XVIᵉ siècle, l'embrassa avec effusion en le traitant de confrère. "Ah! permettez," lui répondit l'autre en se dégageant, "il y a une grande différence entre nous: vous êtes avant tout chrétien, et je suis avant tout historien."—Cherbuliez, *Revue des Deux Mondes*, 1872, i. 537.

[68] Nackte Wahrheit ohne allen Schmuck; gründliche Erforschung des Einzelnen; das Uebrige, Gott befohlen.—*Werke*, xxxiv. 24. Ce ne sont pas les théories qui doivent nous servir de base dans la recherche des faits, mais ce sont les faits qui doivent nous servir de base pour la composition des théories.—Vincent, *Nouvelle Revue de Théologie*, 1859, ii. 252.

neutrality and suspense, and of the useful but subordinate work that was done by beginners who borrowed his wand, thought that too much was made of these obscure preliminaries which a man may accomplish for himself, in the silence of his chamber, with less demand on the attention of the public.[69] That may be reasonable in men who are practised in these fundamental technicalities. We who have to learn them, must immerse ourselves in the study of the great examples.

Apart from what is technical, method is only the reduplication of common sense, and is best acquired by observing its use by the ablest men in every variety of intellectual employment.[70]

---

[69] Die zwanglose Anordnungs—die leichte und leise Andeutungskunst des grossen Historikers voll zu würdigen, hinderte ihn in früherer Zeit sein Bedürfniss nach scharfer begrifflicher Ordnung und Ausführung, später, und in immer zunehmenden Grade, sein Sinn für strenge Sachlichkeit, und genaue Erforschung der ursächlichen Zusammenhänge, noch mehr aber regte sich seine geradherzige Offenheit seine männliche Ehrlichkeit, wenn er hinter den fein verstrichenen Farben der Rankeschen Erzählungsbilder die gedeckte Haltung des klugen Diplomaten zu entdecken glaubte.—HAYM, *Duncker's Leben*, 437. The ground of criticism is indeed, in my opinion, nothing else but distinct attention, which every reader should endeavour to be master of.—HARE, December 1736; *Warburton's Works*, xiv. 98. Wenn die Quellenkritik so verstanden wird, als sei sie der Nachweis, wie ein Autor den andern benutzt hat, so ist das nur ein gelegentliches Mittel—eins unter anderen—ihre Aufgabe, den Nachweis der Richtigkeit zu lösen oder vorzubereiten.—DROYSEN, *Historik*, 18.

[70] L'esprit scientifique n'est autre en soi que l'instinct du travail et de la patience, le sentiment de l'ordre, de la réalité et de la mesure.—PAPILLON, *R. des Deux Mondes*, 1873, v. 704. Non seulement les sciences, mais toutes les institutions humaines s'organisent de même, et sous l'empire des mêmes idées régulatrices.—COURNOT, *Idées Fondamentales*, i. 4. There is no branch of human work whose constant laws have not close analogy with those which govern every other mode of man's exertion. But more than this, exactly as we reduce to greater simplicity and surety any one group of these practical laws, we shall find them passing the mere condition of connection or analogy, and becoming the actual expression of some ultimate nerve or fibre of the mighty laws which govern the moral world.—RUSKIN, *Seven Lamps*, 4. The sum total of all intellectual excellence is good sense and method. When these have

Bentham acknowledged that he learned less from his own profession than from writers like Linnaeus and Cullen; and Brougham advised the student of Law to begin with Dante. Liebig described his *Organic Chemistry* as an application of ideas found in Mill's *Logic*, and a distinguished physician, not to be named lest he should overhear me, read three books to enlarge his medical mind; and they were Gibbon, Grote, and Mill. He goes on to say, "An educated man cannot become so on one study alone, but must be brought under the influence of natural, civil, and moral modes of thought."[71] I quote my colleague's golden words

---

passed into the instinctive readiness of habit, when the wheel revolves so rapidly that we cannot see it revolve at all, then we call the combination genius. But in all modes alike, and in all professions, the two sole component parts, even of genius, are good sense and method.—COLERIDGE, June 1814, *Mem. of Coleorton*, ii. 172. Si l'exercice d'un art nous empêche d'en apprendre un autre, il n'en est pas ainsi dans les sciences: la connoissance d'une vérité nous aide à en découvrir une autre.—Toutes les sciences sont tellement liées ensemble qu'il est bien plus facile de les apprendre toutes à la fois que d'en apprendre une seule en la détachant des autres.—Il ne doit songer qu'à augmenter les lumières naturelles de sa raison, non pour résoudre telle ou telle difficulté de l'école, mais pour que dans chaque circonstance de la vie son intelligence montre d'avance à sa volonté le parti qu'elle doit prendre.—DESCARTES, *Œuvres Choisies*, 300, 301. Règles pour la Direction de l'Esprit. La connaissance de la méthode qui a guidé l'homme de génie n'est pas moins utile au progrès de la science et même à sa propre gloire, que ses découvertes.—LAPLACE, *Système du Monde*, ii. 371. On ne fait rien sans idées préconçues, il faut avoir seulement la sagesse de ne croire à leurs déductions qu'autant que l'expérience les confirme. Les idées préconçues, soumises au contrôle sévère de l'expérimentation, sont la flamme vivante des sciences d'observation; les idées fixes en sont le danger.—PASTEUR, in *Histoire d'un Savant*, 284. Douter des vérités humaines, c'est ouvrir la porte aux découvertes; en faire des articles de foi, c'est la fermer.—DUMAS, *Discours*, i. 123.

[71] We should not only become familiar with the laws of phenomena within our own pursuit, but also with the modes of thought of men engaged in other discussions and researches, and even with the laws of knowledge itself, that highest philosophy.—Above all things, know that we call you not here to run your minds into our moulds. We call you here on an excursion, on an adventure, on a voyage of discovery into

in order to reciprocate them. If men of science owe anything to us, we may learn much from them that is essential.[72] For they can show how to test proof, how to secure fulness and soundness in induction, how to restrain and to employ with safety hypothesis and analogy. It is they who hold the secret of the mysterious property of the mind by which error ministers to truth

---

space as yet uncharted.—ALLBUTT, *Introductory Address at St. George's,* October 1889. Consistency in regard to opinions is the slow poison of intellectual life.—DAVY, *Memoirs,* 68.

[72] Ce sont vous autres physiologistes des corps vivants, qui avez appris à nous autres physiologistes de la société (qui est aussi un corps vivant) la manière de l'observer et de tirer des conséquences de nos observations.—J. B. SAY DE CANDOLLE, 1st June 1827; DE CANDOLLE, *Mémoires,* 567.

and truth slowly but irrevocably prevails.[73] Theirs is the logic

---

[73] Success is certain to the pure and true: success to falsehood and corruption, tyranny and aggression, is only the prelude to a greater and an irremediable fall.—STUBBS, *Seventeen Lectures*, 20. The Carlylean faith, that the cause we fight for, so far as it is true, is sure of victory, is the necessary basis of all effective activity for good.—CAIRD, *Evolution of Religion*, ii. 43. It is the property of truth to be fearless, and to prove victorious over every adversary. Sound reasoning and truth, when adequately communicated, must always be victorious over error.—GODWIN, *Political Justice* (Conclusion). Vice was obliged to retire and give place to virtue. This will always be the consequence when truth has fair play. Falsehood only dreads the attack, and cries out for auxiliaries. Truth never fears the encounter; she scorns the aid of the secular arm, and triumphs by her natural strength.—FRANKLIN, *Works*, ii. 292. It is a condition of our race that we must ever wade through error in our advance towards truth: and it may even be said that in many cases we exhaust almost every variety of error before we attain the desired goal.—BABBAGE, *Bridgewater Treatise*, 27. Les hommes ne peuvent, en quelque genre que ce soit, arriver à quelque chose de raisonnable qu'après avoir, en ce même genre, épuisé toutes les sottises imaginables. Que de sottises ne dirions-nous pas maintenant, si les anciens ne les avaient pas déjà dites avant nous, et ne nous les avaient, pour ainsi dire, enlevées!—FONTENELLE. Without premature generalisations the true generalisation would never be arrived at.—H. SPENCER, *Essays*, ii. 57. The more important the subject of difference, the greater, not the less, will be the indulgence of him who has learned to trace the sources of human error,—of error, that has its origin not in our weakness and imperfection merely, but often in the most virtuous affections of the heart.—BROWN, *Philosophy of the Human Mind*, i. 48, 1824. Parmi les châtiments du crime qui ne lui manquent jamais, à côté de celui que lui inflige la conscience, l'histoire lui en inflige un autre encore, éclatant et manifeste, l'impuissance.—COUSIN, *Phil. Mod.* ii. 24. L'avenir de la science est garanti; car dans le grand livre scientifique tout s'ajoute et rien ne se perd. L'erreur ne fonde pas; aucune erreur ne dure très longtemps.—RENAN, *Feuilles Détachées*, xiii. Toutes les fois que deux hommes sont d'un avis contraire sur la même chose, à coup sûr, l'un ou l'autre se trompe; bien plus, aucun ne semble posséder la vérité; car si les raisons de l'un étoient certaines et évidentes, il pourroit les exposer à l'autre de telle manière qu'il finiroit par le convaincre également.—DESCARTES, *Règles; Œuvres Choisies*, 302. Le premier principe de la critique est qu'une doctrine ne captive ses adhérents que par ce qu'elle a de légitime.—RENAN, *Essais*

de Morale, 184. Was dem Wahn solche Macht giebt ist wirklich nicht er selbst, sondern die ihm zu Grunde liegende und darin nur verzerrte Wahrheit.—FRANTZ, *Schelling's Philosophie*, i. 62. Quand les hommes ont vu une fois la vérité dans son éclat, ils ne peuvent plus l'oublier. Elle reste debout, et tôt ou tard elle triomphe, parce qu'elle est la pensée de Dieu et le besoin du monde.—MIGNET, *Portraits*, ii. 295. C'est toujours le sens commun inaperçu qui fait la fortune des hypothèses auxquelles il se mêle.—COUSIN, *Fragments Phil.* i. 51, Preface of 1826. Wer da sieht, wie der Irrthum selbst ein Träger mannigfaltigen und bleibenden Fortschritts wird, der wird auch nicht so leicht aus dem thatsächlichen Fortschritt der Gegenwart auf Unumstösslichkeit unserer Hypothesen schliessen.—Das richtigste Resultat der geschichtlichen Betrachtung ist die akademische Ruhe, mit welcher unsere Hypothesen und Theorieen ohne Feindschaft und ohne Glauben als das betrachtet werden, was sie sind; als Stufen in jener unendlichen Annäherung an die Wahrheit, welche die Bestimmung unserer intellectuellen Entwickelung zu sein scheint.—LANGE, *Geschichte des Materialismus*, 502, 503. Hominum errores divina providentia reguntur, ita ut saepe male jacta bene cadant.—LEIBNIZ, ed. Klopp, i. p. lii. Sainte-Beuve n'était même pas de la race des libéraux, c'est-à-dire de ceux qui croient que, tout compte fait, et dans un état de civilisation donné, le bien triomphe du mal à armes égales, et la vérité de l'erreur.—D'HAUSSONVILLE, *Revue des Deux Mondes*, 1875, i. 567. In the progress of the human mind, a period of controversy amongst the cultivators of any branch of science must necessarily precede the period of unanimity.—TORRENS, *Essay on the Production of Wealth*, 1821, p. xiii. Even the spread of an error is part of the wide-world process by which we stumble into mere approximations to truth.—L. STEPHEN, *Apology of an Agnostic*, 81. Errors, to be dangerous, must have a great deal of truth mingled with them; it is only from this alliance that they can ever obtain an extensive circulation.—S. SMITH, *Moral Philosophy*, 7. The admission of the few errors of Newton himself is at least of as much importance to his followers in science as the history of the progress of his real discoveries.—YOUNG, *Works*, iii. 621. Error is almost always partial truth, and so consists in the exaggeration or distortion of one verity by the suppression of another, which qualifies and modifies the former.—MIVART, *Genesis of Species*, 3. The attainment of scientific truth has been effected, to a great extent, by the help of scientific errors.—HUXLEY: WARD, *Reign of Victoria*, ii. 337. Jede neue tief eingreifende Wahrheit hat meiner Ansicht nach erst das Stadium der Einseitigkeit durchzumachen.—IHERING, *Geist des R. Rechts*, ii. 22. The more readily we admit the possibility of our own cherished convictions

of discovery,[74] the demonstration of the advance of knowledge and the development of ideas, which as the earthly wants and passions of men remain almost unchanged, are the charter of progress and the vital spark in history. And they often give us invaluable counsel when they attend to their own subjects and address their own people. Remember Darwin taking note only of those passages that raised difficulties in his way; the French philosopher complaining that his work stood still, because he found no more contradicting facts; Baer, who thinks error treated thoroughly nearly as remunerative as truth, by the discovery of new objections; for, as Sir Robert Ball warns us, it is by considering objections that we often learn.[75] Faraday declares that "in

---

being mixed with error, the more vital and helpful whatever is right in them will become.—RUSKIN, *Ethics of the Dust*, 225. They hardly grasp the plain truth unless they examine the error which it cancels.—CORY, *Modern English History*, 1880, i. 109. Nur durch Irrthum kommen wir, der eine kürzeren und glücklicheren Schrittes, als der andere, zur Wahrheit; und die Geschichte darf nirgends diese Verirrungen übergehen, wenn sie Lehrein und Warnerin für die nachfolgenden Geschlechter werden will.—*München Gel. Anzeigen*, 1840, i. 737.

[74] Wie die Weltgeschichte das Weltgericht ist, so kann in noch allgemeinerem Sinne gesagt werden, dass das gerechte Gericht, d.h. die wahre Kritik einer Sache, nur in ihrer Geschichte liegen kann. Insbesondere in der Hinsicht lehrt die Geschichte denjenigen, der ihr folgt, ihre eigene Methode, dass ihr Fortschritt niemals ein reines Vernichten, sondern nur ein Aufheben im philosophischen Sinne ist.—STRAUSS, *Hallische Jahrbücher*, 1839, 120.

[75] Dans tous les livres qu'il lit, et il en dévore des quantités, Darwin ne note que les passages qui contrarient ses idées systématiques.—Il collectionne les difficultés, les cas épineux, les critiques possibles.—VERNIER, *Le Temps*, 6th Décembre 1887. Je demandais à un savant célèbre où il en était de ses recherches. "Cela ne marche plus," me dit-il, "je ne trouve plus de faits contradictoires." Ainsi le savant cherche à se contredire lui-même pour faire avancer sa pensée.—JANET, *Journal des Savants*, 1892, 20. Ein Umstand, der uns die Selbständigkeit des Ganges der Wissenschaft anschaulich machen kann, ist auch der: dass der Irrthum, wenn er nur gründlich behandelt wird, fast ebenso fördernd ist als das Finden der Wahrheit, denn er erzeugt fortgesetzten Widerspruch.—BAER, *Blicke auf die Entwicklung der Wissenschaft*, 120. It is only by virtue of the oppo-

knowledge, that man only is to be condemned and despised who is not in a state of transition." And John Hunter spoke for all of us when he said: "Never ask me what I have said or what I have written; but if you will ask me what my present opinions are, I will tell you."

From the first years of the century we have been quickened and enriched by contributors from every quarter. The jurists brought us that law of continuous growth which has transformed history from a chronicle of casual occurrences into the likeness of something organic.[76] Towards 1820 divines began to recast their doctrines on the lines of development, of which Newman

---

sition which it has surmounted that any truth can stand in the human mind.—ARCHBISHOP TEMPLE; KINGLAKE, *Crimed, Winter Troubles*, app. 104. I have for many years found it expedient to lay down a rule for my own practice, to confine my reading mainly to those journals the general line of opinions in which is adverse to my own.—HARE, *Means of Unity*, i. 19. Kant had a harder struggle with himself than he could possibly have had with any critic or opponent of his philosophy.—GAIRD, *Philosophy of Kant*, 1889, i. p. ix.

[76] The social body is no more liable to arbitrary changes than the individual body.—A full perception of the truth that society is not a mere aggregate, but an organic growth, that it forms a whole, the laws of whose growth can be studied apart from those of the individual atom, supplies the most characteristic postulate of modern speculation.—L. STEPHEN, *Science of Ethics*, 31. Wie in dem Leben des einzelnen Menschen kein Augenblick eines vollkommenen Stillstandes wahrgenommen wird, sondern stete organische Entwicklung, so verhält es sich auch in dem Leben der Völker, und in jedem einzelnen Element, woraus dieses Gesammtleben besteht. So finden wir in der Sprache stete Fortbildung und Entwicklung, und auf gleiche Weise in dem Recht. Und auch diese Fortbildung steht unter demselben Gesetz der Erzeugung aus innerer Kraft und Nothwendigkeit, unabhängig von Zufall und individueller Willkür, wie die ursprüngliche Entstehung.—SAVIGNY, *System*, i. 16, 17. Seine eigene Entdeckung, dass auch die geistige Produktion, bis in einem gewissen Punkte wenigstens, unter dem Gesetze der Kausalität steht, dass jedeiner nur geben kann, was er hat, nur hat, was er irgendwoher bekommen, muss auch für ihn selber gelten.—BEKKER, *Das Recht des Besitzes bei den Römern*, 3, 1880. Die geschichtliche Wandlung des Rechts, in welcher vergangene Jahrhunderte halb ein Spiel des Zufalls und halb ein Werk vernünftelnder Willkür sahen, als gesetzmässige Entwickelung zu beg-

said, long after, that evolution had come to confirm it.[77] Even
the Economists, who were practical men, dissolved their science into liquid history, affirming that it is not an auxiliary, but
the actual subject-matter of their inquiry.[78] Philosophers claim

---

reifen, war das unsterbliche Verdienst der von Männern wie Savigny,
Eichhorn und Jacob Grimm geführten historischen Rechtsschule.
—GIERKE, Rundschau, xviii. 205.

[77] The only effective way of studying what is called the philosophy of
religion, or the philosophical criticism of religion, is to study the history of religion. The true science of war is the history of war, the true
science of religion is, I believe, the history of religion.—M. MÜLLER,
Theosophy, 3, 4. La théologie ne doit plus être que l'histoire des efforts
spontanés tentés pour résoudre le problème divin. L'histoire, en effet,
est la forme nécessaire de la science de tout ce qui est soumis aux lois
de la vie changeante et successive. La science de l'esprit humain, c'est
de même, l'histoire de l'esprit humain.—RENAN, Averroës, Pref. vi.

[78] Political economy is not a science, in any strict sense, but a body
of systematic knowledge gathered from the study of common processes, which have been practised all down the history of the human
race in the production and distribution of wealth.—BONAMY PRICE,
Social Science Congress, 1878. Such a study is in harmony with the best
intellectual tendencies of our age, which is, more than anything else,
characterised by the universal supremacy of the historical spirit. To
such a degree has this spirit permeated all our modes of thinking, that
with respect to every branch of knowledge, no less than with respect to
every institution and every form of human activity, we almost instinctively ask, not merely what is its existing condition, but what were
its earliest discoverable germs, and what has been the course of its
development.—INGRAM, History of Political Economy, 2. Wir dagegen
stehen keinen Augenblick an, die Nationalökonomie für eine reine
Erfahrungswissenschaft zu erklären, und die Geschichte ist uns daher
nicht Hülfsmittel, sondern Gegenstand selber.—ROSCHER, Deutsche
Vierteljahrschrift, 1849, i. 182. Der bei weitem grösste Theil menschlicher Irrthümer beruhet darauf, dass man zeitlich und örtlich Wahres
oder Heilsames für absolut wahr oder heilsam ausgiebt. Für jede Stufe
der Volksentwickelung passt eine besondere Staatsverfassung, die mit
allen übrigen Verhältnissen des Volks als Ursache und Wirkung auf's
Innigste verbunden ist; so passt auch für jede Entwickelungsstufe eine
besondere Landwirthschaftsverfassung.—ROSCHER, Archiv f. p. Oek.
viii. 2 Heft 1845. Seitdem vor allen Roscher, Hildebrand und Knies

that, as early as 1804, they began to bow the metaphysical neck beneath the historical yoke. They taught that philosophy is only the amended sum of all philosophies, that systems pass with the age whose impress they bear,[79] that the problem is to focus the rays of wandering but extant truth, and that history is the source

---

den Werth, die Berechtigung und die Nothwendigkeit derselben unwiderleglich dargethan, hat sich immer allgemeiner der Gedanke Bahn gebrochen, dass diese Wissenschaft, die bis dahin nur auf die Gegenwart, auf die Erkenntniss der bestehenden Verhältnisse und die in ihnen sichtbaren Gesetze den Blick gerichtet hatte, auch in die Vergangenheit, in die Erforschung der bereits hinter uns liegenden wirthschaftlichen Entwicklung der Völker sich vertiefen müsse. —SCHONBERG, *Jahrbücher f. Nationalökonomie und Statistik*, Neue Folge, 1867, i. 1. Schmoller, moins dogmatique et mettant comme une sorte de coquetterie à être incertain, démontre, par les faits, la fausseté ou l'arbitraire de tous ces postulats, et laisse l'économie politique se dissoudre dans l'histoire.—BRETON, *R. de Paris*, ix. 67. Wer die politische Oekonomie Feuerlands unter dieselben Gesetze bringen wollte mit der des heutigen Englands, würde damit augenscheinlich nichts zu Tage fördern als den allerbanalsten Gemeinplatz. Die politische Oekonomie ist somit wesentlich eine historische Wissenschaft. Sie behandelt einen geschichtlichen, das heisst einen stets wechselnden Stoff. Sie untersucht zunächst die besondern Gesetze jeder einzelnen Entwicklungsstufe der Produktion und des Austausches, und wird erst am Schluss dieser Untersuchung die wenigen, für Produktion und Austausch überhaupt geltenden, ganz allgemeinen Gesetze aufstellen können.—ENGELS, *Dührings Umwälzung der Wissenschaft*, 1878, 121.

[79] History preserves the student from being led astray by a too servile adherence to any system.—WOLOWSKI. No system can be anything more than a history, not in the order of impression, but in the order of arrangement by analogy.—DAVY, *Memoirs*, 68. Avec des matériaux si nombreux et si importants, il fallait bien du courage pour résister à la tentation de faire un système. De Saussure eut ce courage, et nous en ferons le dernier trait et le trait principal de son éloge.—CUVIER, Éloge de Saussure, 1810.

of philosophy, if not quite a substitute for it.[80] Comte begins a

[80] C'était, en 1804, une idée heureuse et nouvelle, d'appeler l'histoire au secours de la science, d'interroger les deux grandes écoles rivales au profit de la vérité.—Cousin, *Fragments Littéraires*, 1843, 95, on Dégerando. No branch of philosophical doctrine, indeed, can be fairly investigated or apprehended apart from its history. All our systems of politics, morals, and metaphysics would be different if we knew exactly how they grew up, and what transformations they have undergone; if we knew, in short, the true history of human ideas.—Cliffe Leslie, *Essays in Political and Moral Philosophy*, 1879, 149. The history of philosophy must be rational and philosophic. It must be philosophy itself, with all its elements, in all their relations, and under all their laws represented in striking characters by the hands of time and of history, in the manifested progress of the human mind. —Sir William Hamilton, *Edin. Rev.* l. 200, 1829. Il n'est point d'étude plus instructive, plus utile que l'étude de l'histoire de la philosophie; car on y apprend à se désabuser des philosophes, et l'on y désapprend la fausse science de leurs systèmes.—Royer Collard, *Œuvres de Reid*, iv. 426. On ne peut guère échapper à la conviction que toutes les solutions des questions philosophiques n'aient été développées ou indiquées avant le commencement du dix-neuvième siècle, et que par conséquent il ne soit très difficile, pour ne pas dire impossible, de tomber, en pareille matière, sur une idée neuve de quelque importance. Or si cette conviction est fondée, il s'ensuit que la science est faite.—Jouffroy, in Damiron, *Philosophie du XIXe Siècle*, 363. Le but dernier de tous mes efforts, l'âme de mes écrits et de tout mon enseignement, c'est l'identité de la philosophie et de son histoire.—Cousin, *Cours de* 1829. Ma route est historique, il est vrai, mais mon but est dogmatique; je tends à une théorie, et cette théorie je la demande à l'histoire.—Cousin, *Ph. du XVIIIe Siècle*, 15. L'histoire de la philosophie est contrainte d'emprunter d'abord à la philosophie la lumière qu'elle doit lui rendre un jour avec usure.— Cousin, *Du Vrai*, 1855, 14. M. Cousin, durant tout son professorat de 1816 à 1829, a pensé que l'histoire de la philosophie était la source de la philosophie même. Nous ne croyons pas exagérer en lui prêtant cette opinion.—B. St. Hilaire, *Victor Cousin*, i. 302, Il se hâta de convertir le fait en loi, et proclama que la philosophie, étant identique à son histoire, ne pouvait avoir une loi différente, et était vouée à jamais à l'évolution fatale des quatre systèmes, se contredisant toujours, mais se limitant, et se modérant, par cela même de manière à maintenir l'équilibre, sinon l'harmonie de la pensée humaine.—Vacherot, *Revue des Deux Mondes*, 1868, iii. 957. Er hat überhaupt das unvergängliche

volume with the words that the preponderance of history over

Verdienst, zuerst in Frankreich zu der Erkenntniss gelangt zu sein, dass die menschliche Vernunft nur durch das Studium des Gesetzes ihrer Entwickelungen begriffen werden kann.—LAUSER, *Unsere Zeit*, 1868, i. 459. Le philosophe en quête du vrai en soi, n'est plus réduit à ses conceptions individuelles; il est riche du trésor amassé par l'humanité.—BOUTROUX, *Revue Politique*, xxxvii. 802. L'histoire, je veux dire l'histoire de l'esprit humain, est en ce sens la vraie philosophie de notre temps.—RENAN, Études de Morale, 83. Die Philosophie wurde eine höchst bedeutende Hülfswissenschaft der Geschichte, sie hat ihre Richtung auf das Allgemeine gefördert, ihren Blick für dasselbe geschärft, und sie, wenigstens durch ihre Vermittlung, mit Gesichtspuncten, Ideen, bereichert, die sie aus ihrem eigenen Schoosse sobald noch nicht erzeugt haben würde. Weit die fruchtbarste darunter war die aus der Naturwissenschaft geschöpfte Idee des organischen Lebens, dieselbe auf der die neueste Philosophie selbst beruht. Die seit zwei bis drei Jahrzehnten in der Behandlung der Geschichte eingetretene durchgreifende Veränderung, wie die völlige Umgestaltung so mancher anderen Wissenschaft ... ist der Hauptsache nach ihr Werk.—HAUG, *Allgemeine Geschichte*, 1841, i. 22. Eine Geschichte der Philosophie in eigentlichen Sinne wurde erst möglich, als man an die Stelle der Philosophen deren Systeme setzte, den inneren Zusammenhang zwischen diesen feststellte und— wie Dilthey sagt—mitten in Wechsel der Philosophien ein siegreiches Fortschreiten zur Wahrheit nachwies. Die Gesammtheit der Philosophie stellt sich also dar als eine geschichtliche Einheit.—SAUL, *Rundschau*, February 1894, 307. Warum die Philosophie eine Geschichte habe und haben müsse, blieb unerörtert, ja ungeahnt, dass die Philosophie am meisten von allen Wissenschaften historisch sei, denn man hatte in der Geschichte den Begriff der Entwicklung nicht entdeckt.—MARBACH, *Griechische Philosophie*, 15. Was bei oberflächlicher Betrachtung nur ein Gewirre einzelner Personen und Meinungen zu sein schien, zeigt sich bei genauerer und gründlicherer Untersuchung als eine geschichtliche Entwicklung, in der, alles, bald näher, bald entfernter, mit allem anderen zusammenhängt.—ZELLER, *Rundschau*, February 1894, 307. Nur die Philosophie, die an die geschichtliche Entwickelung anknüpft kann auf bleibenden Erfolg auch für die Zukunft rechnen und fortschreiten zu dem, was in der bisherigen philosophischen Entwickelung nur erst unvollkommen erreicht oder angestrebt worden ist. Kann sich doch die Philosophie überhaupt und insbesondere die Metaphysik ihrer eigenen geschichtlichen Entwickelung nicht entschlagen, sondern hat eine Geschichte der Philosophie als eigene und zwar zugleich historische und

philosophy was the characteristic of the time he lived in.[81] Since Cuvier first recognised the conjunction between the course of inductive discovery and the course of civilisation,[82] science had

---

spekulative Disziplin, in deren geschichtlichen Entwickelungsphasen und geschichtlich aufeinanderfolgenden Systemen der Philosophen die neuere Spekulation seit Schelling und Hegel zugleich die Philosophie selbst als ein die verschiedenen geschichtlichen Systeme umfassendes ganzes in seiner dialektischen Gliederung erkannt hat.—GLOATZ, *Spekulative Theologie*, i. 23. Die heutige Philosophie führt uns auf einen Standpunkt von dem aus die philosophische Idee als das innere Wesen der Geschichte selbst erscheint. So trat an die Stelle einer abstrakt philosophischen Richtung, welche das Geschichtliche verneinte, eine abstrakt geschichtliche Richtung, welche das Philosophische verläugnete. Beide Richtungen sind als überschrittene und besiegte zu betrachten.— BERNER, *Strafrecht*, 75. Die Geschichte der Philosophie hat uns fast schon die Wissenschaft der Philosophie selbst ersetzt.—HERMANN, *Phil. Monatshefte*, ii. 198, 1889.

[81] La siècle actuel sera principalement caractérisé par l'irrévocable prépondérance de l'histoire, en philosophie, en politique, et même en poésie.—COMTE, *Politique Positive*, iii. 1.

[82] The historical or comparative method has revolutionised not only the sciences of law, mythology, and language, of anthropology and sociology, but it has forced its way even into the domain of philosophy and natural science. For what is the theory of evolution itself, with all its far-reaching consequences, but the achievement of the historical method?—PROTHERO, *Inaugural; National Review*, December 1894, 461. To facilitate the advancement of all the branches of useful science, two things seem to be principally requisite. The first is, an historical account of their rise, progress, and present state. Without the former of these helps, a person every way qualified for extending the bounds of science labours under great disadvantages; wanting the lights which have been struck out by others, and perpetually running the risk of losing his labour, and finding himself anticipated.—PRIESTLEY, *History of Vision*, 1772, i., Pref. i. Cuvier se proposait de montrer l'enchainement scientifique des découvertes, leurs relations avec les grands évènements historiques, et leur influence sur les progrès et le développement de la civilisation.—DARESTE, *Biographie Générale*, xii. 685. Dans ses éloquentes leçons, l'histoire des sciences est devenue l'histoire même de l'esprit humain; car, remontant aux causes de leurs progrès et de leurs erreurs, c'est toujours dans les bonnes ou mauvaises routes suivies par l'esprit

its share in saturating the age with historic ways of thought, and subjecting all things to that influence for which the depressing names historicism and historical-mindedness have been devised.

There are certain faults which are corrigible mental defects on which I ought to say a few denouncing words, because they are common to us all. First: the want of an energetic understanding of the sequence and real significance of events, which would be fatal to a practical politician, is ruin to a student of history, who is the politician with his face turned backwards.[83] It is playing at study, to see nothing but the unmeaning and unsuggestive surface, as we generally do. Then we have a curious proclivity to neglect, and by degrees to forget, what has been certainly known. An instance or two will explain my idea. The most popular English writer relates how it happened in his presence that the title of Tory was conferred upon the Conservative party. For it was an opprobrious name at the time, applied to men for whom the Irish Government offered head-money; so that if I have made too sure of progress, I may at least complacently point to this instance of our mended manners. One day, Titus Oates lost his temper with the men who refused to believe

---

humain, qu'il trouve ces causes.—FLOURENS, Éloge de Cuvier, xxxi. Wie keine fortlaufende Entwickelungsreihe von nur Einem Punkte aus vollkommen aufzufassen ist, so wird auch keine lebendige Wissenschaft nur aus der Gegenwart begriffen werden können.—Deswegen ist aber eine solche Darstellung doch noch nicht der gesammten Wissenschaft adäquat, und sie birgt, wenn sie damit verwechselt wird, starke Gefahren der Einseitigkeit, des Dogmatismus und damit der Stagnation in sich. Diesen Gefahren kann wirksam nur begegnet werden durch die verständige Betrachtung der Geschichte der Wissenschaften, welche diese selbst in stetem Flusse zeigt und die Tendenz ihres Fortschreitens in offenbarer und sicherer Weise klarlegt.—ROSENBERGER, *Geschichte der Physik*, iii. p. vi. Die Continuität in der Ausbildung aller Auffassungen tritt um so deutlicher hervor, je vollständiger man sich damit wie sie zu verschiedenen Zeiten waren, vertraut macht.—KOPP, *Entwickelung der Chemie*, 814.

[83] Die Geschichte und die Politik sind Ein und derselbe Janus mit dem Doppelgesicht, das in der Geschichte in die Vergangenheit, in der Politik in die Zukunft hinschaut.—GÜGLER's *Leben*, ii. 59.

him, and, after looking about for a scorching imprecation, he began to call them Tories.[84] The name remained; but its origin, attested by Defoe, dropped out of common memory, as if one party were ashamed of their godfather, and the other did not care to be identified with his cause and character. You all know, I am sure, the story of the news of Trafalgar, and how, two days after it had arrived, Mr. Pitt, drawn by an enthusiastic crowd, went to dine in the city. When they drank the health of the minister who had saved his country, he declined the praise. "England," he said, "has saved herself by her own energy; and I hope that after having saved herself by her energy, she will save Europe by her example." In 1814, when this hope had been realised, the last speech of the great orator was remembered, and a medal was struck upon which the whole sentence was engraved, in four words of compressed Latin: *Seipsam virtute, Europam exemplo.* Now it was just at the time of his last appearance in public that Mr. Pitt heard of the overwhelming success of the French in Germany, and of the Austrian surrender at Ulm. His friends concluded that the contest on land was hopeless, and that it was time to abandon the Continent to the conqueror, and to fall back upon our new empire of the sea. Pitt did not agree with them. He said that Napoleon would meet with a check whenever he encountered a national resistance; and he declared that Spain

---

[84] The papers inclosed, which give an account of the killing of two men in the country of Londonderry; if they prove to be Tories, 'tis very well they are gone.—I think it will not only be necessary to grant those a pardon who killed them, but also that they have some reward for their own and others' encouragement.—ESSEX, *Letters*, 10, 10th January 1675. The author of this happened to be present. There was a meeting of some honest people in the city, upon the occasion of the discovery of some attempt to stifle the evidence of the witnesses.—Bedloe said he had letters from Ireland, that there were some Tories to be brought over hither, who were privately to murder Dr. Oates and the said Bedloe. The doctor, whose zeal was very hot, could never after this hear any man talk against the plot, or against the witnesses, but he thought he was one of these Tories, and called almost every man a Tory that opposed him in discourse; till at last the word Tory became popular.—DEFOE, *Edinburgh Review*, l. 403.

was the place for it, and that then England would intervene.[85]
General Wellesley, fresh from India, was present. Ten years later,
when he had accomplished that which Pitt had seen in the lucid
prescience of his last days, he related at Paris what I scarcely
hesitate to call the most astounding and profound prediction
in all political history, where such things have not been rare.

I shall never again enjoy the opportunity of speaking my
thoughts to such an audience as this, and on so privileged an
occasion a lecturer may well be tempted to bethink himself
whether he knows of any neglected truth, any cardinal proposition, that might serve as his selected epigraph, as a last signal,
perhaps even as a target. I am not thinking of those shining precepts which are the registered property of every school; that is
to say—Learn as much by writing as by reading; be not content
with the best book; seek sidelights from the others; have no
favourites; keep men and things apart; guard against the pres-
tige of great names;[86] see that your judgments are your own, and
do not shrink from disagreement; no trusting without testing;
be more severe to ideas than to actions;[87] do not overlook the

---

[85] La España serà el primer pueblo en donde se encenderá esta
guerra patriotica que solo puede libertar á Europa.—Hemos oido esto
en Inglaterra á varios de los que estaban alli presentes. Muchas veces ha
oido lo mismo al duque de Wellington el general Don Miguel de Alava,
y dicho duque refirió el suceso en una comida diplomatica que dió en
Paris el duque de Richelieu en 1816.—TORENO, *Historia del Levantamiento
de España*, 1838, i. 508.

[86] Nunquam propter auctoritatem illorum, quamvis magni sint nomi-
nis (supponimus scilicet semper nos cum eo agere qui scientiam his-
toricam vult consequi), sententias quas secuti sunt ipse tamquam cer-
tas admittet, sed solummodo ob vim testimoniorum et argumentorum
quibus eas confirmarunt.—DE SMEDT, *Introductio ad historiam critice
tractandam*, 1866, i. 5.

[87] Hundert schwere Verbrechen wiegen nicht so schwer in der Schale
der Unsittlichkeit, als ein unsittliches Princip.—*Hallische Jahrbücher*,
1839, 308. Il faut flétrir les crimes; mais il faut aussi, et surtout, flétrir
les doctrines et les systèmes qui tendent à les justifier.—MORTIMER
TERNAUX, *Histoire de la Terreur*.

strength of the bad cause or the weakness of the good;[88] never be surprised by the crumbling of an idol or the disclosure of a skeleton; judge talent at its best and character at its worst; suspect power more than vice,[89] and study problems in preference to periods; for instance: the derivation of Luther, the scientific influence of Bacon, the predecessors of Adam Smith, the medieval masters of Rousseau, the consistency of Burke, the identity of the first Whig. Most of this, I suppose, is undisputed, and calls for no enlargement. But the weight of opinion is against me when I exhort you never to debase the moral currency or to lower the standard of rectitude, but to try others by the final maxim that governs your own lives, and to suffer no man and no cause to escape the undying penalty which history has the power to inflict on wrong.[90] The plea in extenuation of guilt

---

[88] We see how good and evil mingle in the best of men and in the best of causes; we learn to see with patience the men whom we like best often in the wrong, and the repulsive men often in the right; we learn to bear with patience the knowledge that the cause which we love best has suffered, from the awkwardness of its defenders, so great disparagement, as in strict equity to justify the men who were assaulting it.—STUBBS, *Seventeen Lectures*, 97.

[89] Caeteris paribus, on trouvera tousjours que ceux qui ont plus de puissance sont sujets à pécher davantage; et il n'y a point de théorème de géométrie qui soit plus asseuré que cette proposition.—LEIBNIZ, 1688. ed. Rommel, ii. 197. Il y a toujours eu de la malignité dans la grandeur, et de l'opposition à l'esprit de l'Évangile; mais maintenant il y en a plus que jamais, et il semble que comme le monde va à sa fin, celui qui est dans l'élévation fait tous ses efforts pour dominer avec plus de tyrannie, et pour étouffer les maximes du Christianisme et le règne de Jésus-Christ, voiant qu'il s'approche.—GODEAU, *Lettres*, 423, 27th March 1667. There is, in fact, an unconquerable tendency in all power, save that of knowledge, acting by and through knowledge, to injure the mind of him by whom that power is exercised.—WORDSWORTH, 22nd June 1817; *Letters of Lake Poets*, 369.

[90] I cieli han messo sulla terra due giudici delle umane azioni, la coscienza e la storia.—COLLETTA. Wenn gerade die edelsten Männer um des Nachruhmes willen gearbeitet haben, so soll die Geschichte ihre Belohnung sein, sie auch die Strafe für die Schlechten.—LASAULX, *Philosophie der Künste*, 211. Pour juger ce qui est bon et juste dans la vie

and mitigation of punishment is perpetual. At every step we are met by arguments which go to excuse, to palliate, to confound right and wrong, and reduce the just man to the level of the reprobate. The men who plot to baffle and resist us are, first of all, those who made history what it has become. They set up the principle that only a foolish Conservative judges the present time with the ideas of the past; that only a foolish Liberal judges the past with the ideas of the present.[91]

The mission of that school was to make distant times, and especially the Middle Ages, then most distant of all, intelligible and acceptable to a society issuing from the eighteenth century. There were difficulties in the way; and among others this, that, in the first fervour of the Crusades, the men who took the Cross, after receiving communion, heartily devoted the day to the extermination of Jews. To judge them by a fixed standard, to call them sacrilegious fanatics or furious hypocrites, was to yield a gratuitous victory to Voltaire. It became a rule of policy to praise the spirit when you could not defend the deed. So that we have no common code; our moral notions are always fluid; and you must consider the times, the class from which men sprang, the surrounding influences, the masters in their schools, the preachers in their pulpits, the movement they obscurely obeyed, and so on, until responsibility is merged in numbers, and not a culprit is left for execution.[92] A murderer was no criminal

---

actuelle ou passée, il faut posséder un criterium, qui ne soit pas tiré du passé ou du présent, mais de la nature humaine.—AHRENS, *Cours de Droit Naturel*, i. 67.

[91] L'homme de notre temps! La conscience moderne! Voilà encore de ces termes qui nous ramènent la prétendue philosophie de l'histoire et la doctrine du progrès, quand il s'agit de la justice, c'est-à-dire de la conscience pure et de l'homme rationnel, que d'autres siècles encore que le nôtre ont connu.—RENOUVIER, *Crit. Phil.* 1873, ii. 55.

[92] Il faut pardonner aux grands hommes le marchepied de leur grandeur.—COUSIN, in J. SIMON, *Nos Hommes d'État*, 1887, 55. L'esprit du XVIIIᵉ siècle n'a pas besoin d'apologie: l'apologie d'un siècle est dans son existence.—COUSIN, *Fragments*, iii. 1826. Suspendus aux lèvres éloquentes de M. Cousin, nous l'entendîmes s'écrier que la meilleure cause l'emportait toujours, que c'était la loi de l'histoire, le rhythme

if he followed local custom, if neighbours approved, if he was encouraged by official advisers or prompted by just authority, if he acted for the reason of state or the pure love of religion, or if he sheltered himself behind the complicity of the Law. The depression of morality was flagrant; but the motives were those which have enabled us to contemplate with distressing complacency the secret of unhallowed lives. The code that is greatly modified by time and place, will vary according to the cause. The amnesty is an artifice that enables us to make exceptions,

---

immuable du progrès.—GASPARIN, *La Liberté Morale*, ii. 63. Cousin verurtheilen heisst darum nichts Anderes als jenen Geist historischer Betrachtung verdammen, durch welchen das 19. Jahrhundert die revolutionäre Kritik des 18. Jahrhunderts ergänzt, durch welchen insbesondere Deutschland die geistigen Wohlthaten vergolten hat, welche es im Zeitalter der Aufklärung von seinen westlichen Nachbarn empfangen.—IODL, *Gesch. der Ethik*, ii. 295. Der Gang der Weltgeschichte steht ausserhalb der Tugend, des Lasters, und der Gerechtigkeit.—HEGEL, *Werke*, viii. 425. Die Vermischung des Zufälligen im Individuum mit dem an ihm Historischen führt zu unzähligen falschen Ansichten und Urtheilen. Hierzu gehört namentlich alles Absprechen über die moralische Tüchtigkeit der Individuen, und die Verwunderung, welche bis zur Verzweiflung an göttlicher Gerechtigkeit sich steigert, dass historisch grosse Individuen moralisch nichtswürdig erscheinen können. Die moralische Tüchtigkeit besteht in der Unterordnung alles dessen, was zufällig am Einzelnen unter das an ihm dem Allgemeinen Angehörige.—MARBACH, *Geschichte der Griechischen Philosophie*, 7. Das Sittliche der Neuseeländer, der Mexikaner ist vielmehr ebenso sittlich, wie das der Griechen, der Römer; und das Sittliche der Christen des Mittelalters ist ebenso sittlich, wie das der Gegenwart.—KIRCHMANN, *Grundbegriffe des Rechts*, 194. Die Geschichtswissenschaft als solche kennt nur ein zeitliches und mithin auch nur ein relatives Maass der Dinge. Alle Werthbeurtheilung der Geschichte kann daher nur relativ und aus zeitlichen Momenten fliessen, und wer sich nicht selbst täuschen und den Dingen nicht Gewalt anthun will, muss ein für allemal in dieser Wissenschaft auf absolute Werthe verzichten.—LORENZ, *Schlosser*, 80. Only according to his faith is each man judged. Committed as this deed has been by a pure-minded, pious youth, it is a beautiful sign of the time.—DE WETTE to SAND's Mother; CHEYNE, *Founders of Criticism*, 44. The men of each age must be judged by the ideal of their own age and country, and not by the ideal of ours.—LECKY, *Value of History*, 50.

to tamper with weights and measures, to deal unequal justice to friends and enemies.

It is associated with that philosophy which Cato attributes to the gods. For we have a theory which justifies Providence by the event, and holds nothing so deserving as success, to which there can be no victory in a bad cause; prescription and duration legitimate;[93] and whatever exists is right and reasonable; and as God manifests His will by that which He tolerates, we must conform to the divine decree by living to shape the future after the ratified image of the past.[94] Another theory, less confidently urged, regards History as our guide, as much by showing errors to evade as examples to pursue. It is suspicious of illusions in success, and, though there may be hope of ultimate triumph for what is true, if not by its own attraction, by the gradual exhaustion of error, it admits no corresponding promise for what is ethically right. It deems the canonisation of the historic past more perilous than ignorance or denial, because it would perpetuate the reign of sin and acknowledge the sovereignty of wrong, and conceives it the part of real greatness to know how to stand and fall alone, stemming, for a lifetime, the contemporary flood.[95]

---

[93] La durée ici-bas, c'est le droit, c'est la sanction de Dieu.—GUIRAUD, *Philosophie Catholique de l'Histoire.*

[94] Ceux qui ne sont pas contens de l'ordre des choses ne sçauroient se vanter d'aimer Dieu comme il faut.—Il faut toujours estre content de l'ordre du passé, parce qu'il est conforme à la volonté de Dieu absolue, qu'on connoît par l'évènement. Il faut tâcher de rendre l'avenir, autant qu'il dépend de nous, conforme à la volonté de Dieu présomptive.— LEIBNIZ, *Werke*, ed. Gerhardt, ii. 136. Ich habe damals bekannt und bekenne jetzt, dass die politische Wahrheit aus denselben Quellen zu schöpfen ist, wie alle anderen, aus dem göttlichen Willen und dessen Kundgebung in der Geschichte des Menschengeschlechts.—RADOWITZ, *Neue Gespräche*, 65.

[95] A man is great as he contends best with the circumstances of his age.—FROUDE, *Short Studies*, i. 388. La persuasion que l'homme est avant tout une personne morale et libre, et qu'ayant conçu seul, dans sa conscience et devant Dieu, la règle de sa conduite, il doit s'employer tout entier à l'appliquer en lui, hors de lui, absolument, obstinément, inflexiblement, par une résistance perpétuelle opposée aux autres; et

Ranke relates, without adornment, that William III ordered the extirpation of a Catholic clan, and scouts the faltering excuse of his defenders. But when he comes to the death and character of the international deliverer, Glencoe is forgotten, the imputation of murder drops, like a thing unworthy of notice.[96] Johannes Mueller, a great Swiss celebrity, writes that the British Constitution occurred to somebody, perhaps to Halifax. This

par une contrainte perpétuelle exercée sur soi, voilà la grande idée anglaise.—Tᴀɪɴᴇ; Sᴏʀᴇʟ, *Discours de Réception*, 24. In jeder Zeit des Christenthums hat es einzelne Männer gegeben, die über ihrer Zeit standen und von ihren Gegensätzen nicht berührt wurden.—Bᴀᴄʜᴍᴀɴɴ, *Hengstenberg*, i. 160. Eorum enim qui de iisdem rebus mecum aliquid ediderunt, aut solus insanio ego, aut solus non insanio; tertium enim non est, nisi (quod dicet forte aliquis) insaniamus omnes.—Hᴏʙʙᴇs, quoted by Dᴇ Mᴏʀɢᴀɴ, 3rd June 1858: *Life of Sir W. R. Hamilton*, iii. 552.

[96] I have now to exhibit a rare combination of good qualities, and a steady perseverance in good conduct, which raised an individual to be an object of admiration and love to all his contemporaries, and have made him to be regarded by succeeding generations as a model of public and private virtue.—The evidence shows that upon this occasion he was not only under the influence of the most vulgar credulity, but that he violated the plainest rules of justice, and that he really was the murderer of two innocent women.—Hale's motives were most laudable.—Cᴀᴍᴘʙᴇʟʟ's *Lives of the Chief Justices*, i. 512, 561, 566. It was not to be expected of the colonists of New England that they should be the first to see through a delusion which befooled the whole civilised world, and the gravest and most knowing persons in it.—The people of New England believed what the wisest men of the world believed at the end of the seventeenth century.—Pᴀʟғʀᴇʏ, *New England*, iv. 127, 129 (also speaking of witchcraft). Il est donc bien étrange que sa sévérité tardive s'exerce aujourd'hui sur un homme auquel elle n'a d'autre reproche à faire que d'avoir trop bien servi l'état par des mesures politiques, injustes peut-être, violentes, mais qui, en aucune manière, n'avaient l'intérêt personnel du coupable pour objet.—M. Hastings peut sans doute paraître répréhensible aux yeux des étrangers, des particuliers même, mais il est assez extraordinaire qu'une nation usurpatrice d'une partie de l'Indostan veuille mêler les règles de la morale à celles d'une administration forcée, injuste et violente par essence, et à laquelle il faudrait renoncer à jamais pour être conséquent.—Mᴀʟʟᴇᴛ ᴅᴜ Pᴀɴ, *Mémoires*, ed. Sayous, i. 102.

artless statement might not be approved by rigid lawyers as a faithful and felicitous indication of the manner of that mysterious growth of ages, from occult beginnings, that was never profaned by the invading wit of man;[97] but it is less grotesque than it appears. Lord Halifax was the most original writer of political tracts in the pamphleteering crowd between Harrington and Bolingbroke; and in the Exclusion struggle he produced a scheme of limitations which, in substance, if not in form, foreshadowed the position of the monarchy in the later Hanoverian reigns. Although Halifax did not believe in the plot,[98] he insisted that innocent victims should be sacrificed to content the multitude. Sir William Temple writes: "We only disagreed in one point, which was the leaving some priests to the law upon the accusation of being priests only, as the House of Commons had desired; which I thought wholly unjust. Upon this point Lord Halifax and I had so sharp a debate at Lord Sunderland's lodgings, that he told me, if I would not concur in points which were so necessary for the people's satisfaction, he would tell everybody I was a Papist. And upon his affirming that the plot must be handled as if it were true, whether it were so or no, in those points that were so generally believed." In spite of this accusing passage, Macaulay, who prefers Halifax to all the statesmen of his age, praises him for his mercy: "His dislike of extremes, and a forgiving and compassionate temper which seems to have been natural to him, preserved him from all participation in the worst crimes of his time."

If, in our uncertainty, we must often err, it may be sometimes better to risk excess in rigour than in indulgence, for then at

---

[97] On parle volontiers de la stabilité de la constitution anglaise. La vérité est que cette constitution est toujours en mouvement et en oscillation et qu'elle se prête merveilleusement au jeu de ses différentes parties. Sa solidité vient de sa souplesse; elle plie et ne rompt pas.—BOUTMY, *Nouvelle Revue*, 1878, 49.

[98] This is not an age for a man to follow the strict morality of better times, yet sure mankind is not yet so debased but that there will ever be found some few men who will scorn to join concert with the public voice when it is not well grounded.—*Savile Correspondence*, 173.

least we do no injury by loss of principle. As Bayle has said, it is more probable that the secret motives of an indifferent action are bad than good;[99] and this discouraging conclusion does not depend upon theology, for James Mozley supports the sceptic from the other flank, with all the artillery of Tractarian Oxford. "A Christian," he says, "is bound by his very creed to suspect evil, and cannot release himself.... He sees it where others do not; his instinct is divinely strengthened; his eye is supernaturally keen; he has a spiritual insight, and senses exercised to discern.... He owns the doctrine of original sin; that doctrine puts him necessarily on his guard against appearances, sustains his apprehension under perplexity, and prepares him for recognising anywhere what he knows to be everywhere."[100] There is a popular saying of Madame de Staël, that we forgive whatever we really understand. The paradox has been judiciously pruned

---

[99] Cette proposition: L'homme est incomparablement plus porté au mal qu'au bien, et il se fait dans le monde incomparablement plus de mauvaises actions que de bonnes—est aussi certaine qu'aucun principe de métaphysique. Il est donc incomparablement plus probable qu'une action faite par un homme, est mauvaise, qu'il n'est probable qu'elle soit bonne. Il est incomparablement plus probable que ces secrets ressorts qui l'ont produite sont corrompus, qu'il n'est probable qu'ils soient honnêtes. Je vous avertis que je parle d'une action qui n'est point mauvaise extérieurement.—Bayle, Œuvres, ii. 248.

[100] A Christian is bound by his very creed to suspect evil, and cannot release himself.—His religion has brought evil to light in a way in which it never was before; it has shown its depth, subtlety, ubiquity; and a revelation, full of mercy on the one hand, is terrible in its exposure of the world's real state on the other. The Gospel fastens the sense of evil upon the mind; a Christian is enlightened, hardened, sharpened, as to evil; he sees it where others do not.—Mozley, Essays, i. 308. All satirists, of course, work in the direction of Christian doctrine, by the support they give to the doctrine of original sin, making a sort of meanness and badness a law of society.—Mozley, Letters, 333. Les critiques, même malveillants, sont plus près de la vérité dernière que les admirateurs.—Nisard, Lit. fr., Conclusion. Les hommes supérieurs doivent nécessairement passer pour méchants. Où les autres ne voient ni un défaut, ni un ridicule, ni un vice, leur implacable œil l'aperçoit.—Barbey d'Aurevilly, Figaro, 31st March 1888.

by her descendant, the Duke de Broglie, in the words: "Beware of too much explaining, lest we end by too much excusing."[101] History, says Froude, does teach that right and wrong are real distinctions. Opinions alter, manners change, creeds rise and fall, but the moral law is written on the tablets of eternity.[102] And if there are moments when we may resist the teaching of Froude, we have seldom the chance of resisting when he is supported by Mr. Goldwin Smith: "A sound historical morality will sanction strong measures in evil times; selfish ambition, treachery, murder, perjury, it will never sanction in the worst of times, for these are the things that make times evil.—Justice has been justice, mercy has been mercy, honour has been honour, good faith has been good faith, truthfulness has been truthfulness from the beginning." The doctrine that, as Sir Thomas Browne

---

[101] Prenons garde de ne pas trop expliquer, pour ne pas fournir des arguments à ceux qui veulent tout excuser.—BROGLIE, *Réception de Sorel*, 46.

[102] The eternal truths and rights of things exist, fortunately, independent of our thoughts or wishes, fixed as mathematics, inherent in the nature of man and the world. They are no more to be trifled with than gravitation.—FROUDE, *Inaugural Lecture at St. Andrews*, 1869, 41. What have men to do with interests? There is a right way and a wrong way. That is all we need think about.—CARLYLE to FROUDE, *Longman's Magazine*, December 1892, 151. As to History, it is full of indirect but very effective moral teaching. It is not only, as Bolingbroke called it, "Philosophy teaching by examples," but it is morality teaching by examples.—It is essentially the study which best helps the student to conceive large thoughts.—It is impossible to overvalue the moral teaching of History.—FITCH, *Lectures on Teaching*, 432. Judging from the past history of our race, in ninety-nine cases out of a hundred, war is a folly and a crime.—Where it is so, it is the saddest and the wildest of all follies, and the most heinous of all crimes.—GREG, *Essays on Political and Social Science*, 1853, i. 562. La volonté de tout un peuple ne peut rendre juste ce qui est injuste: les représentants d'une nation n'ont pas le droit de faire ce que la nation n'a pas le droit de faire elle-même.—B. CONSTANT, *Principes de Politique*, i. 15.

says, morality is not ambulatory,[103] is expressed as follows by Burke, who, when true to himself, is the most intelligent of our instructors: "My principles enable me to form my judgment upon men and actions in history, just as they do in common life; and are not formed out of events and characters, either present or past. History is a preceptor of prudence, not of principles. The principles of true politics are those of morality enlarged; and I neither now do, nor ever will admit of any other."[104]

Whatever a man's notions of these later centuries are, such, in the main, the man himself will be. Under the name of History, they cover the articles of his philosophic, his religious, and his political creed.[105] They give his measure; they denote his character: and, as praise is the shipwreck of historians, his preferences betray him more than his aversions. Modern History touches us so nearly, it is so deep a question of life and death, that we are bound to find our own way through it, and to owe our insight to ourselves. The historians of former ages, unapproachable for us in knowledge and in talent, cannot be our limit. We have

---

[103] Think not that morality is ambulatory; that vices in one age are not vices in another, or that virtues, which are under the everlasting seal of right reason, may be stamped by opinion.—SIR THOMAS BROWNE, *Works*, iv. 64.

[104] Osons croire qu'il seroit plus à propos de mettre de côté ces traditions, ces usages, et ces coutumes souvent si imparfaites, si contradictoires, si incohérentes, ou de ne les consulter que pour saisir les inconvéniens et les éviter; et qu'il faudroit chercher non-seulement les éléments d'une nouvelle législation, mais même ses derniers détails dans une étude approfondie de la morale.—LETROSNE, *Réflexions sur la Législation Criminelle*, 137. M. Renan appartient à cette famille d'esprits qui ne croient pas en réalité la raison, la conscience, le droit applicables à la direction des sociétés humaines, et qui demandent à l'histoire, à la tradition, non à la morale, les règles de la politique. Ces esprits sont atteints de la maladie du siècle, le scepticisme moral. —PILLON, *Critique Philosophique*, i. 49.

[105] The subject of modern History is of all others, to my mind, the most interesting, inasmuch as it includes all questions of the deepest interest relating not to human things only, but to divine.—ARNOLD, *Modern History*, 311.

the power to be more rigidly impersonal, disinterested and just than they; and to learn from undisguised and genuine records to look with remorse upon the past, and to the future with assured hope of better things; bearing this in mind, that if we lower our standard in History, we cannot uphold it in Church or State.

6

BEGINNING OF THE MODERN STATE[*]

M odern History tells how the last four hundred years have modified the medieval conditions of life and thought. In comparison with them, the Middle Ages were the domain of stability, and continuity, and instinctive evolution, seldom interrupted by such originators as Gregory VII or St. Francis of Assisi. Ignorant of History, they allowed themselves to be governed by the unknown Past; ignorant of Science, they never believed in hidden forces working onwards to a happier future. The sense of decay was upon them; and each generation seemed so inferior to the last, in ancient wisdom and ancestral virtue, that they found comfort in the assurance that the end of the world was at hand.

Yet the most profound and penetrating of the causes that have transformed society is a medieval inheritance. It was late in the thirteenth century that the psychology of Conscience was closely studied for the first time, and men began to speak of it as the audible voice of God, that never misleads or fails, and that ought to be obeyed always, whether enlightened or darkened, right or wrong. The notion was restrained, on its appearance,

---

[*] Published in Lord Acton, *Lectures on Modern History*, ed. John Neville Figgis and Reginald Vere Laurence (London: Macmillan, 1906), 31–51.

by the practice of regarding opposition to Church power as equivalent to specific heresy, which depressed the secret monitor below the public and visible authority. With the decline of coercion the claim of Conscience rose, and the ground abandoned by the inquisitor was gained by the individual. There was less reason then for men to be cast of the same type; there was a more vigorous growth of independent character, and a conscious control over its formation. The knowledge of good and evil was not an exclusive and sublime prerogative assigned to states, or nations, or majorities. When it had been defined and recognised as something divine in human nature, its action was to limit power by causing the sovereign voice within to be heard above the expressed will and settled custom of surrounding men. By that hypothesis, the soul became more sacred than the state, because it receives light from above, as well as because its concerns are eternal, and out of all proportion with the common interests of government. That is the root from which liberty of Conscience was developed, and all other liberty needed to confine the sphere of power, in order that it may not challenge the supremacy of that which is highest and best in man.

The securities by which this purpose has been attempted compose the problem of all later history, and centuries were spent in ascertaining and constructing them. If in the main the direction has been upward, the movement has been tardy, the conflict intense, the balance often uncertain. The passion for power over others can never cease to threaten mankind, and is always sure of finding new and unforeseen allies in continuing its martyrology. Therefore, the method of modern progress was revolution. By a series of violent shocks the nations in succession have struggled to shake off the Past, to reverse the action of Time and the verdict of success, and to rescue the world from the reign of the dead. They have been due less to provocation by actual wrong than to the attraction of ideal right, and the claims that inspired them were universal and detached. Progress has imposed increasing sacrifices on society, in behalf of those who can make no return, from whose welfare it derives no equivalent benefit, whose existence is a burden, an evil, eventually a peril to the community. The mean duration of life, the compendious test of improvement, is prolonged by all the chief agents of civilisation, moral and material, religious and scientific, working together, and depends on preserving, at infinite cost, which is infinite loss, the crippled child and the victim of accident, the idiot and the madman, the pauper and the culprit, the old and infirm, curable and incurable. This growing dominion of disinterested motive, this liberality towards the weak, in social life, corresponds to that respect for the minority, in political life, which is the essence of freedom. It is an application of the same principle of self-denial, and of the higher law.

Taking long periods, we perceive the advance of moral over material influence, the triumph of general ideas, the gradual amendment. The line of march will prove, on the whole, to have been from force and cruelty to consent and association, to humanity, rational persuasion, and the persistent appeal to common, simple, and evident maxims. We have dethroned necessity, in the shape both of hunger and of fear, by extending the scene from Western Europe to the whole world, so that all shall contribute to the treasure of civilisation, and by taking into partnership in the enjoyment of its rewards those who are far off as well as those who are below. We shall give our attention to much that has failed and passed away, as well as to the phenomena of progress, which help to build up the world in which we live. For History must be our deliverer not only from the undue influence of other times, but from the undue influence of our own, from the tyranny of environment and the pressure of the air we breathe. It requires all historic forces to produce their record and submit to judgment, and it promotes the faculty of resistance to contemporary surroundings by familiarity with other ages and other orbits of thought.

In these latter days the sum of differences in international character has been appreciably bound down by the constant process of adaptation and adjustment, and by exposure to like influences. The people of various countries are swayed by identical interests, they are absorbed in the same problems, and thrill with the same emotions; their classics are interchangeable, authorities in science are nearly alike for all, and they readily combine to make experiments and researches in common.

Towards 1500, European nations, having been fashioned and composed out of simple elements during the thousand years between the fall of the Roman Empire and that of its successor in the East, had reached full measure of differentiation. They were estranged from each other, and were inclined to treat the foreigner as the foe. Ancient links were loosened, the Pope was no longer an accepted peacemaker; and the idea of an international code, overriding the will of nations and the authority of sovereigns, had not dawned upon philosophy. Between the old order that was changing and the new that was unborn, Europe had an inorganic interval to go through.

Modern History begins under stress of the Ottoman Conquest. Constantinople fell, after an attempt to negotiate for help, by the union of the Greek and Latin Churches. The agreement come to at Florence was not ratified at home; the attempt was resented, and led to an explosion of feeling that made even subjugation by the Turk seem for the moment less intolerable, and that hastened the catastrophe by making Western Christians slow to sacrifice themselves for their implacable brethren in the East. Offers of help were made, conditional on acceptance of the Florentine decree, and were rejected with patriotic and theological disdain. A small force of papal and Genoese mercenaries shared the fate of the defenders, and the end could not have been long averted, even by the restoration of religious unity. The Powers that held back were not restrained by dogmatic arguments only. The dread of Latin intolerance was the most favourable circumstance encountered by the Turks in the Eastern Empire, and they at once offered protection and immunities to the patriarch and his prelates. The conquest of the entire peninsula, with the islands, occupied a generation, and it was good policy meanwhile to do nothing that would diminish the advantage or awaken alarm of persecution. Their system required the increase rather than the conversion of Christian subjects, for the tribute of gold as well as the tribute of blood. The Janissaries were selected among the sons of Christian parents, who became renegades, and who, having neither home nor family, no life but in camp, no employment but arms, became not only the best professional soldiers in the world, but a force constantly active to undo the work of pacific statesmen and to find fresh occasion for war. There were occasional outbreaks of blind ferocity, and at all times there was the incapacity of an uncivilised race to understand the character and the interest of alien subjects more cultivated than themselves. But there was not at first the sense of unmitigated tyranny that arose later; and there was not so great a contrast with life as it was under Italian despots as to make Christians under the Sultan passionately long for deliverance.

From the perjury of Varna, in 1446, when the Christians broke the treaty just concluded at Sregedin, it was understood that they could never be trusted to keep engagements entered into with people of another religion. It seemed a weak-minded exaggeration of hypocrisy to abstain from preying on men so furiously divided, so full of hatred, so incapable of combining in defence of their altars and their homes, so eager in soliciting aid and intervention from the infidel in their own disputes. The several principalities of the circumference, Servia, Bosnia, Wallachia, the Morea, and the islands, varying in nationality and in religion, were attacked separately, and made no joint defence. In Epirus, Scanderbeg, once a renegade, then in communion with Rome, drawing his supplies from the opposite coast of Apulia, which his sentinels on Cape Linguetta could see at sunrise, maintained himself for many years victoriously, knowing that his country would perish with him. John Hunyadi had defended Christendom on the Hungarian frontier so well that the monarchy of his son stemmed the tide of invasion for seventy years. While the Turkish outposts kept watch on the Danube, Mahomet seized Otranto, and all the way upwards to the Alps there was no force capable of resisting him. Just then, he died, Otranto was lost, and the enterprise was not renewed. His people were a nation of soldiers, not a nation of sailors. For operations beyond sea they relied on the seamen of the Aegean, generally Christians, as they had required the help of Genoese ships to ferry them over the Hellespont.

Under Bajazet, the successor, there was some rest for Europe. His brother, who was a dangerous competitor, as the crown went to the one who survived, fled for safety to the Christians, and was detained as a hostage, beyond the possibility of ransom, by the Knights of St. John, and then by the Pope. The Sultan paid, that he might be kept quiet.

For years the Turks were busy in the East. Selim conquered Syria and part of Persia. He conquered Arabia, and was acknowledged by the Sheriff of Mecca caliph and protector of the holy shrine. He conquered Egypt and assumed the prerogative of the Imaum, which had been a shadow at Cairo, but became, at Constantinople, the supreme authority in Islam. Gathering up the concentrated resources of the Levant, Solyman the Magnificent turned, at last, against the enemy who guarded the gates of civilised Europe. Having taken Belgrade, he undertook, in 1526, the crowning campaign of Turkish history. At the battle of Mohacs Hungary lost her independence. The Turks found a Transylvanian magnate who was willing to receive the crown from them; and the broad valley of the Danube continued to be their battlefield until the days of Sobieski and Eugene. But the legitimate heir of King Ladislas, who fell at Mohacs, was Ferdinand, only brother of Charles V; and Hungary, with the vast region then belonging to the Bohemian crown, passing to the same hands as the ancient inheritance of the Habsburgs, constituted the great Austrian monarchy which extended from the Adriatic to the far Sarmatian plain, and Solyman's victory brought him face to face with the first Power able to arrest his progress. The Turks were repulsed at Vienna in 1529, at Malta in 1564. This was their limit in Western Europe; and after Lepanto, in 1571, their only expansion was at the expense of Poland at Muscovy. They still wielded almost boundless resources; the entire seaboard from Cattaro all round by the Euxine to the Atlantic was Mahomedan, and all but one-fourth of the Mediterranean was a Turkish lake. It was long before they knew that it was not their destiny to be masters of the Western as well as of the Eastern world.

While this heavy cloud overhung the Adriatic and the Danube, and the countries within reach of the Turk were in peril of extinction, the nations farther west were consolidating rapidly into unity and power. By the marriage of Ferdinand and Isabella, by their conquest of Granada and the rise of a new hemisphere at their command, Spain for the first time became a great Power; while France, having expelled the English, having instituted a permanent army, acquired vast frontier provinces, and crushed the centrifugal forces of feudalism, was more directly formidable and more easily aggressive. These newly created Powers portended danger in one direction. Their increase was not in comparison with England or with Portugal, so much as in contrast with Italy. England, by the Tudors, had achieved internal tranquillity; and Portugal was already at the head of Europe in making the ocean tributary to trade. But Italy was divided, unwarlike, poor in the civic virtues that made Switzerland impregnable, rich in the tempting luxuries of civilisation, an inexhaustible treasure-house of much that the neighbours greatly needed and could never find elsewhere. The best writers and scholars and teachers, the most consummate artists, the ablest commanders by land and sea, the deepest explorers of the mystery of State that have been known before or since, all the splendours of the Renaissance, and the fruits of a whole century of progress were there, ready to be appropriated and employed for its own benefit by a paramount Power.

It was obvious that the countries newly strengthened, the countries growing in unity and concentration and superfluous forces, should encroach upon those that were demoralised and weakened. By strict reason of State, this was not the policy of France; for the French frontiers were assigned by nature everywhere but in the northeast. There the country was open, the enemy's territory approached the capital; and the true line of expansion was towards Antwerp, or Liège, or Strasburg. But the French were invited into Italy with promise of welcome, because the Angevin claim to Naples, defeated in 1462, had passed to the King of France. The Aragonese, who had been successful in resisting it, was not legitimate, and had been compelled again to struggle for existence by the Rising of the Barons. The rising was suppressed; the discontented Neapolitans went into exile; and they were now in France, prophesying easy triumphs if Charles VIII would extend his hand to take the greatness that belonged to the heir of the house of Anjou. They were followed by the most important of the Italian Cardinals, Della Rovere, nephew of a former Pope, himself afterwards the most famous pontiff who had appeared for centuries. Armed with the secrets of the Conclave, the Cardinal insisted that Alexander VI should be deposed, on the ground that he had paid for the papacy in ascertainable sums of money and money's worth; whereas spiritual office obtained in that way was *ipso facto* void.

The advent of the French, heralded by the passionate eloquence of Savonarola, was also hailed by Florence and its dependencies, in their impatience of the Medicean rule, now that it had dropped from the hands of the illustrious Lorenzo, into those of his less competent son. Lodovico Sforza, the Regent of Milan, was also among those who called in the French, as he had a family quarrel with Naples. His father, Francesco, the most successful of the Condottieri, who acquired the Milanese by marriage with a Visconti, is known by that significant saying: "May God defend me from my friends. From my enemies I can defend myself." As the Duke of Orleans also descended from the Visconti, Lodovico wished to divert the French to the more alluring prospect of Naples.

In September 1494 Charles VIII invaded Italy by the Mont Genèvre, with an army equal to his immediate purpose. His horsemen still displayed the medieval armour, wrought by the artistic craftsmen of the Renaissance. They were followed by artillery, the newer arm which, in another generation, swept the steel-clad knight away. French infantry was not thought so well of. But the Swiss had become, in their wars with Burgundy, the most renowned of all foot-soldiers. They were unskilled in manoeuvres; but their pikemen, charging in dense masses, proved irresistible on many Italian fields; until it was discovered that they would serve for money on either side, and that when opposed to their countrymen they refused to fight. At Pavia they were cut down by the Spaniards and their fame began to wane. They were Germans, hating Austria, and their fidelity to the golden lilies is one of the constant facts of French history, until the Swiss guard and the white flag vanished together, in July 1830.

Charles reached Naples early in 1495, having had no resistance to overcome, but having accomplished nothing, and having manifested no distinct purpose on his way, when he found himself, for a moment, master of Florence and of Rome. The deliverance of Constantinople was an idea that occurred inevitably to a man of enterprise who was in possession of Southern Italy. It was the advanced post of Europe against the East, of Christendom against Islam; the proper rendezvous of Crusaders; the source of supplies; the refuge of squadrons needing to refit. The Sultan was not an overwhelming warrior, like his father; he had not, like Selim, his successor, control of the entire East, and he was held in check by the existence of his brother, whom Charles took with him, on leaving Rome, with a view to ulterior service, but whom he lost soon after.

Charles VIII was not a man ripened by experience of great affairs, and he had assumed the title of King of Jerusalem, as a sign of his crusading purpose. But he also called himself King of Sicily, as representing the Anjous, and this was not a disused and neglected derelict. For the island belonged to the King of Aragon, the most politic and capable of European monarchs. Before starting for Italy, Charles had made terms with him, and Ferdinand, in consideration of a rectified frontier, had engaged, by the treaty of Barcelona, to take no unfriendly advantage of his neighbour's absence. The basis of this agreement was shattered by the immediate unexpected and overwhelming success of the French arms. From his stronghold in the South it would be easy for Charles to make himself master of Rome, of Florence, of all Italy, until he came in sight of the lion of St. Mark. So vast and sudden a superiority was a serious danger. A latent jealousy of Spain underlay the whole expedition. The realm of the Catholic kings was expanding, and an indistinct empire, larger, in reality, than that of Rome, was rising out of the Atlantic. By a very simple calculation of approaching contingencies, Ferdinand might be suspected of designs upon Naples. Now that the helplessness of the Neapolitans had been revealed, it was apparent that he had made a false reckoning when he allowed the French to occupy what he might have taken more easily himself, by crossing the Straits of Messina. Ferdinand joined the Italians of the North in declaring against the invader, and his envoy Fonseca tore up the Treaty of Barcelona before the face of the French king.

Having been crowned in the Cathedral, and having garrisoned his fortresses, Charles set out for France, at the head of a small army. As he came over the Apennines into Lombardy, at Fornovo he was met by a larger force, chiefly provided by Venice, and had to fight his way through. A fortnight after his departure the Spaniards, under Gonsalvo of Cordova, landed in Calabria, as auxiliaries of the dethroned king. The throne was once more occupied by the fallen family, and Charles retained nothing of his easy and inglorious conquests when he died in 1498.

His successor, Louis XII, was the Duke of Orleans, who descended from the Visconti, and he at once prepared to enforce his claim on Milan. He allied himself against his rival, Sforza, with Venice, and with Pope Alexander. That he might marry the widowed queen, and preserve her duchy of Brittany for the Crown, he required that his own childless marriage should be annulled. Upon the Legate who brought the necessary documents the grateful king bestowed a principality, a bride of almost royal rank, and an army wherewith to reconquer the lost possessions of the Church in Central Italy. For the Legate was the Cardinal of Valencia, who became thenceforward Duke of Valentinois, and is better known as Caesar Borgia. The rich Lombard plain, the garden of Italy, was conquered as easily as Naples had been in the first expedition. Sforza said to the Venetians: "I have been the dinner; you will be the supper"; and went up into the Alps to look for Swiss levies. At Novara, in 1500, his mercenaries betrayed him and he ended his days in a French prison. On their way home from the scene of their treachery, the Swiss crowned their evil repute by seizing Bellinzona and the valley of the Ticino, which has remained one of their cantons.

Louis, undisputed master of Milan and Genoa, assured of the Roman and the Venetian alliance, was in a better position than his predecessor to renew the claim on the throne of Naples. But now, behind Frederic of Naples, there was Ferdinand of Aragon and Sicily, who was not likely to allow the king for whom he had fought to be deposed without resistance. Therefore it was a welcome suggestion when Ferdinand proposed that they should combine to expel Frederic and to divide his kingdom. As it was Ferdinand who had just reinstated him, this was an adaptation to the affairs of Christendom of the methods which passed for justice in the treatment of unbelievers, and were applied without scruple by the foremost men of the age, Albuquerque and Cortez. Frederic turned for aid to the Sultan, and this felonious act was put forward as the justification of his aggressors. The Pope sanctioned the Treaty of Partition, and as the Crown of Naples was technically in his gift, he deprived the king on the ground stated by the allies. The exquisite significance of the plea was that the Pope himself had invited Turkish intervention in Italy, and now declared it a cause of forfeiture. In 1501 French and Spaniards occupied their allotted portions, and then quarrelled over the distribution of the spoil. For a time Gonsalvo, "the great Captain," was driven to bay at Barletta on the Adriatic; but at the end of 1503 he won a decisive victory, and the defeated French, under Bayard, withdrew from the Garigliano to the Po. Naples remained a dependency of Spain, for all purposes, in modern history.

In the midst of foreign armies, and of new combinations disturbing the established balance of Italian Powers, the lesser potentates were exposed to destruction; and there were forces about sufficient, under capable guidance, to remodel the chaotic centre of Italy, where no strong government had ever been constituted. Caesar Borgia recognised the opportunity as soon as the French were at Milan; the Pope was growing old and was clay in his terrible hands. His sister just then became Duchess of Ferrara, on the border of the defenceless region which he coveted; and the dominions of the King of France, his patron and ally, extended to the Adda and the Po. Never had such advantages been united in such a man. For Caesar's talents were of the imperial kind. He was fearless of difficulties, of dangers, and of consequences; and having no preference for right or wrong, he weighed with an equal and dispassionate mind whether it was better to spare a man or to cut his throat. As he did not attempt more than he could perform, his rapid success awakened aspirations for a possible future. He was odious to Venice, but a Venetian, who watched his meteoric course, wonders, in his secret diary, whether this unerring schemer was to be the appointed deliverer. He was a terror to Florence, yet the Florentine secretary, to whom he confided his thoughts in certain critical hours, wrote of him as men have written of Napoleon, and erected a monument to his memory that has secretly fascinated half the politicians in the world.

With his double equipment as a lieutenant of the French king and as a *condottiere* of the Pope, he began by reviving the dormant authority of Rome, where nominal feudatories held vicarious sway. In the place of many despots struggling not for objects of policy, but for their own existence, there appeared a single state, reaching from sea to sea, from the Campagna to the salt-marshes by the delta of the Po, under a papal prince and *gonfaloniere*, invested with rights and prerogatives to protect the Holy See, and with power to control it. Rome would have become a dependency of the reigning house of Borgia, as it had been of less capable vassals, and the system might have lasted as long as the brain that devised it. Lorenzo de' Medici once said that his buildings were the only works that would outlast him; and it is common in the secular characters of that epoch, unlike the priesthood, not to believe in those things that are abiding, and not to regard organisations that are humble and obscure at first and bloom by slow degrees for the use of another age.

Caesar's enterprise was not determined or limited by the claims of the Vatican. He served both Pope and king, and his French alliance carried farther than the recovery of the Romagna. Florence became tributary by taking him into pay. Bologna bought him off with a heavy ransom. Venice inscribed his name in the illustrious record of its nobility. None could tell where his ambition or his resources would end, how his inventive genius would employ the rivalry of the invaders, what uses he would devise for the Emperor and the Turk. The era of petty tyranny was closed by the apparition of one superior national tyrant, who could be no worse than twenty, for though his crimes would be as theirs, they would not be useless to the nation, but were thoughtfully designed and executed for the sake of power, the accepted object of politics in a country where the right was known by the result. Caesar was not an unpopular master, and his subjects were true to him in his falling fortunes. The death of Alexander and the decline of the French cause in the South cut short his work in the autumn of 1503. Della Rovere, Cardinal Vincula, whose title came from the Church of St. Peter in Chains, the inflexible enemy of the Borgias, was now Julius II; and after a brief interval he was strong enough to drive Caesar out of the country; while the Venetians, entering the Romagna under ill omens for the Republic, occupied the remnant of his many conquests.

Julius had resisted Alexander, as a man unfit for his function, and it soon appeared that this was not a private feud, but a total reversal of ideas and policy. The change was not felt in religious reform or in patronage of learning, but first in the notion of territorial politics. Caesar had rebuilt the duchy of Romagna in the service of the papacy; and it was the essence of the schemes of Julius that it should be secured for the Holy See, together with all else that could be claimed by right, or acquired by policy and war. The Borgias had prevailed by arms, and Julius would not consent to be their inferior and to condemn his whole career. He must draw the sword; but, unlike them, he would draw it in the direct interest of the Church. He had overthrown the conqueror, not that the conquests might be dissolved, or might go to Venice, but in order that he himself and his successors might have power in Italy, and through Italians, over the world. Upon this foundation he instituted the temporal power, as it subsisted for three centuries. The jealous municipal spirit of the Middle Ages had dissolved society into units, and nothing but force could reverse the tradition and weld the fragments into great communities. Borgia had shown that this could be done; but also that no victorious *condottiere*, were he even his own son, could be trusted by a Pope. Julius undertook to command his army himself, and to fight at the head of his troops. Letting his white beard grow, putting on armour, and proudly riding his war-horse under fire, he exhibited the most picturesque and romantic figure of his time.

The Venetians, commanding the seaboard with their galleys, were not easy to dislodge from the towns they occupied. Essentially a maritime and commercial Power, their centre of gravity lay so far east that it was once proposed to move the capital from the Lagoons to the Bosphorus. When the advancing Turk damaged their trade and threatened their Colonial empire, they took advantage of Italian disintegration to become a continental state, and the general insecurity and oppression of miniature potentates made it a happy fate to be subject to the serene and politic government, whose three thousand ships still held the sea, flying the Christian flag. Renouncing non-intervention on the mainland, they set power above prosperity, and the interest of the State above the welfare and safety of a thousand patrician houses. Wherever there were troubled waters, the fisher was Venice. All down the Eastern Coast, and along the Alpine slopes to the passes which were the trade route to Northern Europe, and still farther, at the expense of Milan and Naples, the patriarch of Aquileia and the Duke of Ferrara, the Emperor and the Pope, the Queen of the Adriatic extended her intelligent sway. It was under the long administration of the Doge Foscari, Byron's hero, that it dawned upon the Venetians that it might be their mission to supersede the frail and helpless governments of the Peninsula; and their famous politician and historian, Paruta, believed that it was in their power to do what Rome had done. Their ambition was evident to their neighbours, and those whom they had despoiled, under every plausible pretext, awaited the opportunity of retribution.

Julius, taking counsel with Machiavelli, found it easy to form a league composed of their enemies. As it was not the interest of the empire, France and Spain, to spite Venice by strengthening each other, the Venetians imagined they could safely hold their ground, leaving the dependent cities to make their own terms with the enemy. Padua held out victoriously against Maximilian, but the battle of Agnadello was lost against the French in the same year 1509, in which, fighting under the Crescent in the Indian Ocean, the Venetians were defeated by the Portuguese, and lost their Eastern trade. They soon obtained their revenge. Having gained his ends by employing France against Venice in the League of Cambray, Julius now allied himself with the Venetians to expel the French from Milan. He had recovered the papal possessions, he had broken the Venetian power, and in this his third effort to reconstitute Italy, he still succeeded, because he had the support of the Venetians and the Swiss. The French gave battle to the Spaniards at Ravenna and to the Swiss at Novara, and then they evacuated the Milanese.

Louis XII swore that he would wreak vengeance on the papacy, and, in conjunction with the Emperor, opened a Council at Pisa, which was attended by a minority of cardinals. Julius met the attack by calling a general Council to meet at the Lateran, which was the first since the great reforming Council, and was still sitting when Julius died in 1513. Like the Council at Pisa, it was regarded at Rome as a move in the great game of Politics, and it made no serious attempt to heal the long-standing and acknowledged wounds of the Church. Its action spread the belief that the reigning diseases were known, but that the remedy was refused, and that reforms that might help religion were not to be expected from Church or State. Julius II died without having expelled the barbarians, as he had promised. The French were gone, but the Spaniards remained unshaken, and were still the pivot of the operations of the Holy See. The investiture of Naples was granted to Ferdinand of Aragon, and the fairest region in Europe bound Spain irrevocably to the Popes.

Although the Italian scheme of Julius was left half-way, his Roman scheme was completed; the intermittent suzerainty of the Middle Ages was straitened out into effective sovereignty over the half of Central Italy, where anarchy used to reign, and the temporal power was fixed on foundations solid enough to bear the coming diminution of spiritual power. The added splendours of modern royalty, round which cardinals of reigning houses—Medici, Este, Farnese, Gonzaga—displayed the pomp and ceremony of semi-regal state, in palaces built by Bramante and Michelangelo, with the ambassadors and protectors of the Powers, and the heads of princely families that had worn the tiara, made Rome the magnetic pole of aristocratic society. As the capital of an absolute monarchy, as others were, it became associated with principles which, in the Middle Ages, it resisted with spiritual and secular weapons; and the magnitude of the change was apparent when Leo X, by the Concordat of Bologna, conceded to Francis I the choice of bishops and the higher patronage of the Church of France. For Francis on his accession sent an army into Italy, the last work of Julius II was overthrown at Marignano, and France again was master of the Milanese.

The final struggle was to come at the vacancy of the Imperial throne. Ferdinand of Aragon was dead, and Naples passed to the King of undivided Spain. It was the unswerving policy of Rome that it should not be united with the Empire, and against that fixed axiom the strongest dynasty of emperors went to pieces. The Reformation had just begun in Germany, and Leo wished one of the Northern Electors to be chosen as Maximilian's successor. In conformity with the political situation, he would have preferred Frederic of Saxony, the protector of Luther. The election of Charles, in 1519, was a defiance of the Balance of Power, a thing not to the taste of the Middle Ages, but becoming familiar in those days. France, unable formerly to keep Naples against Spain, had now to defend Lombardy against Spain, supported by Germany, Naples, and the Netherlands. Francis maintained the unequal struggle for four years, although his most powerful vassal, Bourbon, brought the enemy to the gates of Marseilles. The decisive action of the long Italian war was fought at Pavia in June 1525, where Francis was taken prisoner, and was compelled to purchase his release by cruel sacrifices.

The years that followed are only a phase in the permanent subjugation of Italy, but they are memorable in another connection. For the triumph of Pavia brought the suppression of the Lutherans within the range of practical politics. The Peasants' War had damaged their position; the Emperor was able now to execute the Imperial decree of Worms, and there were some in Germany who desired it. He made it a condition of his prisoners' deliverance that he should assist in destroying them; and Francis readily offered to do it by coming in person, and bearing half the charge. Charles proposed to take him at his word, when he learnt that the Pope was at the head of a great alliance against him. Pope Clement was advised by the best ecclesiastic in his court, the *Datario* Giberti, to try one more struggle before the chains were riveted, and before he became, as they said, a Spanish chaplain. It is a war, said Giberti, not for power or dominion, but for the redemption of Italy from perpetual bondage; and he placed his master, for the moment, at the head of the nation. Clement concluded a treaty with the Emperor's enemies at Cognac, released Francis from his oath to observe the Treaty of Madrid, and endeavoured to make Pescara, the victor of Pavia, turn traitor by the prospect of the throne of Naples.

In this way Charles was compelled to turn his arms against Rome. He protested that he would risk all his crowns for the sake of revenge, and appealed to Germany, with its Lutherans, for support. Tell them, he wrote, that they are wanted against the Turk. They will know what Turk we mean. They knew it so well that the lands-knechts came provided with silken nooses for the necks of cardinals, besides a gold-thread one for the Pope. He issued a detailed manifesto against him, the work of Valdes, one of the rare Lutherans of Spain; and those who were in the secret expected that the shrift would be short. Francis had intended from the first moment to break his word, and to execute no conditions injurious to France, but he came too late. A large body of Germans poured over the Alps and joined the Spaniards in Lombardy. It was observed afterwards that the Spaniards were the most vindictive, but it was the Germans who made the push for Rome; and Bourbon, on the plea of economy, as he could not pay them, led them through the passes of the Apennines, overthrowing the Medici at Florence on the way. Rome was taken almost without resistance, and Clement shut himself up in St. Angelo, while the city was given over to unmerciful pillage, the prelates were held to ransom, and all the secret treasure was got at by torture. That month of May 1527, with its awful experience, was an end to the pride and the hope and the gladness of the pagan revival; a severe and penitential spirit came over society, preparing to meet the Reformation by reform, and to avert change in doctrine by a change in morality. The sack of Rome, said Cardinal Cajetan, was a just judgment on the sufferers. The city was now the Emperor's, by right of conquest, to bestow as he chose, and the Romans were not unwilling that it should be his capital. Some said that the abolition of the temporal power would secure peace among the Powers, whilst others thought that the consequence would be a patriarch in France, if not in England as well. The last effort of the French being spent, and Doria having gone over to the Emperor, taking with him Genoa, the key of French influence, the chain of transactions which began with the Neapolitan expedition of 1494, concluded in 1530 with the siege of Florence. Charles made peace with France at Cambray, and with the Pope at Barcelona, and received the Imperial crown at Bologna.

This was the consummation of the Italian wars, by which the main conditions of modern politics were determined. The conflicts which had lasted for a generation, and the disorder and violence which were older still, were at an end; Italy obtained repose from her master, and spent for centuries her intellect in his service. Pescara, Ferrante Gonzaga, Philibert Emanuel, Spinola, were the men who made Spain the first of military powers. And Parma's invincible legions, which created Belgium, wrested Antwerp from the Dutch, delivered Paris against Henry IV, and watched the signals of the Armada that they might subdue England, were thronged with Italian infantry. Excepting Venice, strong in her navy and her unapproachable lagoon, Spain dominated thenceforward over Italy, and became, by her ascendency in both Sicilies, a bulwark against the Turks.

Italy passed out of general politics, and was a force in Europe only through Rome. The Conclave, and the creation of cardinals to compose the Conclave, made it a constant school of negotiation and intrigue for the best diplomacy in the world. By favour of the Habsburgs, the papacy obtained a fixed dominion, secure against all comers, requiring no military defence, no wasting and profitless expenditure, nothing to dissolve the mirage of an ideal government, under spiritual and converted men. The pontificates became steadily longer, averaging six years in the sixteenth century, eight in the seventeenth, twelve in the eighteenth, sixteen in the nineteenth, and by the original and characteristic institution which is technically known as nepotism, the selection of a Prime Minister, not from the College of the ecclesiastical aristocracy, but from the family of the reigning sovereign, the tonsured statesmen introduced a dynastic infusion into the fluctuations of elective monarchy.

The triumph and coronation of the Emperor Charles V, when he was superior to all that Europe had beheld since

Charlemagne, revived the ancient belief in a supreme authority elevated on alliance with the priesthood, at the expense of the independence and the equipoise of nations. The exploits of Magellan and Cortez, upsetting all habits of perspective, called up vain dreams of the coming immensity of Spain, and roused the phantom of universal empire. The motive of domination became a reigning force in Europe; for it was an idea which monarchy would not willingly let fall after it had received a religious and an international consecration. For centuries it was constantly asserted as a claim of necessity and of right. It was the supreme manifestation of the modern state according to the image which Machiavelli had set up, the state that suffers neither limit nor equality, and is bound by no duty to nations or to men, that thrives on destruction, and sanctifies whatever things contributed to increase of power.

This law of the modern world, that power tends to expand indefinitely, and will transcend all barriers, abroad and at home, until met by superior forces, produces the rhythmic movement of History. Neither race, nor religion, nor political theory has been in the same degree an incentive to the perpetuation of universal enmity and national strife. The threatened interests were compelled to unite for the self-government of nations, the toleration of religions, and the rights of men. And it is by the combined efforts of the weak, made under compulsion, to resist the reign of force and constant wrong, that, in the rapid change but slow progress of four hundred years, liberty has been preserved, and secured, and extended, and finally understood.

7

THE NEW WORLD*

G reater changes than those which were wrought by governments or armies on the battlefield of Italy were accomplished at the same time, thousands of miles away, by solitary
adventurers, with the future of the world in their hands. The
Portuguese were the first Europeans to understand that the
ocean is not a limit, but the universal waterway that unites mankind. Shut in by Spain, they could not extend on land, and had
no opening but the Atlantic. Their arid soil gave little scope to
the territorial magnate, who was excluded from politics by the
growing absolutism of the dynasty, and the government found
it well to employ at a distance forces that might be turbulent
at home.

The great national work of exploration did not proceed from
the State. The Infante Henry had served in the African wars,
and his thoughts were drawn towards distant lands. He was not
a navigator himself; but from his home at Sagres, on the Sacred
Promontory, he watched the ships that passed between the great
maritime centre at the mouth of the Tagus and the regions that

---

* Published in Lord Acton, *Lectures on Modern History*, ed. John Neville
Figgis and Reginald Vere Laurence (London: Macmillan, 1906), 52–70.

were to compose the Portuguese empire. As Grandmaster of the Order of Christ he had the means to equip them, and he rapidly occupied the groups of islands that lie between Africa and mid-Atlantic, and that were a welcome accession to the narrow territory of Portugal. Then he sent his mariners to explore the coast of the unknown and dreaded continent. When they reached the Senegal and the Gambia, still more, when the coast of Guinea trended to the East, they remembered Prester John, and dreamed of finding a way to his fictitious realm which would afford convenient leverage for Christendom, at the back of the dark world that faced the Mediterranean.

As the trade of the country did not cover the outlay, Henry began in 1442 to capture Negroes, who were imported as slaves, or sold with advantage to local chiefs. In five years, 927 blacks from Senegambia reached the Lisbon market; and, later on, the Guinea coast supplied about a thousand every year. That domestic institution was fast disappearing from Europe when it was thus revived; and there was some feeling against the Infante, and some temporary sympathy for his victims. On the other side, there were eminent divines who thought that the people of hot countries may properly be enslaved. Henry the Navigator applied to Rome, and Nicholas V issued Bulls authorising him and his Portuguese to make war on Moors and pagans, seize their possessions, and reduce them to perpetual slavery, and prohibiting all Christian nations, under eternal penalties, from trespassing on the privilege. He applauded the trade in Negroes, and hoped that it would end in their conversion. Negro slavery struck no deep root in Europe. But the delusion, says Las Casas, lasted to his own time, when, half a century after the death of its founder, it began to control the destinies of America.

Henry's brother, the Regent Dom Pedro, had visited the courts of Europe, and brought Marco Polo's glowing narrative of his travels in the Far East, still, in Yule's edition, one of the most fascinating books that can be found. Emmanuel the Great, in the Charter rewarding Vasco da Gama, affirms that, from 1433, the Infante pursued his operations with a view to India. After his death, in 1460, they were carried on by the State, and became a secondary purpose, dependent on public affairs. Africa was farmed out for some years, on condition that an hundred leagues of coast were traced annually. There was a moment of depression, when the Guinea coast, having run eastward for a thousand miles and more, turned south, apparently without end. Toscanelli of Florence was a recognised authority on the geography of those days, and he was asked what he thought of the situation. No oracle ever said anything so wise as the answer of the Tuscan sage. For he told them that India was to be found not in the East, but in the West; and we shall see what came of it twenty years later, when his letter fell into predestined hands. The Portuguese were not diverted from their aim. They knew quite well that Africa does not stretch away forever, and that it needed only a few intrepid men to see the end of it, and to reach an open route to Eastern Asia. They went on, marking their advance beyond the Congo, and erected crosses along the coast to signify their claim; but making no settlements, for Africa was only an obstruction on the way to the Indies.

Each successive voyage was made under a different commander, until 1486, when the squadron of Bartholomew Diaz was blown offshore, out into the Atlantic. When the storm fell he sailed east until he had passed the expected meridian of Africa, and then, turning northward, struck land far beyond Cape Agulhas. He had solved the problem, and India was within his reach. His men soon after refused to go farther, and he was forced to renounce the prize. On his way back he doubled the Cape, which, from his former experience, he called the Cape Tempestuous, until the king, showing that he understood, gave it a name of better omen. Nevertheless, Portugal did no more for ten years, the years that were made memorable by Spain. Then, under a new king, Emmanuel the Fortunate, Vasco da Gama went out to complete the unfinished work of Diaz, lest Columbus, fulfilling the prophecy of Toscanelli, should reach Cathay by a shorter route, and rob them of their reward. The right man had been found. It was all plain sailing; and he plucked the ripe fruit. Vasco da Gama's voyage to the Cape was the longest ever made till then. At Malindi, on the equatorial east coast of Africa, he found a pilot, and, striking across the Indian Ocean by the feeble monsoon of 1497, sighted the Ghats in May. The first cargo from India covered the expenses many times over. The splendour of the achievement was recognised at once, and men were persuaded that Emmanuel would soon be the wealthiest of European monarchs. So vast a promise of revenue required to be made secure by arms, and a force was sent out under Cabral.

The work thus attempted in the East seemed to many too much for so small a kingdom. They objected that the country would break its back in straining so far; that the soil ought first to be cultivated at home; that it would be better to import labour from Germany than to export it to India. Cabral had not been many weeks at sea when these murmurs received a memorable confirmation. Following the advice of Da Gama to avoid the calms of the Gulf of Guinea, he took a westerly course, made the coast of South America, and added, incidentally and without knowing it, a region not much smaller than Europe to the dominions of his sovereign.

The Portuguese came to India as traders, not as conquerors, and desired, not territory, but portable and exchangeable commodities. But the situation they found out there compelled them to wage war in unknown seas, divided from supports, and magazines, and docks by nearly half the globe. They made no attempt on the interior, for the Malabar coast was shut off by a range of lofty mountains. Their main object was the trade of the Far East, which was concentrated at Calicut, and was then carried by the Persian Gulf to Scanderoon and Constantinople, or by Jeddah to Suez and Alexandria. There the Venetians shipped the products of Asia to the markets of Europe. But on the other side of the isthmus the carrying trade, all the way to the Pacific, was in the hands of Moors from Arabia and Egypt. The Chinese had disappeared before them from Indian waters, and the Hindoos were no mariners. They possessed the monopoly of that which the Portuguese had come to take, and they were enemies of the Christian name. The Portuguese required not their share in the trade, but the monopoly itself. A deadly conflict could not be avoided. By the natives, they were received at first as friends; and Vasco da Gama, who took the figures of the Hindoo Pantheon for saints of the Catholic Calendar, reported that the people of India were Christians. When this illusion was dispelled, it was a consolation to find the Nestorians settled at Cochin, which thus became a Portuguese stronghold, which their best soldier, Duarte Pacheco, held against a multitude. Calicut, where they began operations, has disappeared like Earl Godwin's estate. Forbes, who was there in 1772, writes: "At very low water I have occasionally seen the waves breaking over the tops of the highest temples and minarets." It was an international city, where 1500 vessels cleared in a season, where trade was open and property secure, and where the propagation of foreign religion was not resented.

The Zamorin, as they called the Rajah of Calicut, ended by taking part with the old friends from the Arabian Seas, who supplied his country with grain, against the visitors who came in questionable shape. The Portuguese lacked the diplomatic graces, and disregarded the art of making friends and acquiring ascendency by the virtues of humanity and good faith. When it came to blows, they acquitted themselves like men conscious that they were the pioneers of History, that their footsteps were in the van of the onward march, that they were moulding the future, and making the world subservient to civilisation. They were Crusaders, coming the other way, and robbing the Moslem of their resources. The shipbuilding of the Moors depended on the teak forests of Calicut; the Eastern trade enriched both Turk and Mameluke, and the Sultan of Egypt levied duty amounting to £290,000 a year. Therefore he combined with the Venetians to expel the common enemy from Indian waters. In 1509 their fleet was defeated by the Viceroy Almeida near Diu, off the coast of Kattywar, where the Arabian seaman comes in sight of India. It was his last action before he surrendered power to his rival, the great Albuquerque. Almeida sought the greatness of his country not in conquest but in commerce. He discouraged expeditions to Africa and to the Moluccas; for he believed that the control of Indian traffic could be maintained by sea power, and that land settlements would drain the resources of the nation. Once the Moslem traders excluded, Portugal would possess all it wanted, on land and sea.

Almeida's successor, who had the eye of Alexander the Great for strategic points and commercial centres, was convinced that sea-power, at six months from home, rests on the occupation of seaports, and he carried the forward policy so far that Portugal possessed fifty-two establishments, commanding 15,000 miles of coast, and held them, nominally, with 20,000 men. Almeida's victory had broken the power of the Moors. Albuquerque resolved to prevent their reappearance by closing the Persian Gulf and the Red Sea. With Aden, Ormuz, and Malacca, he said, the Portuguese are masters of the world. He failed in the Red Sea. When Socotra proved insufficient, he attacked Aden, and was repulsed. There was a disconcerting rumour that no Christian vessel could live in the Red Sea, as there was a loadstone that extracted the nails. Albuquerque succeeded in the Persian Gulf, and erected a fortress at Ormuz, and at the other end of the Indian world he seized Malacca, and became master of the narrow seas, and of all the produce from the vast islands under the equator. He made Goa the impregnable capital of his prodigious empire, and the work that he did was solid. He never perceived the value of Bombay, which is the best harbour in Asia, and did not see that the key of India is the Cape of Good Hope. His language was sometimes visionary. He beheld a cross shining in the heavens, over the kingdom of Prester John, and was eager for an alliance with him. He wished to drain the Nile into the Red Sea. He would attack Mecca and Medina, carry off the bones of the prophet, and exchange them for the Holy Sepulchre. The dependency was too distant and too vast. The dread proconsul in his palace at Goa, who was the mightiest potentate between Mozambique and China, was too great a servant for the least of European kings. Emmanuel was suspicious. He recalled the victorious Almeida, who perished on the way home; and Albuquerque was in disgrace, when he died on his quarter-deck, in sight of the Christian city which he had made the capital of the East.

The secret of Portuguese prosperity was the small bulk and the enormous market value of the particular products in which they dealt. In those days men had to do without tea, or coffee, or chocolate, or tobacco, or quinine, or coca, or vanilla, and sugar was very rare. But there were the pepper and the ginger of Malabar; cardamoms in the damp district of Tellicherry; cinnamon and pearls in Ceylon. Beyond the Bay of Bengal, near the equator, there was opium, the only conqueror of pain then known; there were frankincense and indigo; camphor in Borneo; nutmeg and mace in Amboyna; and in two small islands, only a few miles square, Ternate and Tidor, there was the clove tree, surpassing all plants in value. These were the real spice islands, the enchanted region which was the object of such passionate desire; and their produce was so cheap on the spot, so dear in the markets of Antwerp and London, as to constitute the most lucrative trade in the world. From these exotics, grown on volcanic soil, in the most generous of the tropical climates, the profit was such that they could be paid for in precious metals. When Drake was at Ternate in 1579, he found the Sultan hung with chains of bullion, and clad in a robe of gold brocade rich enough to stand upright. The Moluccas were of greater benefit to the Crown than to the Portuguese workman. About twenty ships, of 100 to 550 tons, sailed for Lisbon in the year. A voyage sometimes lasted two years, out and home, and cost, including the ship, over £4000. But the freight might amount to £150,000. Between 1497 and 1612 the number of vessels engaged in the India trade was 806. Of these, ninety-six were lost. After the annexation by Philip II, Lisbon was closed to countries at war with Spain. Dutch and English had to make their own bargains in the East, and treated Portugal as an enemy. Their empire declined rapidly, and the Dutch acquired the islands long before the English succeeded on the mainland of India.

The Portuguese acknowledged no obligations of international law towards Asiatics. Even now, many people know of no law of nations but that which consists in contracts and conventions; and with the people of the East there were none. They were regarded as outlaws and outcasts, nearly as Bacon regarded the Spaniards and Edmund Burke the Turks. Solemn instruments had declared it lawful to expropriate and enslave Saracens and other enemies of Christ. What was right in Africa could not be wrong in Asia. Cabral had orders to treat with fire and sword any town that refused to admit either missionary or merchant. Barros, the classic historian of Portuguese Asia, says that Christians have no duties towards pagans; and their best writers affirm to this day that such calculated barbarities as they inflicted on women and children were justified by the necessity of striking terror. In the Commentaries of the great Albuquerque, his son relates with complacency how his father caused the Zamorin to be poisoned. These theories demoralised the entire government. St. Francis Xavier, who came out in 1542, found an organised system of dishonesty and plunder, and wrote home that no official in India could save his soul. By him and his brethren many converts were made, and as intermarriages were frequent, the estrangement grew less between the races. Just then, the Inquisition was introduced into Portugal, and sent a branch to Goa. One of the governors afterwards reported that it had helped to alienate the natives, whose temples were closed. But the solid structure of Almeida and Albuquerque was strong enough to defeat a second expedition from Egypt, after Egypt had become a province of Turkey, and an Indian war and insurrection. It declined with the decline of Portugal under Sebastian, in the latter part of the sixteenth century, but it perished through its association with Spain, at the hands of enemies not its own, and not from internal causes.

While the Asiatic empire was built up by the sustained and patient effort of a nation, during seventy years, the discovery of the West was due to one eager and original intellect, propelled by medieval dreams. Columbus had sailed both North and South; but the idea which changed the axis of the globe came to him from books. He failed to draw an inference favourable to his design from the driftwood which a tropical current carries to Iceland, and proceeded on the assurance of Pierre d'Ailly and of Toscanelli, that Asia reaches so far east as to leave but a moderate interval between Portugal and Japan. Although he rested his case on arguments from the classics and the prophets, his main authority was Toscanelli; but it is uncertain whether, as he affirmed, they had been in direct correspondence, or whether Columbus obtained the letter and the Chart of 1474 by means which were the cause of his disgrace.

Rejected by Portugal, he made his way into Spain. He was found, starving, at the gate of a Franciscan convent; and the place where he sank down is marked by a monument, because it is there that our modern world began. The friar who took him in and listened to his story soon perceived that this ragged mendicant was the most extraordinary person he had known, and he found him patrons at the court of Castile. The argument which Columbus now laid before the learned men of Spain was this: The eastern route, even if the Portuguese succeed in finding it, would be of no use to them, as the voyage to Cipango, to Cathay, even to the spice islands, would be too long for profit. It was better to sail out into the West, for that route would be scarcely 3000 miles to the extremity of Asia; the other would be 15,000, apart from the tremendous circuit of Africa, the extent of which was ascertained by Diaz while Columbus was pursuing his uphill struggle. The basis of the entire calculation was that the circumference of the earth is 18,000 miles at the equator, and that Asia begins, as is shown in Toscanelli's chart, somewhere about California. Misled by his belief in cosmographers, he blotted out the Pacific, and estimated the extent of water to be traversed at one-third of the reality. The Spaniards, who were consulted, pointed out the flaw, for the true dimensions were known; but they were unable to demonstrate the truths against the great authorities cited on the other side. The sophisms of Columbus were worth more than all the science of Salamanca. The objectors who called him a visionary were in the right, and he was obstinately wrong. To his auspicious persistency in error Americans owe, among other things, their existence.

A majority reported favourably—a majority composed, it would appear, of ignorant men. Years were spent in these preliminaries, and then the war with Granada absorbed the resources and the energies of the Crown. Columbus was present when the last Moorish king kissed the hand of Isabella, and he saw the cross raised over the Alhambra. This victory of Christendom was immediately followed by the expulsion of the Jews, and then the Catholic queen gave audience to the Genoese projector. His scheme belonged to the same order of ideas, and he was eloquent on its religious aspect. He would make so many slaves as to cover all expenses, and would have them baptized. He would bring home gold enough in three years to reconquer Palestine. He had one impressive argument which was not suggested by the situation at Court. Toscanelli had been at Rome when envoys came from the Grand Khan, petitioning for missionaries to instruct his people in the doctrines of Christianity. Two such embassies were sent, but their prayer was not attended to. Here were suppliants calling out of the darkness: Come over and help us. It was suitable that the nation which conquered the Moslem and banished the Jews should go on to convert the heathen. The Spaniards would appear in the East, knowing that their presence was desired. In reality they would come in answer to an invitation, and might look for a welcome. Making up by their zeal for the deficient enterprise of Rome, they might rescue the teeming millions of Farthest Asia, and thus fulfil prophecy, as there were only a hundred and fifty-five years to the end of the world. The conversion of Tartary would be the crowning glory of Catholic Spain.

All this was somewhat hypothetical and vague; but nothing could be more definite than the reward which he demanded. For it appeared that what this forlorn adventurer required for himself was to be admiral of the Atlantic, ranking with the constable of Castile, Viceroy, with power of life and death, in the regions to be occupied, and a large proportion of the intended spoil. And he would accept no less. None divined what he himself knew not, that the thing he offered in return was dominion over half the world. Therefore, when he found that this would not do, Columbus saddled his mule and took the road to France. In that superb moment he showed what man he was, and the action was more convincing than his words had been. An Aragonese official, Santangel, found the money, the £1500 required for the expedition, and the traveller was overtaken by an alguazil a couple of leagues away, and recalled to Granada. Santangel was, by descent, a Jew. Several of his kindred suffered under the Inquisition, before and after, and he fortified himself against the peril of the hour when he financed the first voyage of Columbus. Granada fell on the 2nd of January 1492. The Jews were expelled on the 20th of March. On the 17th of April the contract with Columbus was signed at Santa Fe. The same crusading spirit, the same motive of militant propagandism, appears in each of the three transactions. And the explorer, at this early stage, was generally backed by the clergy. Juan Perez, the hospitable Franciscan, was his friend; and Mendoza, the great cardinal of Toledo, and Deza, afterwards Archbishop of Seville. Talavera, the Archbishop of Granada, found him too fanciful to be trusted.

Sailing due west from the Canaries he crossed the Atlantic in its widest part. The navigation was prosperous and uneventful until, changing their course to follow the flight of birds, they missed the continent and came upon the islands. It was the longest voyage that had ever been attempted in the open sea; but the passage itself, and the shoals and currents of the West Indies, were mastered with the aid of nautical instruments from Nuremberg, and of the *Ephemerides* of Regiomontanus. These were recent achievements of the Renaissance, and without them the undertaking was impossible. Even with the new appliances, Columbus was habitually wrong in his measurements. He put Cuba 18° too far to the west; he thought San Domingo as large as Spain; and he saw mountains 50,000 feet high in Yucatan. Indeed, he protested that his success was not due to science, but to the study of the prophet Isaiah. Above all things, he insisted that Cuba was part of the Asiatic continent, and obliged his companions to testify to the same belief, although there is evidence that he did not share it.

He had promised Cathay. If he produced an unknown continent instead, a continent many thousands of miles long, prohibiting approach to Cathay, he would undo his own work; the peasants who had exposed his fallacies would triumph in his failure, and the competing Portuguese would appropriate all that he had undertaken to add to the crown of Castile. Without civilisation and gold his discoveries would be valueless; and there was so little gold at first that he at once proposed to make up for it in slaves. His constant endeavour was not to be mistaken, for the man who discovered the new world. Somewhere in the near background he still beheld the city with the hundred bridges, the crowded bazaar, the long train of caparisoned elephants, the palace with the pavement of solid gold. Naked savages skulking in the forest, marked down by voracious cannibals along the causeway of the Lesser Antilles, were no distraction from the

quest of the Grand Khan. The facts before him were uninterest-
ing and provisional, and were overshadowed by the phantoms
that crowded his mind. The contrast between the gorgeous and
entrancing vision and the dismal and desperate reality made
the position a false one. He went on seeking gold when it was
needful to govern, and proved an incapable administrator.
Long before his final voyage he had fallen into discredit, and
he died in obscurity.

Many miserable years passed after his death before America
began, through Cortez, to weigh perceptibly in the scales of
Europe. Landing at Lisbon from his first expedition, Columbus,
in all his glory, had an audience of the king. It was six years since
Diaz proved that the sea route to India was perfectly open, but no
European had since set eyes on the place where Table Mountain
looks down on the tormented Cape. Portugal apparently had
renounced the fruits of his discovery. It was now reported that
a Spanish crew had found in the West what the Portuguese
had been seeking in the East, and that the Papal privilege had
been infringed. The king informed Columbus that the regions
he had visited belonged to Portugal. It was evident that some
limit must be drawn separating the respective spheres. Rome
had forbidden Spain from interfering with the expeditions
of Portugal, and the Spaniards accordingly demanded a like
protection. On the surface, there was no real difficulty. Three
Bulls were issued in 1493, two in May and one in September,
admonishing Portuguese mariners to keep to the east of a line
drawn about 35° west of Greenwich. That line of demarcation
was suggested by Columbus, as corresponding with a point he
had reached on 13th September, an hundred leagues beyond
the Azores. On that day the needle, which had pointed east of
the Pole, shifted suddenly to the west. There, he reckoned, was
the line of No Variation. At that moment, the climate changed.
There was a smooth sea and a balmy air; there was a new heaven
and a new earth. The fantastic argument did not prevail, and in
the following year Spain and Portugal agreed, by the treaty of
Tordesillas, to move the dividing meridian farther west, about
midway between the most westerly island of the Old World and
the most easterly island of the New. By this agreement, supersed-

ing the Papal award, Portugal obtained Brazil. When the lines of demarcation were drawn in 1493 and 1494, nobody knew where they would cut the equator on the other side of the globe. There also there was matter for later negotiation.

After the fall of Malacca, Albuquerque sent a squadron to examine the region of islands farther east. One of his officers, Serrano, remained out there, and after as many adventures as Robinson Crusoe, he found his way to the very heart of the Moluccas, to Ternate, the home of the clove. In describing his travels to a friend, he made the most of the distance traversed in his eastward course. Magellan, to whom the letter was addressed, was out of favour with his commander Albuquerque, and on his return home found that he was out of favour with King Emmanuel. For the country which had repelled Columbus repelled the only navigator who was superior to Columbus. Magellan remembered Serrano's letter, and saw what could be made of it. He told the Spaniards that the spice islands were so far east that they were in the Spanish hemisphere, and he undertook to occupy them for Spain. He would sail, not east, but west, in the direction which was legally Spanish. For he knew a course that no man knew, and America, hitherto the limit of Spanish enterprise, would be no obstacle to him.

It seemed an apparition of Columbus, more definite and rational, without enthusiasm or idealism, or quotations from Roger Bacon, and Seneca, and the greater prophets. Cardinal Adrian, the Regent, refused to listen, but Fonseca, the President of the Board of Control, became his protector. Magellan wanted a good deal of protection; for his adventure was injurious to his countrymen, and was regarded by them as the intrigue of a traitor. Vasconcellos, Bishop of Lamego, afterwards Archbishop of Lisbon, advised that he should be murdered; and at night he was guarded in the streets of Valladolid by Fonseca's men. Magellan was not the first to believe that America comes to an end somewhere. Vespucci had guessed it; the extremity is marked on a globe of 1515; and a mercantile house that advanced funds is supposed to have been on the track.

Without a chart Magellan made his way through the perilous straits that perpetuate his name in twelve days' sailing.

Drake, who came next, in 1577, took seventeen days, and Wallis, one hundred and sixteen. And then, at Cape Deseado, the unbroken highway to the fabled East, which had been closed against Columbus, opened before him. The Spaniards discovered Cape Horn five years later, but it was doubled for the first time in 1616 by the Dutchman who gave his name to it. From the coast of Chili, Magellan sailed north-west for three months, missing all the Pacific Islands until he came to the Ladrones. He was killed while annexing the Philippines to the Crown of Spain, and his lieutenant Delcano, the first circumnavigator, brought the remnant of his crew home by the Cape. On the 9th of September 1522, thirteen wasted pilgrims passed barefoot in procession through the streets of Seville, not so much in thanksgiving for that which had not been given to man since the Creation, as in penance for having mysteriously lost a day, and kept their feasts and fasts all wrong. Magellan's acquisition of the Philippines lasted to the present year, but his design on the Moluccas was given up. Nobody knew, until the voyage of Dampier, to whom, by the accepted boundary, they belonged; and in 1529 Spain abandoned its claim for 350,000 ducats. The Portuguese paid that price for what was by right their own; for Magellan was entirely wrong both as to the meridian and as to the South American route, which was much the longest, and was not followed by sailors.

For more than twenty years Spain struggled vainly with the West Indian problem. Four large islands and forty small ones, peopled by barbarians, were beyond the range of Spanish experience in the art of government. Grants of land were made, with the condition that the holder should exercise a paternal rule over the thriftless inhabitants. It was thought to pay better to keep them underground, digging for gold, than to employ them on the surface. The mortality was overwhelming; but the victims awakened little sympathy. Some belonged to that Arcadian race that was the first revealed by the landfall of Columbus, and they were considered incurably indolent and vicious. The remainder came from the mainland and the region of the Orinoco, and had made their way by the Windward Islands as far as San

Domingo, devouring the people they found there. Neither the stronger nor the weaker race withstood the exhausting labour to which they were put by taskmasters eager for gold. Entire villages committed suicide together; and the Spaniards favoured a mode of correction which consisted in burning Indians alive by a slow fire. Las Casas, who makes these statements, and who may be trusted for facts and not for figures, affirms that fifty millions perished in his time, and fifteen millions were put to death.

Without a fresh labour supply, the colony would be ruined. It was the office of the clergy to prove that this treatment of the natives was short-sighted and criminal, and their cause was taken up by the Dominican missionaries. In 1510 the preacher Montesino, taking for his text the words, "I am the voice of one crying in the wilderness," denounced the practice. Their mouthpiece with the Home Government, their immortal mouthpiece with posterity, is Las Casas, whose narrative is our authority. The government was anxious to preserve conquests that began to yield some profit. They appointed Commissions to advise, and followed sometimes one report, sometimes the other, taking generally the line of least resistance. The most important Commission of all, in which Las Casas asserted the duties of Christians and the rights of savages, against Sepulveda, who denied them, never came to a decision.

Failing the native supply, the Spaniards substituted Negroes. The slaves forwarded by Columbus had been sent back with tokens of the queen's displeasure, and Ximenes would not permit the importation of Africans. But the traffic went on, and the Indies were saved. Under Charles V 1000 slaves were allotted to each of the four islands. It did not seem an intolerable wrong to rescue men from the devil-worshippers who mangled their victims on the Niger or the Congo. Las Casas himself was one of those who advised that the Negro should be brought to the relief of the Carib, and he would have allowed twelve slaves to each settler. He survived half a century, lived to lament his error, and declared his repentance to the world. He repented from motives of humanity rather than from principle; his feelings were more sensitive than his conscience, and he resembled the imperious Parliaments of George III which upheld the slave trade until imaginations were steeped in the horrors of the Middle Passage.

The supreme moment in the conquest of America is the landing of Cortez at Vera Cruz in 1521. He was an insubordinate officer acting in defiance of orders, and the governor of Cuba, in just indignation, despatched a force under Narvaez to bring him back. Cortez came down from the interior to the coast, deprived Narvaez of his command, and took possession of his men. With this unexpected reinforcement he was able to conquer Mexico, the capital of an illimitable empire. There was plenty of hard fighting, for the dominant race about the king was warlike. They were invaders, who reigned by force, and as they worshipped beings of the nether world who were propitiated with human sacrifice, they took their victims from the subject people, and their tyranny was the most hateful upon earth. The Spaniards, coming as deliverers, easily found auxiliaries against the government that practised unholy rites in the royal city. When Mexico fell Cortez sent a report to Charles V, with the first-fruits of his victory. Then, that no protesting narrative might follow and weaken his own, that his men might have no hope except in his success, he took the most daring resolution of his life, and scuttled his ships. Fonseca had signed the order for his arrest, when the most marvellous tale in that sequence of marvels reached his hands, and the disgraced mutineer was found to have added to the Emperor's dominions a region many times vaster and wealthier than all that he possessed in Europe. In 1522 the accumulated treasure which had been extracted from Mexican mines since the beginning of ages came pouring into the imperial exchequer, and the desire of so many explorers during thirty unprofitable years was fulfilled at last.

Cortez was not only the most heroic of the Conquistadors, for there was no lack of good soldiers, but he was an educated man, careful to import the plants and quadrupeds needed for civilisation, and a statesman capable of ruling mixed races without help from home. From the moment of his appearance the New World ceased to be a perplexing burden to Spain, and began to foreshadow danger and temptation to other nations. And a man immeasurably inferior to him, a man who could not write his name, whose career, in its glory and its shame, was a servile imitation, almost a parody, of his own, succeeded thereby in establishing a South American empire equal to that of Cortez in the North. One of the ships sailing from the islands to the isthmus carried a stowaway hidden in a cask, whose name was Balboa, and who discovered the Pacific.

The third name is Francisco Pizarro. He stood by and listened while a native described a mighty potentate, many days to the south, who reigned over the mountains and the sea, who was rich in gold, and who possessed a four-footed beast of burden, the only one yet encountered, which was taken at first for a camel. He waited many years for his opportunity. Then, with 168 armed men, and with aid from an associate who risked his money in the business, he started for the Andes and the civilised and prosperous monarchy in the clouds, which he had heard of when he was the lieutenant of Balboa. The example of Cortez, the fundamental fact of American history, had shown what could be done by getting hold of the king, and by taking advantage of internal dissension. How much could be accomplished by treachery and unflinching vigour Pizarro knew without a teacher. Whilst he established his power in the highlands under the equator, Almagro occupied the coast in the temperate zone, 1000 miles farther. Together they had conquered the Pacific. Then, as no man had the ascendency of Cortez, the time that succeeded the occupation was disturbed by internal conflict, in which both the conquerors perished. They had done even more for the Spanish empire than their greater rival. There were 4,600,000 ducats in the treasury of the Inca, and he filled his prison with gold as high as he could reach for the ransom which did not save his life. The mines were soon in working order; and, as the expanse of fertile soil was 3000 miles long, it was clear that Peru, added to Mexico, constituted an important factor in European finance.

As time carried away the tumult of conquest, and the evil generation that achieved it, Spanish America became the seat of such abundance and profusion as was not found in any European capital; and the natives, instructed and regulated by the missionaries, were the object of an elaborate protective legislation, which gave reason for attachment to the mother country. The prodigality of nature was too much for tropical society, and it accomplished nothing of its own for the mind of man. It influenced the position of classes in Europe by making property obtained from afar, in portable shape, predominate over property at home. Released from the retarding pressure of accumulated years, it developed towards revolution; and all the colonies founded by the Conquistadors on the continent of America became Republics. These events shifted the centre of political gravity from land to sea. The resources of the ocean world extended the physical basis of modern History; and increase of wealth involving increase of power, depended thenceforward on the control of distant regions. Vasco da Gama created a broad channel for the pursuit of Empire, and Columbus remodelled the future of the world. For History is often made by energetic men, steadfastly following ideas, mostly wrong, that determine events.

8

THE RISE OF THE WHIGS[*]

The Liberal ideas bred in sectarian circles, here and in America, did not become the common property of mankind until they were detached from their theological root, and became the creed of a party. That is the transition which occupies the reign of Charles II. It is the era in which parties took the place of churches as a political force.

A gentleman has written to remind me that the Independents did not jointly or corporately renounce the connection between Church and State, or assert religious liberty as a principle of government. They did individually that which they never did collectively, and such individuals were acting conformably to the logic of the system. In the Petition of 1616 they say, "We deny also a national, a provincial, and diocesan church under the Gospel to be a true, visible, political church." John Robinson writes: "It is the Church of England, or State Ecclesiastical, which we account Babylon, and from which we withdraw in spiritual communion." In 1644 we are told: "Godwin is a bitter enemy to

---

[*] Published in Lord Acton, *Lectures on Modern History*, ed. John Neville Figgis and Reginald Vere Laurence (London: Macmillan, 1906), 206–18. Reprinted in *Selected Writings of Lord Acton*, ed. J. Rufus Fears, 3 vols. (Indianapolis: Liberty Fund, 1985–88), 1:98–108.

presbytery, and is openly for a full liberty of conscience, to all sects, even Turks, Jews, Papists." The author of the tract, *What the Independents Would Have*, writes that he thinks it a sin either to follow an erring conscience or to go against it; but to oppose it the greater sin, for he that will do the least sin against conscience is prepared in disposition to do the greatest. Therefore he reckons liberty of conscience to be England's chiefest good.

When I said that the English exiles in Holland came in contact with the most spiritual remnant of the Reformers, I meant the German Anabaptists. The English Baptists and the Quakers were as much opposed to the principle of persecution as the Independents I have quoted.

Only two conditions were imposed on Charles II before he came over. One of these was liberty of conscience. Cromwell had died without leaving behind him an established Constitution, and his lieutenants succeeded no better than his son. The army refused to obey a parliament of their own creating, the remnant which remained when Pride expelled the majority. It was a parliament founded not on law but on violence, on the act of men thirsting for the king's blood. The simplest solution was to restore the Long Parliament, to give power to the Presbyterian majority, which had been excluded, and was not responsible for the miscarriages and the constitutional instability of the last eleven years. The idea was so obvious that it occurred to everybody—to Monk in Scotland, to Fairfax at York, and to the army which Lambert collected to meet Monk at Newcastle, and which dispersed without fighting for its own imperial supremacy.

It is worthwhile to study, in the second volume of Guizot's *Richard Cromwell*, the consummate policy with which Monk prepared the desired result. For the recall of the excluded members was the restoration to power of men who had persisted in negotiating with Charles I, of men who had been Royalists in season and out of season. They were no friends of arbitrary government; but it was certain that they would restore the monarchy. A premature rising of incautious Royalists was put down; and the object of Monk was to gain time, until the blindest could perceive what was inevitable. His hand was forced by Fairfax, who was ill with gout, but had himself lifted into the saddle, and raised Yorkshire for a free parliament. Under that flag he crossed the Tweed at Coldstream on New Year's Day. He was already the master of England, and met with no resistance on the way to Westminster. The Republicans, in their extremity, offered him the crown, which Monk refused. He likewise refused the offers of the king, who would have made him chancellor and grand constable, besides making lavish grants of money, which the general was believed to like. He knew that he was sure of his reward when the time came. It came quickly. The Long Parliament made way for a Convention Parliament, which renewed the fundamental laws, and finally abolished the feudal rights of the crown. Whilst these bills were being voted, Charles issued the Declaration of Breda, proposed by Monk, and resumed the crown without a struggle.

The nation was glad to escape from the misgovernment of the Republic, which had weighed heavily on numerous classes, and believed that the crown had received a lesson which could not be forgotten. The new government was not imposed by a victorious monarchy. It was an expression of the national wish. Parliament retained control, and there was no political reaction.

The changes now introduced went to strengthen not the Prerogative, but the gentry, who were the governing class. They were relieved from the payment of feudal dues, by means of a tax which fell on other classes; members were taken from the towns and added to the country districts; and the militia, which was to protect society from the parliamentary army, was placed in the hands of the gentry. The new order of things was the work not of a party, but of a class. The dominant cavaliers were willing to refuse a share in their power to the old Puritan enemy, and passed every measure for inflicting disabilities on the Nonconformists. They were excluded from all offices, in the Church and in the State, even in the municipalities. In this way, by a religious test, the class that consisted mainly of Churchmen secured all political authority for themselves. They, however, added a political test. They imposed an oath in favour of non-resistance. Nobody could hold office who was not what was afterwards known as a Tory. This was Anglican doctrine; and the clergy set to work to rule the country in conjunction with the conservative country gentlemen, on a basis of principles laid down by Hobbes, the philosopher of the day, who denied the rights, and even the existence of conscience.

Clarendon was minister; and it was an ingenious and politic thing in his eyes to suppress the Roundhead by suppressing the Presbyterian. He had reflected more deeply than any man then living on the problem of Church and State; and he did not believe in the sacred fixity of divisions founded on schemes of Church government only. Archbishop Ussher had made great concessions to the Presbyterians. Baxter had made concessions to Prelacy. The see of Hereford was offered to him, and it was thought he might accept it. Leighton, who was as much the greatest Puritan divine in Scotland as Baxter in England, did accept the offer of a mitre, and became Archbishop of Glasgow. The restored government was intolerant, because, by intolerance, it could exercise political repression. This did not apply to the Catholics. Clarendon had pledged himself that they should profit by the indulgence which was afterwards promised at Breda. When he adopted the policy of coercion against the Puritans, he was unable to keep his promise. The unnatural situation could not last after his fall. The Puritans had made war upon the throne, and the Catholics had defended it. When it was restored, they proclaimed their principles in a series of voluntary declarations which dealt with the customary suspicions and reproaches, and fully satisfied the purpose aimed at by the oath of allegiance. No people could be more remote from the type of Allen and Parsons than the English Benedictines and the Irish Franciscans who hailed the revived monarchy. Against such men the old argument of Elizabethan persecutors was vain.

After the fall of Clarendon a different policy was attempted. The rigid exclusiveness of the Puritans had bequeathed one sinister vice to the English people. They were complacent in their insularity, and had a prejudice against the foreigner. It had been directed against Spain, for the sake of Plate fleets to seize and coasts to pillage; and now it was strongest against the Dutch, who were dangerous rivals by sea, both in peace and war. It was least, at that time, against France, whose great statesman,

Mazarin, had made terms with the Republic, and retained the friendship of the restored king. A trivial dispute on the Guinea Coast was fanned into a quarrel by the Duke of York, who was a sailor, and who hoped to strengthen his position at home by his professional skill, in which he only partially succeeded. This is the war that terminated in the memorable change of front of the Triple Alliance, uniting the Dutch, the English, and the Swedes against France. It was a popular but totally ineffective measure; and in 1669 England abandoned her allies and went over to France. Louis XIV accomplished this important diplomatic success by the Treaty of Dover, the first in the process of events that overthrew the Stuart monarchy, and brought in the modern type of Constitution.

Soon after his return to England, Charles opened negotiations with Rome, which were carried on through one of his sons, born before Monmouth, who became a Jesuit; and he vainly endeavoured to obtain supplies from Alexander VII. Later on, he sought them in France. It was impossible, he said, to restore the royal authority unless it was done through the restoration of Catholicism. That could be secured, if Louis would make him independent of the House of Commons. The scheme was prepared in January 1669, Arlington consenting, for a bribe of £12,000. It was decided to restore the Catholic Church in England by such a display of force as should be sufficient to raise the crown above the restraints of parliament. In execution of the design Louis advanced £80,000, and undertook, in case of resistance, to furnish a force of 6000 men, to be a French garrison in England, for the repression of Protestants. The sum was much less than Charles demanded, for the object of the French king was not to strengthen, but to weaken him. The second point in the Treaty was that England engaged to support France in any claims she might have upon Spain. Lastly, England was to help her ally against Holland, in return for further payments and the annexation of Walcheren. But it was agreed to postpone the Dutch war until the year 1672. That is the solid substance of the phantom which is called the Popish Plot.

It was, in reality, a plot, under cover of Catholicism, to introduce absolute monarchy, and to make England a dependency of France, not only by the acceptance of French money, but by submission to a French army. Charles I and his ministers had gone to the block for less than this.

If the thing should become known, nobody could foretell the consequences. Turenne was told, because he would be wanted if it came to blows; and Turenne told a lady of his aquaintance, who proved indiscreet. The king, in a fury, asked him how he could be such a fool. The marshal, not unaccustomed to the experience of being under fire, replied that he was not the only man who had been made a fool of by a woman, and King Louis XIV did not see his way to pursue the conversation. His political object was secured, even if nothing should be done in England to fulfil the agreement. He had Charles completely in his power. The secret text only needed to be divulged, in order to raise the country against him. He never again could be formidable. If all other devices for dividing him from his people were insufficient, this one could not fail. Many years later Louis caused a book to be printed, by an Italian adventurer, in which the secret was revealed. The book was suppressed and the author imprisoned, for the sake of appearances. But one hundred and fifty-five copies were in circulation, and the culprit was released after six days. It became dangerous for Charles to meet parliament. The facts became known to Shaftesbury long before, and determined his course from the time of his dismissal from office, in November 1673. The scheme laid down in the Dover Treaty was a dangerous one, and after the beginning of the Dutch war there were no French troops to spare.

Charles tried another way to gain his purpose. Both he and his brother desired to establish Catholicism for its own sake. They were not converts, but they intended to be before they died. The difference was that James was ready to make some sacrifice for his religion, Charles was not. They both regarded it as the only means of putting the crown above the law. This could be done more safely by claiming the right to dispense from penalties and disabilities imposed by parliament. The idea, entertained as early as 1662, ripened ten years later, when the Penal Laws, as well as the intolerant legislation of Clarendon against the Puritans, which had been considered the safeguard of monarchy, were declared inoperative. The ministers, including Shaftesbury, expected to obtain the support of Nonconformists. This calculation proved delusive. The Dissenters, on an assurance that they would be relieved by parliament if they resisted the offers of the king, refused to accept them. The object of his declaration was too apparent, and was indeed too openly avowed. Just then the Duke of York became a Catholic, and although the fact was not made public, it was suspected. Ministers advised Charles to maintain his offer of indulgence and his claim to the dispensing power. Charles gave way and accepted his defeat. He gave way because Louis advised it, and promised him more French regiments than had been stipulated for, as soon as he was again at peace with the Dutch.

The House of Commons followed up its victory by passing the Test Act, excluding Catholics from office. The Duke of York resigned his post as Lord High Admiral. It was, he said, the beginning of the scheme for depriving him of the succession to the throne. In November 1673 Shaftesbury, who had promoted the Declaration of Indulgence, was dismissed from office and went into opposition, for the purposes of which Louis sent him £10,000. He learnt from Arlington the main particulars of the Treaty of Dover, and in the following month of January the secret was substantially made public in a pamphlet, which is reprinted in the *State Tracts*. From that moment he devoted himself to the exclusion of James.

In 1676 the Duke of York made it known that he had become a Catholic. This was so gratuitous that people took it to mean that he was strong in the support which the French king gave him. He was still true to the policy of the Dover Treaty, which his brother had abandoned, and still watched his opportunity to employ force for the restoration of his Church. All this was fully understood, and his enemy, Shaftesbury, was implacable.

When he had been five years out of office, in September 1678, Titus Oates appeared. Who the people were who brought him forward, with the auxiliary witnesses, Bedloe, Dangerfield, and Turberville, the one who received £600 for his evidence against

Stafford, is still unknown. Shaftesbury was not the originator. He would not have waited so many years. His part in the affair was to employ the public alarm for the destruction of the Duke of York. Therefore, from the summer of 1678 there was a second plot. The first, consisting in the Treaty of Dover, drawn up by the Catholic advisers, Arundel, Bellasis, the historian Belling, and Leighton, the great archbishop's brother. The second was the Protestant plot against the Catholics, especially the Duke of York. The indignation against the real plot, that of Dover, was essentially political.

In February 1675 the opposition proposed to James to restore his offices if he would abandon Louis. When the imperial ambassador, in July 1677, complained of the No Popery cry, they replied that there was no question of religion, but of liberty. In the case of Oates and his comrades, the political motive faded into insignificance beside the religious. At first the evidence was unsubstantial. Oates was an ignorant man, and he obtained credit only by the excitement and distrust caused by the discovery of the premeditated *coup d'état*. Godfrey, the magistrate who conducted the inquiry, warned James that the secretary of the Duchess of York was implicated. His name was Coleman, and he had time to destroy his papers. Some of them were seized. They spoke of a great blow which was being prepared against the Protestants. It appeared also that he was in the pay of Louis, and had solicited his confessor, Père La Chaise, for a sum of £300,000 in order to get rid of parliament. It was argued that if such things were found in the papers he had not burnt, there must have been worse still in those which had perished. It showed that the scheme of Dover was still pursued, was still a danger. At that moment the magistrate who sent the warning disappeared. After some days his dead body was found at the foot of Green Berry Hill, now Primrose Hill; and one of the most extraordinary coincidences, so interesting in the study of historical criticism, is the fact that the men hanged for the murder were named Green, Berry, and Hill. It was of course suspected that Godfrey had perished because he knew too much.

For some time the excitement rose very high. On the day when two Jesuits were executed, one of the Catholic envoys writes that nothing else could have saved the lives of all the Catholics in London. Taking advantage of the state of public feeling, Shaftesbury proposed that James should be excluded from the succession for his religion. The crown was to go to the next heir, the Princess of Orange. This was thrown out by the Lords. Meantime the second Test Act expelled the Catholic peers from the House of Lords. James withdrew from the council, from the palace, and at last from the kingdom.

The second Exclusion Bill was founded, not on his religion, but on his politics, that is, his treasonable connection with the King of France. The opponents of exclusion proposed limitation of the royal power, in a manner such as that which has since prevailed. Charles preferred this amendment to the Constitution rather than an Act which enabled parliament to regulate the succession. William of Orange vigorously opposed it, as the same restraints might be retained when his wife came to the throne. Halifax, who defeated the Exclusion Bill and defended the Limitation Bill, assured the prince that it would never be applied, as James had no chance whatever of succeeding his brother. His only purpose in proposing his Bill was to preserve the succession, according to law, from parliamentary control.

In order to obtain evidence that should ruin James's prospects, it was resolved now to put the Catholic peers on their trial. Stafford came first. He had not been in the secret of the fatal Treaty. But the plans this time were cleverly laid. Although Lord Stafford was entirely innocent, Count Thun, the Austrian envoy, was profoundly impressed by the weight of the case against him and the weakness of the defence. He was beheaded amid shrieks of execration and exultation. Arundel was to come next; and Arundel did know enough to compromise the duke. But the plan had failed. Nothing had been discovered in Stafford's trial that could help the exclusion; and a revulsion of popular feeling followed. Monmouth was now put forward. If James could not be excluded he must make way for Monmouth, if Monmouth was legitimate. The king was pressed to acknowledge him. A black box was said to contain the necessary evidence of his mother's marriage. A bishop was spoken of who knew all about it. Monmouth himself accepted the idea. When the

Duke of Plymouth died he refused to wear mourning. He would not mourn, he said, for a brother who was illegitimate. After the Test Act, the Exclusion Bill, the succession of Monmouth, the indefatigable Shaftesbury had still one resource. He tried an insurrection. When he found it impossible to draw the line between insurrection and murder, he thought the position dangerous, and went abroad. Russell and Sidney were put to death. Charles was victorious over his enemies. He owed his victory to the French king, who gave him £700,000, and enabled him to exist without a parliament for three years.

It was during this struggle against the overshadowing suspicion of the Dover Treaty that the Habeas Corpus Act was passed, and that Party took shape in England. In general, the old cavalier families, led by the clergy and the lawyers, acquiesced in the royal prerogative, the doctrine of passive obedience, the absolute and irresistible authority of that which Hobbes called Leviathan, meaning the abstract notion of the State. They had a passion for order, not for oppression; good government was as dear to them as to their opponents, and they believed that it would not be secured if the supreme authority was called in question. That was the Court Party, known as Tories. As time went on, after the Revolution, they underwent many developments. But at first they were simply defenders of royal authority against aggression, without any original ideas.

The Country Party was the party of reform. They were the people excluded from the public service by the oath in favour of non-resistance. They believed in the rightfulness of the war which the Long Parliament waged against the king, and were prepared, eventually, to make war against Charles II. That was the essential distinction between them and the Tories. They dreaded revolution, but, in an extreme case, they thought it justifiable. "Acts of tyranny," said Burnet, "will not justify the resistance of subjects, yet a total subversion of their constitution will." When Burnet and Tillotson urged this doctrine on Lord Russell, he replied that he did not see a difference between a legal and a Turkish Constitution, upon this hypothesis.

Whig history exhibits a gradual renunciation of Burnet's mitigated doctrine, that resistance is only justified by extreme provocation, and a gradual approach to the doctrine of Russell, on which the American Revolution proceeded. The final purpose of the Whigs was not distinct from that of their fathers in the Long Parliament. They desired security against injustice and oppression. The victors in the Civil War sought this security in a Republic, and in this they conspicuously failed. It was obvious that they made a mistake in abolishing the monarchy, the Established Church, and the House of Lords. For all these things came back, and were restored as it were by the force of Nature, not by the force of man.

The Whigs took this lessen of recent experience to heart. They thought it unscientific to destroy a real political force. Monarchy, Aristocracy, Prelacy, were things that could be made innocuous, that could be adjusted, limited, and preserved. The very essence of the new Party was compromise. They saw that it is an error to ride a principle to death, to push things to an extreme, to have an eye for one thing only, to prefer abstractions to realities, to disregard practical conditions. They were a little disappointing, a little too fond of the half-way house. Their philosophy, or rather their philosopher, John Locke, is always reasonable and sensible, but diluted and pedestrian and poor. They became associated with great interests in English society, with trade, and banking, and the city, with elements that were progressive, but exclusive, and devoted to private, not to national ends. So far as they went, they were in the right, ethically as well as politically. But they proceeded slowly beyond the bare need of the moment. They were a combination of men rather than a doctrine, and the idea of fidelity to comrades was often stronger among them than the idea of fidelity to truths. General principles were so little apparent in the system that excellent writers suppose that the Whigs were essentially English, Nonconformists, associated with limited monarchy, unfit for exportation over the world. They took long to outgrow the narrow limits of the society in which they arose. A hundred years passed before Whiggism assumed the universal and scientific character. In the American speeches of Chatham and Camden, in Burke's writings from 1778 to 1783, in the *Wealth of Nations*, and the tracts of Sir William Jones, there is an immense development.

The national bounds are overcome. The principles are sacred, irrespective of interests. The charter of Rhode Island is worth more than the British Constitution, and Whig statesmen toast General Washington, rejoice that America has resisted, and insist on the acknowledgment of independence. The progress is entirely consistent; and Burke's address to the colonists is the logical outcome of the principles of liberty and the notion of a higher law above municipal codes and constitutions, with which Whiggism began.

It is the supreme achievement of Englishmen, and their bequest to the nations; but the patriarchs of the doctrine were the most infamous of men. They set up the monument to perpetuate the belief that the Catholics set fire to London. They invented the Black Box and the marriage of Lucy Waters. They prompted, encouraged, and rewarded the murderer Oates. They proclaimed that the Prince of Wales came in the warming pan. They were associated with the Rye House assassins; that conspiracy was their ruin. Charles triumphed, and did not spare his enemies. When he died, in spite of the Dover Treaty, of his paid subserviency to France, of the deliberate scheme to subvert the liberties of England, James, the chief culprit, succeeded, with undiminished power. The prostrate Whigs were at the mercy of Jeffreys.

But forty years of agitation produced the leaven that has leavened the world. The revolutionary system was saved, because the king threw away his advantage. The Whig party became supreme in the State by a series of events which are the most significant in English History.

9

THE LIFE AND TIMES OF EDMUND BURKE[*]

This is a book especially interesting to Catholics, both on account of the subject and of the manner of treating it; for Burke was the wisest, the most sincere, and the most disinterested of all the advocates of the Catholic cause; and Mr. Macknight is the most impartial and unprejudiced of his biographers. Of the many who have preceded him, none can be said to have been equal to the subject. The memoir published immediately after the death of Burke, together with the *Observations on the Conduct of the Minority,* is a mere sketch of seventy pages; but it contains much accurate information, and has been made the foundation of the article in Knight's *English Cyclopaedia,* the most satisfactory account of Burke yet published. M'Cormick's *Memoirs,* written in the dissenting and revolutionary interest, are a storehouse of all the calumnies ever uttered against him. Bisset's *Life of Burke* was successful at the time, and was even translated into French; but although Mr. Macknight declares that it is far from being the worst book on the subject, it is certainly not the best, and is

[*] Published as "The Life and Times of Edmund Burke," review of *History of the Life and Times of Edmund Burke,* by Thomas Macknight, *Rambler* 9, no. 52 (April 1858): 268–73. Reprinted in *Selected Writings of Lord Acton,* ed. J. Rufus Fears, 3 vols. (Indianapolis: Liberty Fund, 1985–88), 1:135–40.

now almost as completely forgotten as his *History of George III*. A life by Mr. Peter Burke is a book of moderate pretensions, and of still less value. Dr. Croly's *Memoirs* are only remarkable as an attempt to extract a system of Tory politics from the writings of the great Whig statesman. Prior's popular but dull biography contains in the last edition a tolerable account of Burke's personal history. Its chief defect is, that in the case of such a man as Burke this is not enough. In order to be fully understood, his life must be viewed as a part of the history of the times whose chief ornament he was, and which he so greatly influenced. The lives of all great public men are inseparable from their times, and a biography which refuses to be a history is inevitably imperfect. Mr. Macknight's horizon is far wider than Mr. Prior's; and he has not only written well on the history of George III, but he has also shown great industry in collecting minute facts relating to Burke's private life. He refutes, for instance, the report of Burke's having been an unsuccessful candidate for the professorship of logic at Glasgow; and he zealously vindicates his character from the imputations cast upon it by his acquaintance with the celebrated Peg Woffington. The care bestowed on these minute and not very necessary investigations, and the habit of speaking fully of all persons and events that Burke was in any way connected with, have occasioned an excessive diffuseness, which would be a blemish if it were possible to complain of the length of a biography of our greatest statesman, which is considerably exceeded by the lives of such persons as Dr. Chalmers and Hannah More. But we must also regret a certain pompous grandiloquence, and some errors of taste which we should hardly have expected in so practised a writer.

Mr. Macknight is at great pains to vindicate for Burke the authorship of several works that are not generally understood to be his. He considers the *Account of the European Settlements in America*, which is included in the American edition of Burke's works, to be almost entirely by him. When the Seven-Years' War was over, *A Compleat History of the late War* was published, consisting of extracts from the Annual Register of the six preceding years. This was unquestionably Burke's. That he was the originator, and for many years the chief compiler, of the *Annual Register*, is well known. Mr. Macknight affirms that the historical portion was for the most part written by him, at least till the close of the American war; but M'Cormick, who was his contemporary, states that his connection with it lasted till 1789, when the work passed into the hands of his friends Dr. Laurence and Dr. King. The extraordinary richness and energy of Burke's mind bestow a particular value upon every fragment that remains of his writings. We must therefore re-echo Mr. Macknight's wish for a more complete collection of his works, which would, in our opinion, be of greater service than the most elaborate biography. It ought to contain twice as much as any of the existing editions. Besides a judicious selection from the *Annual Register,* and the various pamphlets and essays which have not yet been collected, it would include all the speeches, of which so many fragments remain in the Parliamentary History and the Cavendish Debates. Many of these short and imperfectly reported speeches, as well as some of his private letters, give an idea of his genius at least as high as his greater works. Some of his later speeches, which were not published by him, and some of the letters in the collection which appeared in 1844, are more profound than anything that can be found in his *Reflections.* That work, on which his popular fame chiefly rests, does not fairly represent his genius. It was written in a style calculated to produce a great immediate effect, and was in this respect eminently successful. It would probably have been less effective if it had been more original and more profound. In these qualities Burke's subsequent writings are greatly superior to it.

Mr. Macknight, who is himself chiefly known as a pamphleteer, has given most prominence to Burke's political writings, and has scarcely done justice to his most remarkable literary production, the *Abridgment of English History.* The most learned of all the writers on the same subject, Lappenberg, says, speaking of this book, that if Burke had devoted himself continuously to historical pursuits, England might have possessed a history worthy to rank with the masterpieces of the Attic and the Tuscan historians. If we may believe the story that Burke desisted from the undertaking because Hume had taken up the same subject, it must ever be regretted that the reverse did not occur, and that the philosopher did not give way to the politician. We should certainly have had a much better History of England; for there is very little doubt that as Burke was our greatest statesman, so he would have been the first of our historians. In that part of the work which he completed, he speaks of medieval institutions with an intelligence and appreciation which in his time were almost equally rare among Catholics, Protestants, and infidels. The great ecclesiastical writers of the preceding age, such as Bossuet and Fleury, had about as little sympathy with the Middle Ages as Mosheim or Voltaire. Leibniz alone had written about them in a tone which would not now be contemptible. The vast compilations of great scholars, of Ducange, Mabillon and Muratori, had not yet borne fruit on the Continent; and in England the rise of a better school of historians was still more remote. Several generations of men were still to follow, who were to derive their knowledge of the Middle Ages from the Introduction to Robertson's *Charles V,* to study ecclesiastical history in the pages of Gibbon, and to admire Hume as the prince of historians. At the age of thirty, Burke proved himself superior to that system of prejudice and ignorance which was then universal, and which is not yet completely dissipated. Mr. Macknight's remarks on the book, though not quite just, are sufficiently characteristic of himself to deserve being quoted:

> Though scarcely a history, this work is excellent as a disquisition. Written in 1757, it has none of that illiberal liberality which was then so much in fashion. The services of the Catholic Church, and even of the monastic system, to the cause of civilisation in the dark ages, are fully admitted. There is no sneering at the monks, no bewailing the superstitions and prejudices of the people, no raptures at the lights of the eighteenth century.

It is remarkable that so many of our public men should have written history. Our historians are more often great historical actors than great historical writers. Their works are generally remarkable for every quality excepting learning. It is characteristic of the English mind that we should so long have been without regular learned histories. In the most essential qualities our professional historians cannot compete with those of other countries; and we have nobody who will bear a comparison with Niebuhr, or Hurter, or Ranke, any more than with Thucydides or Tacitus. Gibbon, Lingard, Grote are not equal to the moderns in learning: Hume and Macaulay are inferior in art to the ancients. In the Middle Ages great deeds were performed by men who could not write; and they were recorded by men who had not seen, and could not understand, them. Many of the greatest historians of the present day write from the seclusion of their libraries concerning events of which they have no experience. But the prevailing character of the English historians has been neither that of the monastic chronicler nor of the German professor. The catalogue is crowded with names distinguished in another sphere, Bacon, Raleigh, Milton, Clarendon, Burnet, Swift, Fox, and Mackintosh. This connection between historical studies and political life has been more beneficial in developing the qualities of the statesman than of the historian. Our historical literature was long in emancipating itself from the traditional falsehoods which are so dear to the popular mind, and consequently such studies have not yet exercised that powerful influence for good which is so conspicuous abroad. But Burke was free both from vulgar prejudice and from pedantry; and no other man was so well fitted to adorn history with the attainments of a great scholar, and the reality and vigour derived from personal experience of public affairs.

Mr. Macknight deserves great credit for having traced the growth of Burke's ideas respecting the Catholic religion, and for pointing out all the causes which contributed to produce those enlightened views by which he was so remarkably distinguished. After tracing his obscure ancestry, he says:

> Burke certainly never forgot that his forefathers had been Catholics. He never forgot that their religion was proscribed in the country he so much loved. Though himself by education and by conviction a sincere member of the Church of England, he ever respected the creed of the mother who had cherished him in his helpless

infancy, of Mrs. Crotty the nurse who had borne him in her arms, and of his uncle Garret, whom he believed to be the best and kindest of human beings. So powerful an influence had this association on his whole life, that, unless it is steadily borne in mind, much of his history and political career must be quite unintelligible.

Burke's mother was a Catholic, and he seems to have continued extremely attached to her even during the time of his estrangement from his father. When a boy, he was much with his Catholic uncles. Besides these early influences, the same generous hatred of oppression which afterwards displayed itself on another field in the impeachment of Hastings seems to have incited in him a warm sympathy with the oppressed Irish; and in his last years there is no doubt that his familiarity with many of the exiled clergy of France operated in the same manner. Many absurd stories have been circulated to account for the favour with which he treated Catholics. In his time the Duke of Newcastle suspected him of being a Catholic; and we learn from a notice of Mr. Macknight's book in a well-known weekly contemporary, that there are still persons foolish enough to believe it. Dr. Nugent, Burke's father-in-law, was a Catholic; and the same has often been said of Mrs. Burke herself. The evidence which makes Mr. Macknight think this not improbable is exceedingly weak. All these reports originate only in the necessity of accounting for the absence of intolerance in Burke, which is to many people still incomprehensible. There is, however, no reason to suppose that he would have been prepossessed in favour of the Church by one who did not bring up her children in her own faith, and who certainly did not habitually fulfil her religious duties. There is no reason to doubt that Mrs. Burke was a Presbyterian, like her mother. In fact, there was much that was essentially Catholic in Burke's mind, and which appears quite as distinctly in his general political views as in his conduct towards the Catholics. We will make room for one more passage on this point:

> As the first of Burke's efforts against oppression, his wishes, thoughts, and intentions at this time (1763) in

favour of the Catholics have been far too little understood. In his old age he appealed to those who knew
what his sentiments were while he was in Ireland, during Lord Halifax's administration, and declared that
they had not in any manner been changed, but were
then just as much matured in his mind as at any later
period. There were then no Catholic associations, no
Catholic agitators, no politicians in England prepared
to temporise with Catholic Emancipation. Grattan was
yet a schoolboy. William Pitt was a mere child. Charles
Fox was at Eton, and writing French verses in praise of
Lord Bute. Canning was not yet born. Holland House,
instead of being the citadel of liberalism, was the noi-
some receptacle of political corruption. To the great man
whose life and works are the subject of these pages, is
due the honour of having, in season and out of season,
continued the warfare with more consistency, ardour,
and perseverance, than any other statesman of his time,
or of the succeeding generation. We have seen that this
fragment on the penal laws, his first work on practical
politics, was in favour of his oppressed countrymen. We
shall see that the last letter he dictated on political affairs,
reclining on a couch, with his strength exhausted, with
his last hour fast approaching, and in hasty intervals during the cessation of pain, had the same sacred object.

Mr. Macknight's two volumes, however, do not come down so
far. They stop in 1783. Hitherto Burke is a brilliant partisan, a
popular leader in a popular cause. The task of his Whig biographer has been comparatively easy. The most interesting, but far
the most difficult, portion of his life remains, in which from the
leader of a party he became a teacher of mankind. The writings
of these latter years cannot be judged by the narrow standard
of party politics; and his biographer, in order to be equal to his
great argument, will need to put aside all party views, and to
recognise the universal principles of political philosophy which
Burke so eloquently upheld at the close of his life, and which
led to the secession of 1791.

10

THE AMERICAN REVOLUTION

The rational and humanitarian enlightenment of the eighteenth century did much for the welfare of mankind, but little to promote the securities of freedom. Power was better employed than formerly, but it did not abdicate.

In England, politically the most advanced country, the impetus which the Revolution gave to progress was exhausted, and people began to say, now that the Jacobite peril was over, that no issue remained between parties which made it worthwhile for men to cut each others' throats. The development of the Whig philosophy was checked by the practical tendency to compromise. Compromise distinguished the Whig from the Roundhead, the man who succeeded from the man who failed, the man who was the teacher of politics to the civilised world from the man who left his head on Temple Bar.

The Seven Years' War renewed the interrupted march by involving America in the concerns of Europe, and causing the colonies to react on the parent state. That was a consequence

---

*Published in Lord Acton, *Lectures on Modern History*, ed. John Neville Figgis and Reginald Vere Laurence (London: Macmillan, 1906), 305–14. Reprinted in Lord Acton, *Selected Writings of Lord Acton*, ed. J. Rufus Fears, 3 vols. (Indianapolis: Liberty Fund, 1985–88), 1:189–97.

which followed the Conquest of Canada and the accession of George III. The two events, occurring in quick succession, raised the American question. A traveller who visited America some years earlier reports that there was much discontent, and that separation was expected before very long. That discontent was inoperative whilst a great military power held Canada. Two considerations reconciled the colonists to the disadvantages attending the connection with England. The English fleet guarded the sea against pirates; the English army guarded the land against the French. The former was desirable; the latter was essential to their existence. When the danger on the French side disappeared, it might become very uncertain whether the patrol of the Atlantic was worth the price that America had to pay for it. Therefore Montcalm foretold that the English, if they conquered the French colonies, would lose their own. Many Frenchmen saw this, with satisfaction; and the probability was so manifest that Englishmen saw it too. It was their interest to strengthen their position with new securities, in the place of that one supreme security which they had lost by their victory at Quebec. That victory, with the vast acquisition of territory that followed, would be no increase of imperial power if it loosened the hold on Atlantic colonies. Therefore, the policy of the hour was to enforce the existing claims and to obtain unequivocal recognition of English sovereignty. The most profitable method of doing it was in the shape of heavier taxation; but taxes were a small matter in comparison with the establishment of undisputed authority and unquestioning submission. The tax might be nominal, if the principle was safe. Ways and means would not be wanting in an empire which extended from Hudson's Bay to the Gulf of Mexico. For the moment the need was not money but allegiance. The problem was new, for the age of expansion had come suddenly, in East and West, by the action of Pitt; and Pitt was no longer in office, to find the solution.

Among the Whigs, who were a failing and discredited party, there were men who already knew the policy by which since then the empire has been reared—Adam Smith, Dean Tucker, Edmund Burke. But the great mass went with the times, and held that the object of politics is power, and that the more dominion is extended, the more it must be retained by force. The reason why free trade is better than dominion was a secret obscurely buried in the breast of economists.

Whilst the expulsion of the French from their Transatlantic empire governed the situation, the immediate difficulty was brought on by the new reign. The right of searching houses and ships for contraband was conveyed by certain warrants called Writs of Assistance, which required no specified designation, no oath or evidence, and enabled the surprise visit to be paid by day or night. They were introduced under Charles II, and had to be renewed within six months of the demise of the crown. The last renewal had been at the death of George II; and it was now intended that they should be efficacious, and should protect the revenue from smugglers. Between 1727 and 1761 many things had changed, and the colonies had grown to be richer, more confident, more self-respecting. They claimed to extend to the Mississippi, and had no French or Spaniards on their borders. Practically, there was no neighbour but England, and they had a patrimony such as no Englishman had dreamt of. The letter of the law, the practice of the last generation, were no argument with the heirs of unbounded wealth and power, and did not convince them that they ought to lose by the aid which they had given against France. The American jurists argued that this was good by English law, but could not justly be applied to America, where the same constitutional safeguards did not exist—where the cases would be tried by judges without a jury, by judges who could be dismissed at pleasure, by judges who were paid by fees which increased with the amount of the property confiscated, and were interested in deciding against the American importer, and in favour of the revenue. That was a technical and pedestrian argument which every lawyer could understand, without passing the limits of accustomed thought.

Then James Otis spoke, and lifted the question to a different level, in one of the memorable speeches in political history. Assuming, but not admitting, that the Boston customhouse officers were acting legally, and within the statute, then, he said, the statute was wrong. Their action might be authorised by parliament; but if so, parliament had exceeded its authority, like Charles with his shipmoney, and James with the dispensing power. There are principles which override precedents. The laws of England may be a very good thing, but there is such a thing as a higher law.

The court decided in favour of the validity of the writs; and John Adams, who heard the judgment, wrote long after that in that hour the child Independence was born. The English view triumphed for the time, and the governor wrote home that the murmurs soon ceased. The States, and ultimately the United States, rejected general warrants; and since 1817 they are in agreement with the law of England. On that point, therefore, the colonies were in the right.

Then came the larger question of taxation. Regulation of external traffic was admitted. England patrolled the sea and protected America from the smuggler and the pirate. Some remuneration might be reasonably claimed; but it ought to be obtained in such a way as not to hamper and prohibit the increase of wealth. The restrictions on industry and trade were, however, contrived for the benefit of England and to the injury of her colonies. They demanded that the arrangement should be made for their mutual advantage. They did not go so far as to affirm that it ought to be to their advantage only, irrespective of ours, which is our policy with our colonies at the present time. The claim was not originally excessive. It is the basis of the imputation that the dispute, on both sides, was an affair of sordid interest. We shall find it more just to say that the motive was empire on one side and self-government on the other. It was a question between liberty and authority, government by consent and government by force, the control of the subject by the State, and the control of the State by the subject. The issue had never been so definitely raised. In England it had long been settled. It had been settled that the legislature could, without breach of any ethical or constitutional law, without forfeiting its authority or exposing itself to just revolt, make laws injurious to the subject for the benefit of English religion or English trade. If that principle was abandoned in America it could not well be maintained in Ireland, and the green flag might fly on Dublin Castle.

This was no survival of the dark ages. Both the oppression of Ireland and the oppression of America was the work of the modern school, of men who executed one king and expelled another. It was the work of parliament, of the parliaments of Cromwell and of William III. And the parliament would not consent to renounce its own specific policy, its right of imposing taxes. The crown, the clergy, the aristocracy, were hostile to the Americans; but the real enemy was the House of Commons. The old European securities for good government were found insufficient protection against parliamentary oppression. The nation itself, acting by its representatives, had to be subjected to control. The political problem raised by the New World was more complicated than the simple issues dealt with hitherto in the Old. It had become necessary to turn back the current of the development of politics, to bind and limit and confine the State, which it was the pride of the moderns to exalt. It was a new phase of political history. The American Revolution innovated upon the English Revolution, as the English Revolution innovated on the politics of Bacon or of Hobbes. There was no tyranny to be resented. The colonists were in many ways more completely their own masters than Englishmen at home. They were not roused by the sense of intolerable wrong. The point at issue was a very subtle and refined one, and it required a great deal of mismanagement to make the quarrel irreconcilable.

Successive English governments shifted their ground. They tried the Stamp Act; then the duty on tea and several other articles; then the tea duty alone; and at last something even less than the tea duty. In one thing they were consistent: they never abandoned the right of raising taxes. When the colonists, instigated by Patrick Henry, resisted the use of stamps, and Pitt rejoiced that they had resisted, parliament gave way on that particular measure, declaring that it retained the disputed right. Townshend carried a series of taxes on imports, which produced about three hundred pounds, and were dropped by Lord North. Then an ingenious plan was devised, which would enforce the right of taxation, but which would not be felt by American pockets, and would, indeed, put money into them, in the shape of a bribe. East Indiamen were allowed to carry tea to American ports without paying toll in England. The Navigation Laws were suspended, that people in New England might drink cheap tea, without smuggling. The duty in England was a shilling a pound. The duty in America was threepence a pound. The shilling was remitted, so that the colonies had only a duty of threepence to pay instead of a duty of fifteenpence. The tea-drinker at Boston got his tea cheaper than the tea-drinker at Bristol. The revenue made a sacrifice, it incurred a loss, in order to gratify the discontented colonials. If it was a grievance to pay more for a commodity, how could it be a grievance to pay less for the same commodity? To gild the pill still further, it was proposed that the threepence should be levied at the British ports, so that the Americans should perceive nothing but the gift, nothing but the welcome fact that their tea was cheaper, and should be spared entirely the taste of the bitterness within. That would have upset the entire scheme. The government would not hear of it. America was to have cheap tea, but was to admit the tax. The sordid purpose was surrendered on our side, and only the constitutional motive was retained, in the belief that the sordid element alone prevailed in the colonies.

That threepence broke up the British empire. Twelve years of renewed contention, ever coming up in altered shape under different ministers, made it clear that the mind of the great parent State was made up, and that all variations of party were illusory. The Americans grew more and more obstinate as they purged the sordid question of interest with which they had begun. At first they had consented to the restrictions imposed under the Navigation Laws. They now rejected them. One of the tea ships in Boston harbour was boarded at night, and the tea chests were flung into the Atlantic. That was the mild beginning of the greatest Revolution that had ever broken out among civilised men. The dispute had been reduced to its simplest expression, and had become a mere question of principle. The argument from the Charters, the argument from the Constitution, was discarded. The case was fought out on the ground of the Law of Nature, more properly speaking, of Divine Right. On that evening of 16th December 1773, it became, for the first time, the reigning force in History. By the rules of right, which had been obeyed till then, England had the better cause. By the principle which was then inaugurated, England was in the wrong, and the future belonged to the colonies.

The revolutionary spirit had been handed down from the seventeenth-century sects, through the colonial charters. As early as 1638 a Connecticut preacher said: "The choice of public magistrates belongs unto the people, by God's own allowance. They who have the power to appoint officers and magistrates, it is in their power, also, to set the bounds and limitations of the power and place unto which they call them." In Rhode Island, where the Royal Charter was so liberal that it lasted until 1842, all power reverted annually to the people, and the authorities had to undergo re-election. Connecticut possessed so finished a system of self-government in the towns, that it served as a model for the federal Constitution. The Quakers of Pennsylvania managed their affairs without privilege, or intolerance, or slavery, or oppression. It was not to imitate England that they went into the desert. Several colonies were in various ways far ahead of the mother country; and the most advanced statesman of the Commonwealth, Vane, had his training in New England.

After the outrage on board the *Dartmouth* in Boston harbour the government resolved to coerce Massachusetts, and a continental Congress met to devise means for its protection. The king's troops were sent to destroy military stores that had been collected at Concord; and at Lexington, on the outward march, as well as all the way back, they were assailed by militia. The affair at Lexington, 19th April 1775, was the beginning of the War of Independence, which opened with the siege of Boston. Two months later the first action was fought at Bried's Hill, or Bunker Hill, which are low heights overlooking the town, and the colonials were repulsed with very little loss.

The war that followed, and lasted six years, is not illustrious in military annals, and interests us chiefly by the result. After the first battle the colonies declared themselves independent. Virginia, acting for herself only, led the way. Then the great revolutionist, who was the Virginian leader, Jefferson, drew up the Declaration of Independence, which was adopted by the remaining states. It was too rhetorical to be scientific; but it recited the series of ideas which the controversy had carried to the front.

Thirty thousand German soldiers, most of them from Hesse Cassel, were sent out, and were at first partially successful; for they were supported by the fleet, which the estuaries carried far inland. Where the European army had not that advantage things went badly. The Americans attacked Canada, expecting to be welcomed by the French inhabitants who had been so recently turned into British subjects. The attack failed dramatically by the death of General Montgomery, under the walls of Quebec, and the French colonists remained loyal. But an expedition sent from Canada against New York, under Burgoyne, miscarried. Burgoyne had scarcely reached the Hudson when he was forced to surrender at Saratoga. The Congress of the States, which feebly directed operations, wished that the terms of surrender should not be observed, and that the 5000 English and German prisoners, instead of being sent home, should be detained until they could be exchanged. Washington and his officers made known that if this was done they would resign.

The British defeat at Saratoga is the event which determined the issue of the conflict. It put an end to the vacillation of France. The French government had to recover the position it had lost in the last war, and watched the course of events for evidence that American resistance was not about to collapse. At the end of 1777 the victory of Saratoga supplied the requisite proof. Volunteers had been allowed to go over, and much war material was furnished through the agency of a comic poet. Now a treaty of alliance was concluded, a small army was sent to sea, and in March 1778 England was informed that France was at war with her. France was followed by Spain, afterwards by Holland.

It was evident from the first that the combination was more than England could hope to meet. Lord North at once gave way. He offered to satisfy the American demands, and he asked that Chatham should take office. From the moment that his old enemy, France, appeared on the scene, Chatham was passionately warlike. The king agreed that he should be asked to join the ministry, but refused to see him. America declined the English overtures, in fulfilment of her treaty with France. The negotiation with Chatham became impossible. That was no misfortune, for he died a few weeks later, denouncing the government and the opposition.

Then came that phase of war during which the navy of France, under d'Orvilliers in the Channel, under Suffren in the east, under d'Estaing and De Grasse in the west, proved itself equal to the navy of England. It is by the fleet, not by the land forces, that American independence was gained. But it is by the army officers that American ideas, sufficient to subvert every European state, were transplanted into France. When De Grasse drove the English fleet away from Virginian waters, Cornwallis surrendered the army of the south at Yorktown, as Burgoyne had surrendered with the northern army at Saratoga.

The Whigs came in and recognised the independence of the colonies, as North would have done four years earlier, when France intervened. Terms of peace with European Powers were made more favourable by the final success of Rodney at Dominica and of Elliot at Gibraltar; but the warlike repute of England fell lower than at any time since the Revolution.

The Americans proceeded to give themselves a Constitution which should hold them together more effectively than the Congress which carried them through the war, and they held a Convention for the purpose at Philadelphia during the summer of 1787. The difficulty was to find terms of union between the three great states—Virginia, Pennsylvania, Massachusetts—and the smaller ones, which included New York. The great states would not allow equal power to the others; the small ones would not allow themselves to be swamped by mere numbers. Therefore one chamber was given to population, and the other, the Senate, to the states on equal terms. Every citizen was made subject to the federal government as well as to that of his own state. The powers of the states were limited. The powers of the federal government were actually enumerated, and thus the states and the union were a check on each other. That principle of division was the most efficacious restraint on democracy that has been devised; for the temper of the Constitutional Convention was as conservative as the Declaration of Independence was revolutionary.

The Federal Constitution did not deal with the question of religious liberty. The rules for the election of the president and for that of the vice-president proved a failure. Slavery was deplored, was denounced, and was retained. The absence of a definition of State Rights led to the most sanguinary civil war of modern times. Weighed in the scales of Liberalism the instrument, as it stood, was a monstrous fraud. And yet, by the development of the principle of Federalism, it has produced a community more powerful, more prosperous, more intelligent, and more free than any other which the world has seen.

ABOUT LORD ACTON

John Emerich Edward Dalberg Acton, First Baron (1834–1902) was an English Catholic historian, politician, and writer. He was educated at Oscott under Cardinal Wiseman and then at Edinburgh. He then studied with Ignaz Döllinger at Munich. He served briefly in the House of Commons as a Liberal MP representing the Irish borough of Carlow. He edited the *Rambler* and later the *Home and Foreign Review* and was also published in the *North British Review, Quarterly Review,* and the *English Historical Review.* Acton was awarded honorary degrees from Munich University, Cambridge, and Oxford. He was made a lord-in-waiting by Prime Minister Gladstone in 1892 and was appointed Regius Professor of Modern History at Cambridge in 1895. There he lectured on the French Revolution and modern history. *The Cambridge Modern History* was planned under his editorship but he did not live to see its completion. Although Acton wrote and lectured widely throughout his life, he never wrote a book. In addition to his lectures, essays, and reviews he left a large body of learned personal correspondence and notes as well as an extensive library full of his own annotations now housed at the University of Cambridge.

ABOUT THE EDITOR

Daniel J. Hugger is librarian and research associate at the Acton Institute for the Study of Religion & Liberty. He studied history at Hillsdale College and earned a State of Michigan teaching certificate at Calvin College, where he completed a thesis on the role of the imagination in the writings of St. Ignatius of Loyola. For his work in history at Calvin he was nominated for a Lilly Fellowship. He has taught history, English, and economics at public schools in the Grand Rapids area and has lectured on Lord Acton.

Made in the USA
Lexington, KY
03 June 2017